THE SILENT ESCAPE

THE SILENT ESCAPE

ESCAPE

Three Thousand Days in Romanian Prisons

LENA CONSTANTE

Translation by
Franklin Philip

Introduction by
Gail Kligman

UNIVERSITY OF CALIFORNIA PRESS
Berkeley   Los Angeles   London

Published as *L'évasion silencieuse: Trois mille jour seule dans les prisons roumaines* in 1990 by Éditions La Découverte, Paris

The publisher gratefully acknowledges the contribution provided by the Literature in Translation Endowment Fund, which is supported by a generous gift from Joan Palevsky.

University of California Press
Berkeley and Los Angeles, California

University of California Press
London, England

Library of Congress Cataloging-in-Publication Data
Constante, Lena
    [Evasion silencieuse. English]
    The silent escape: three thousand days in Romanian prisons /
Lena Constante; translation by Franklin Philip; introd. by Gail Kligman.
        p. cm.—(Society and culture in East Central Europe)
    Translation of: L'évasion silencieuse.
    ISBN 0–520–08209–5
    1. Constante, Lena.   2. Political prisoners—Romania—Biography.
I. Title.   II. Series: Societies and culture in East-Central Europe.
HV9772.5.C6613A3   1995
365'.45'092—dc20   94–10627
    [B]   CIP

Printed in the United States of America

1 2 3 4 5 6 7 8 9

The paper used in this publication meets the minimum requirements of American National Standard for Information Sciences—Permanence of Paper for Printed Library Materials, ANSI Z39.48-1984 ⊚

In loving memory of my husband, Harry Brauner

Contents

Introduction

Lena Constante spent twelve arduous years incarcerated in Romanian prisons. She had been accused and convicted of participating in the "espionage conspiracy" organized by Lucreţiu Pătrăşcanu, the popular communist Minister of Justice who became a principal scapegoat of Romania's Stalinist-era show trials. Lena Constante, an artist, came into close association with Pătrăşcanu through her work with the minister's wife, Elena Pătrăşcanu. In 1945, Lena Constante joined Mrs. Pătrăşcanu in her efforts to create the first puppet theater in Bucharest. Little did these two women realize that they themselves would take part in one of the most sinister forms of "puppet" theater—the Stalinist show trial.

In Eastern Europe, these trials took place between 1948 and 1954.[1] Although directed from Moscow, the show trials were scripted in the respective satellite countries. There was a basic plot structure that required elaboration. "Plausible" conspiracies had to be concocted in which espionage for imperialist powers was a central element. Loyal communists in good standing—such as Lucreţiu Pătrăşcanu—were vilified as deviationists, bourgeois nationalists, and traitors. Those accused were painstakingly obliged to "learn" their designated roles for the "show trial" during the investigation period, more accurately termed *interrogation* period.

For the Pătrăşcanu affair, this lasted five years. The participants were uncooperative and often uncomprehending of what was expected of them. The conspiracy plot was repeatedly reworked by one of the accused in this scenario.[2] The secret show trial was held from April 6 to 14, 1954. As predetermined, Lucreţiu Pătrăşcanu was condemned to death; he was executed sometime between dusk on April 16, 1954 and the dawn of April 17, 1954. Lena Constante, like her companion Harry Brauner, received a sentence of twelve years. By the time her conviction was secured, she had already served five of these years. There were seven more to endure. She did, and was released in the early part of her final year in 1961. In 1968, all of those tried and convicted in the Pătrăşcanu show trial, including the deceased, were exonerated and fully rehabilitated.[3]

The Silent Escape is Lena Constante's recounting of the first eight years of her imprisonment. Why these particular years? Her response paid tribute to all of those who had been forced to waste too much of their lives in Romanian jails. Some prisoners never emerged from the depths of these living hells; instead, they perished within the confines of the prison walls, the stony guardians of many of Stalinism's dark secrets. There was nothing especially distinctive about spending twelve years in prison. Many others "did more time."[4] However, what Lena Constante feels to be unique about her experience is that she is the only woman political prisoner to have endured eight years of solitary confinement in Romanian prisons. These eight years are the subject of her telling.[5] It is an extraordinary account.

Lena Constante was born in Bucuresti in 1909. Her father was a patriotic Romanian-Macedonian from Skopje; her mother, of a petite bourgeois family from Bucharest. Lena was the second of three sisters. During the first World War, the family moved to Iasi, a town overpopulated with refugees.[6] After the armistice, the family began a lengthy homeward odyssey which took them through Odessa, and then London, and on to Paris, where they remained for several years before returning to Bucharest. At home, she completed her studies in fine arts. In spite of the difficulties that familial financial insecurity added to the traumas of those war-torn years, Lena Constante has fond memories of her childhood. "I believe that is why I get along well with children, even though I don't have any of my own." Her fondness for the young at heart has found creative expression in books that she has illustrated for children, puppet plays that she composed (and which helped her discipline her mind against the insanity that threatened to engulf her throughout those eight lonely years), folk dolls clad in "traditional" village dress which she fashioned, and greeting cards using folk motifs which she designed. Such creations were often the products of necessity, enabling her to eke out a meager living in the midst of hard times, of which there have been many.

As a child, Lena Constante recalls struggling with "extraordinary" questions that she was unable to resolve: "What is truth?" or "Which is real life—that which I experience during my waking hours, or that which occupies my dreams?" or "Mother taught me that the grass is green, the sky is blue. But how do I know that what she sees is the same as what I see?" or "I would notice that sometimes my parents would tell what could be called social lies. There was this very tiresome family friend to whom we had to be very polite when she visited. Yet I overheard my parents talking together, commenting about how stupid this person was. I wanted to know what they really thought! When were they telling the truth? When not?" These concerns about truth, about public representations and private thoughts, about social justice, and human frailties—these have confronted Lena Constante throughout her life's experiences.

As a teenager, she remembers commenting on what today would be labeled "feminist" tendencies. During a spirited discussion at home, Lena interjected into an adult conversation about women and politics that she thought women would not make the same mistakes of judgment as did men. Lena also decided that she did not want to marry before the age of forty. She knew that in Romania, a married woman would not be able to pursue her artwork; she would have too many familial obligations. Circumstances were such that she and her longtime partner and fellow "accomplice" in the Pătrășcanu conspiracy, Harry Brauner, did not marry until they were released from prison. Lena was then fifty.

Lena Constante met Harry Brauner while he was working as the assistant to the Romanian ethnomusicologist, Constantin Brăiloiu. Brailoiu was responsible for the popular (or folk) music component of the village monographic studies organized by the Romanian sociologist, Dimitrie Gusti. Lena's older sister, a sociologist, was engaged in these reseach projects and invited her to visit. It was then that she met Harry with whom a lasting friendship and partnership developed.[7] Brauner, a Jew, was handsome, spiritual, popular, and talented. He loved the richness and diversity of Romanian folk music, to which he devoted his life's work as an ethnomusicologist and folklorist. Together, he and Lena traveled throughout Romanian villages as opportunity permitted, both before and after their imprisonments. These shared interests in the popular arts of Romania had profound consequences, positive and negative, for their lives.

As mentioned above, Lena Constante participated in Mrs. Pătrăşcanu's project to create a puppet theater in Bucuresti. The Pătrăşcanus became intimate friends with Lena Constante and her partner, Harry Brauner.[8] With Lucreţiu Pătrăşcanu's assistance, Brauner was able to create the Institute of Folklore in Bucuresti, which in 1948 was not a state institution.[9] This detail was later used against them as evidence of their conspiratorial activities. Foreigners came to the Institute of Folklore, which in the script for the show trial was transformed into a meeting place for spies. This was its "real" purpose, and was why Pătrăşcanu aided Brauner in his efforts to form it. For her part, Lena Constante was accused of being a spy, among other things. The source of these kernels of truth distorted into rewritten histories was Belu Zilber, the other person among those accused known to Lena Constante.[10] She had met Zilber in the early thirties. During the second World War, he and other Jewish intellectuals often came to her apartment to listen to classical music.[11] Some years later, he would by and large author the Romanian version of the Stalinist show trial that "legitimated" the death of his formerly close friend Lucreţiu Pătrăşcanu,[12] and the guilt of the others accused, including himself. It was a slow process; it took the "puppet" prisoners nearly five years to "recognize" what Zilber had written and to learn their roles properly. In the end, at the trial, Pătrăşcanu did not acquiesce. He believed that communism could not be built on lies, and that he could not engage in them. With or without confession of his "crimes," Pătrăşcanu's fate had been sealed long before the trial.[13] Most of the others eventually found their way out into the world beyond the walls again.

Upon release, Lena Constante was not allowed immediately to live in Bucuresti. Neither was Harry Brauner, who was subject to another two years of probation with forced residence in a small locale in the Baragan, the plains of Southeast Romania. It was there that the couple married. After their return to Bucuresti, they each attempted to become reengaged in their respective professional lives: Brauner, in ethnomusicology and folklore; Constante, in popular art.[14] In 1968, they were fully rehabilitated. This official declaration (ritualized throughout the socialist world) vindicated them of any wrongdoing, and enabled them to resume their lives as "normal" citizens.

It was partially a consequence of this special status that I was able to meet them in 1975, and to continue to do so throughout my years of cultural anthropological research in Romania.[15] At the time, Lena Constante was embroiled in another fabricated conspiracy of sorts in which the themes of national identity, representation, and "truth" were again, if differently, involved. Beginning in 1963, Lena Constante collected pieces of the richly enbroidered sleeves and bodices of the stunning peasant blouses worn in a remote village of Hunedoara. When the blouses were too faded or torn, the women would either sell them by the kilogram to a mill for "recycling" or they would use them as rags.[16] Lena Constante arranged to have some of the peasant women send these "rags" to her. She then began making them into tapestries. An exhibit of these stunning creations was held in Bucuresti in 1974. However, Romanian nationalism a la Ceausescu was quietly burgeoning at this time, and so began another saga.[17] In 1975, a law about the national cultural patrimony was introduced. Nothing of national value was allowed to be removed from the country. Constante was later accused of destroying these embroideries (of national value) for which it was suggested she be arrested![18] She was not; nonetheless, false accusations were again made in the self-interests of others. Among the "conspiracy" theories offered was that she profited from her Jewish folklorist husband Harry Brauner's discovery of this treasure of embroidered blouses in Hunedoara. He then hid them "who knows where, to later give them to me to cut them up!"[19] The scandal eventually died down. Yet again, Lena Constante had found herself in the vortex of a conspiracy about which she had to become informed, but which affected her everyday life's tranquility (or lack thereof). The consequences of this "episode" were, however, little more than aggravating.

Lena Constante finished writing *The Silent Escape* in 1985. The original is handwritten in French, in a tiny scrawl. In 1990, she gave the manuscript to a publisher in France. Since then, she has finished the second volume about her years of incarceration.[20] Both of these books differ from the more customary prison memoirs because hers are not primarily political reflections. Instead, Lena Constante draws us into the practical and emotional experiences of everyday life in Romanian prisons: how "interrogations" proceeded, what methods were employed to persuade, punish, and torture prisoners. She opens up the emotional and "thoughtful" world of prison life. This is an entirely human account about endless days, hours, and minutes of gripping despair, of pain from the physical and psychological means employed to control prisoners. Her style of writing underscores the unrelenting presence of time. Lena Constante re-creates the rituals of daily life, the habits of the heart and mind that saw her, and many others, through these ordeals. She writes of her artistic compositions, usually formulated in her thoughts and committed to memory, her attempts to engage (and discipline) her mind so as not to lose it to the temptations of fear, submission, and so on. She, like so many others, was not always successful in her resolve to maintain her "dignity." Personal and existential concerns about human frailty and human dignity are more easily tackled in the classroom or in the cafe than they are in the bowels of a prison where the machinations of torturers test the human will and spirit beyond comprehension.

Eight years of solitary confinement—that is also beyond everyday comprehension. As the years progressed, Lena Constante became fluent in the "language of the walls," the method of communication that enabled prisoners to "talk" with each other through a kind of Morse code tapped through the walls. Few accounts written about the sufferings of too many of the world's peoples explicate this critical feature of prison life as vividly as does Lena Constante's. While prison routine, particularly during the Stalinist era, was rigidly structured in time and space, this secretive communication through the walls was not. It was not a mode of communicative exchange predicated on familiar time frames. She describes the characteristics of the walls that had to be mastered so as to avoid drawing the attention of the guards. (Of course, some abused this mode of "talking" in the interest of informing on fellow prisoners.) This type of communication opened up a world of active social communication. In Lena Constante's particular case, her sheer pleasure, derived from involvement in the "secrets of prison life," from her reengagement in a social world, brings the rigors of her solitary experience more sharply into focus.

Lena Constante also introduces us to prison life for women in general, about which there is relatively little known. As she writes, "These women, all admirable and miserable, they were all in solidarity with each other." She tells us about the affective relations between women prisoners, about sexual desire, about friendships that would have been unthinkable "outside." There are profoundly touching passages about her growing relationships "through the walls" with fellow prisoners.

Lena Constante experienced and underlines for us that in spite of excessive privation of all sorts, the lack of elementary hygiene, the incidence of illness and the inadequacy of treatment—indeed, prison doctors determined the limits of torture for those who were ill so as not to provoke an "accidental" death due to maltreatment—in spite of all of this, everyday life in prison was characterized by an extraordinary female solidarity in the face of hardship, harshness, and suffering. Lena Constante offers us an eloquent rendering of this female solidarity, of the will to survive, and of human dignity. Yet, ever respectful of an essential humanism, she also reminds us that "we were not the only to suffer. The majority of the Romanian people were crushed under the weight of an inhuman and aberrant regime." In this deeply moving account, Lena Constante has graced the too often brutal pages of history with the eloquence of her humanity.

Gail Kligman

Notes

1. For readers wanting more background on these trials, see G. Hodos, *Show Trials: Stalinist Purges in Eastern Europe, 1948–1954* (New York: Praeger, 1987). The discussion of the Pătrășcanu affair is one of the few accounts available in English. See chapter 10, "The Reinterpreted Show Trials in Romania."

2. Belu Zilber, Pătrășcanu's friend, succumbed to the persuasiveness of torture. He essentially wrote the script for the show trial that his fellow accused had to learn to "recognize." See A. Șerbulescu, *Monarhie de Drept Dialectic. A doua versiune a memoriilor lui Belu Zilber* (București: Humanitas, 1991). (Șerbulescu was Zilber's pen alias.) Constante discusses him at greater length in her second book, *Evaderea Imposibila* (Bucuresti: Fundatia Culturala Româna, 1993).

3. The factionalist struggles in the Romanian Communist Party made Pătrășcanu an ideal candidate to be sacrificed in the show trial. Pătrășcanu was Gheorghe Gheorghiu-Dej's most formidable rival. The former was always suspect because of a general characteristic of intellectuals: a lack of sufficient dogmatism. Pătrășcanu and the others accused with him were rehabilitated by Nicolae Ceaușescu, Gheorghiu-Dej's successor. Again, factionalist rivalries motivated Ceaușescu's reconsideration of this case.

4. Corneliu Coposu, leader of the National Christian-Democratic Peasant Party, spent seventeen years in prison. After the collapse of communism in Romania—that is, after the fall of the Ceauşescu regime—an "Association of Former Political Prisoners" was formed. This Association belongs to the "Democratic Convention," a political umbrella of opposition Parties and groups in postcommunist Romania.

5. A second volume about the last years of her imprisonment has been published in Romania. See footnote 2. Lena Constante was transferred from solitary confinement and integrated into "normal" prison life.

6. During the war, the government retreated to Iaşi. Lena's father worked in the government as the equivalent of a civil servant. The family moved with him.

7. Lena was so taken with Harry Brauner that she resorted to a folk practice to assure the fruition of their relationship. He was a handsome and popular man. With a laugh, she tells of how she asked the village "witch" to cast a spell that would bind them for life. Lena was told to bring something of his. Not knowing exactly how to acquire such an item, she made up a story about having a men's shirt and needing a tie to wear with it. Brauner lent her one, which she took to the sorceress who then chanted over it; she also had a bottle with basil (a holy and magical plant) and water. Lena didn't know what the witch did or said, but obviously it worked!

8. Many people assume that Lena and Harry were a married couple sharing a residence during this period. That was not the case, although, fortuitously, they lived in the same neighborhood. They found this arrangement stimulating for what she termed a relationship of "art in process."

They had become close friends of the Pătrăşcanus. Elena Pătrăşcanu (known to friends as Saşa—a nickname given to her by Constante) was Jewish; Pătrăşcanu, Christian. Constante describes him as an idealist, and like most idealists, naive in many ways. While talking about Pătrăşcanu, she commented wistfully about how complexly intertwined everything seemed to have been; how it had been possible to "rework" events that changed innocent persons' lives.

9. Precious collections that had been hidden during the war needed to be catalogued and properly placed in archives. However, for Pătrăşcanu to help Brauner in this endeavor, Brauner had to join the Communist Party. Neither the Institute of Folklore nor the Puppet Theater was founded in 1949, the official year of their opening. This was the year when these both became state institutions.

Both Brauner and Pătrăşcanu were Romanian "nationalists" of different sorts. Harry Brauner loved the expressive cultures of Romania. Lucreţiu Pătrăşcanu, a committed communist, was committed first to his country's interests (and not dogmatically to international communism). Brauner and Pătrăşcanu, both intellectuals, would pay dearly for their different but related efforts on behalf of Romania.

10. Constante claims to have met most of the other coconspirators at the secret trial itself. One of the standard elements of conspiracies is the ever-expanding network of persons often unknown to each other, but known to a

central figure. "Belu" is the name by which Herbert Zilber was popularly known.

11. Jews were not supposed to have radios during the war, so they came to visit Constante, who was not Jewish.

12. Remus Koffler was also sentenced to death. The others received punishments varying from twelve years to life imprisonment. (Belu Zilber was sentenced to the latter.) Following their rehabilitation in 1968, all sentences were commuted to freedom for those still alive and imprisoned. Koffler and Pătrășcanu were not among them.

13. Although the circumstances bear no comparison, there is a disturbing resemblance between the executions of Pătrășcanu and Ceaușescu, whose secret trials differently represent travesties of "due process."

14. In 1964, Harry's brother, the painter Victor Brauner, who was established in Paris, tried to "buy" Harry out of Romania. At the time, this did not work (although by the eighties, this was a customary practice; Jews and Germans could be bought out with "hard" currency). Victor Brauner died in 1966 before the opening of his art exhibit, to which Harry had been invited. With pressure from the French Government, a visa was obtained. Harry and Lena assumed that the Romanians wanted to show that former prisoners had the same rights as all citizens. ("Show" this was, because years later, most Romanians—unlike former political prisoners with the ironically "privileged" status of having been rehabilitated—did not have the right to travel.) In fact, thereafter, Brauner and Constante traveled frequently, invited by friends and family, especially in France and Switzerland. They always returned home to Romania.

15. After their rehabilitation, Brauner taught at the Conservatory of Music. He also continued his folklore collections and wrote about the "Pollution of Folklore" that was introduced by Ceaușescu through the mass cultural festival system, "The Singing of Romania." The pollution (through homogenization and standardization) of expressive cultural practices was anathema to Harry. Sadly, Harry Brauner died in 1988 before the fall of Ceaușescu.

It would have been much more difficult for me to visit Harry Brauner and Lena Constante after 1978 when the interdictions against meeting with foreigners became ever more stringent under Ceaușescu's rule. However, given their status (and their publicly known work in culture), it was possible. Much, however, remained unsaid between us, particularly in-depth discussion of their prison years.

16. I was not surprised to hear that these peasant women would use their seemingly faded yet exquisitely hand-embroidered blouses as rags. I encountered this in villages in Oltenia; this was at a time when the "folkloric" machine-sewn embroidered blouses of Romania were all the rage in the West. While Romanian peasants discarded what they considered to be worn-out shirts, westerners were paying high prices for poor facsimiles.

17. These works are not tapestries in the classic sense, although they are closest to them. Lena's creations are compositions in the style of tapestries in which the embroidered pieces are creatively arranged by her. It is beyond the scope of this introduction to discuss this ongoing episode in detail. The

noted philosopher Constantin Noica wrote the following lines about her tapestries: "Four hundred embroidered blouses met Lena Constante: 'They are going to throw us away, dear lady!' they said to her. 'They are going to throw us away!' Then she took them in her hand, passed them through her soul, and sent them to Heaven!" And, "When we reach the end like old, worn shirts, when everyone who has seen Lena Constante's tapestries come to the end, some of us will think, perhaps: if she is there, one day, with her deft hands, may she transform us into tapestries for the Great Collector." (I copied and translated these texts presented to Lena Constante; they were signed by Noica, April 1, 1974.)

18. Underlying some of this dispute about the public domain and art was the basic interest in preventing citizens from receiving payment in hard currency. Over the years, various exhibits of her work did occur, but with the agreement that she would not sell privately except to cover her travel expenses. There is a fundamental irony in this case: Constante was accused of destroying the national patrimony (when she salvaged and reworked worn-out blouses whose creators were destroying them themselves) during the period when the state was engaged in "destroying" cultural practices through the homogenization and standardization of "Cîntarea România" (The Singing of Romania). Since the fall of the Ceauşescu regime, her work has again been exhibited in France, Switzerland, and elsewhere.

19. In a letter written by a villager to Constante regarding the accusations against her, the peasant woman wrote: ". . . those that think that we've cut up our new blouses for you are either stupid . . . we thought that only we Pădureni and peasants are stupid, but the professors and directors are stupider than us! Would they destroy their new clothes? Nor do we!"

20. Since 1990, she has not worked much on her tapestries. This is partly because she no longer has the strength or the sharp eyesight needed to repair, design, and sew these inspired creations.

I have been sentenced to twelve years in prison. The trial lasted six days. The preliminary investigation, five years. So I've already served five years. Alone. In a cell not quite fifty-four square feet. For 1,827 days. Alone. For 43,848 hours. In a cell where each hour inexorably had sixty minutes, each minute sixty seconds. One, two, three, four, five seconds. Six, seven, eight, nine, ten seconds, a thousand seconds, a hundred thousand seconds. I have lived, alone, in a cell, 157,852,800 seconds of solitude and fear. Cause for screaming! They sentence me to live yet another 220,838,400 seconds! To live them or to die from them.

During the final days of the investigation, they had raised my hopes of being released once the trial was over. Little by little I'd come to believe them.

The shock at these seven additional years of detention shatter my brain. I feel nothing. For two or three days, perhaps even four, I lie on my straw-filled mattress. Unconscious.

Each day, midday and evening, they bring me a bowl of blackish liquid and a thin slice of bread. I cannot swallow them. I don't even see them. My eyes are closed. Behind my eyelids, all is black. I don't feel my arms. I don't feel my legs. I am coming apart.

About four o'clock in the morning they make me leave my cell. It is April 15, 1954, of that I am certain. They order me to sign a document. I sign it. I don't know what it is I am signing. A sheet of white paper covers the words.

They push me outside. I am still wearing my prison glasses. The lenses are an opaque black. I feel the air. It is cold. They are still pushing me . . . making me go up two steps . . . They make me get into a police car.

I leave behind five years of detention. In those five years, they have made me change prisons four times. In each of these prisons, several changes of cell.

PART ONE

January 1950–April 1954

1 | First Prison

My first prison had only seventeen cells. I was there from January 17, 1950, the date I was arrested, until the end of April. It was a special prison. Secret. I had no way of knowing what went on in that large two- or three-story building whose basement had been converted into a prison. I knew only the four cells I occupied one after the other. The jail. The shower room used also as a punishment room. An interrogation room on the floor above, toilets, and a stairwell.

They had rung my doorbell at eleven at night. I knew right away it was them. Motionless, holding my breath, I heard them ringing. I could have tried to get away. Slip from my balcony to the one next door. But then what? Wake up the neighbors? Go through their apartment? Go down the service stairway? And then what? Even if I managed to reach the street without being seen, where would I go? Where would I hide? At my parents' house? That would be the first place they'd look. They would hunt down all my friends. They would never give up. I'd be caught all the same and everyone who'd helped me would be done for.

I lived on the seventh floor. For a few minutes I hesitated. Throw myself through the window? At the door, they were getting impatient. They knew I was there. The hall porter had seen me come in. He must have told them. My windows were lit. They must have seen them from below. I walked slowly to the door. It was midnight.

I don't remember that first night in jail. I must have slept.

Day 1 of detention—January 19, 1950

Interrogation. A militiaman has me sit in front of a small table. Across from me, a large desk. A man is there. Bull-necked. He asks me several questions. I don't know the answers. He speaks with a foreign accent. I don't know the people he's talking about. I tell him so. He accuses me of lying. Suggests in an authoritative tone that I confess everything. Confess . . . what?

I thought I was in luck. Knowing nothing, I could give nothing away. I'd never heard some of the names he was talking about. He also mentioned a few names I did know, but they were those of my best friends. All estimable and respected. This was no problem for me, and I could in all sincerity answer "no." I was extremely surprised to see he didn't believe me. He persisted. Urged me to tell the truth. This went on for quite some time. Then he got angry. Shouted. Claimed he had proof that my denials were false. I become frightened. He seems sure of himself. He says it is for my own good that he is wasting his time persuading me to confess. He gives me time to think. All the time I need. I am overcome with fear.

Days 2, 3, 4, 5 of detention—January 23, 1950

One interrogation follows another. Several days go by in this unequal contest. His tone grows more and more menacing. I have only a jumbled memory of all this. I have all but forgotten the cell, the stairs, the office. I wouldn't recognize this man now. My memory has clung only to the sensation of my fear.

I was no longer a person. I was nothing. My truth was no longer the truth. My truth was not their truth. But what *was* their truth? It took me a long time to grasp it.

Every interrogator has the right, within limits, to use certain gambits. I knew this. The tactics may include gaining the accused person's trust, misleading him, even threatening him. Hope and fear are the interrogator's weapons. He can thus put them to use. Within limits. To go beyond these limits is inhuman. To go from threats to torture is inhuman. To strike a person's flesh is criminal.

In those first days of interrogation, I didn't doubt the investigator's good faith. I took his questions to be sincere. Honest questions, from his point of view. A correct attitude, from his profession's point of view. Back in my cell, I racked my brains. What arguments could I come up with to persuade him? To show him his mistake. I really had nothing to tell him. Not about myself nor about the others.

My denials are fruitless. All they do is infuriate him. He studies me with eyes filled with hate. The eyes of a madman. I am beginning to doubt myself. Have I lost my mind? My fear is compounded by a new torture.

The guards hustle me into the office several times a day. At any hour. Even in the middle of the night. The stairs, the interrogator, the questions, the threats, the fear.

He embellishes his sadism with words designed to trap me. He speaks of duty, mission, the public good. It is easy to trip over these words. To be skinned alive by them. Shed blood, or even die from them. For him, anything goes. For him, everything is permissible. To impose "his" truth becomes his singular goal. For this madman, the law doesn't exist, because he is the law. And he is justice, too. And vengeance. He is God.

After a few days, he punishes me.

Days 6, 7, 8 of detention—January 25, 1950

As usual, after the wake-up call, the guard opens the door and takes me to the toilet. In the corridor, a small sink, a sliver of soap, a dirty hand towel, a grimy comb with broken-off teeth, full of hair. This is where I wash my hands and face. I feel soiled.

The guard always has me follow him. This time, he doesn't take me back to my cell. He stops where the corridor makes a right angle, and he opens a door, motioning me inside. He shuts the door. The key turns. It's just a cubicle, three by six feet. The steeply pitched ceiling comes down to about three feet above the floor. There is only a square yard of floor space where it's possible to stand up straight. A cement floor. In the far wall is an opening to the outside. About a foot high and two feet wide. This dormer window is boarded over. I can't see it, but I feel it with my hands. The guard slides open the tiny judas window. Warns me that I am forbidden to sit on the floor. I must remain standing.

It is January. Our winters are severe. The cubicle is unheated. Through the chinks come gusts of wind, icy blasts. I am wearing only a thin pleated skirt, a blouse, and woolen jacket. I'm cold. I cross my arms over my chest. Press my legs together. I'm cold. I don't have room to walk. I can take only one step. When I attempt another, I bang my head on the sloping roof. I do some exercises. This is even worse. My whole body is freezing. I manage to loop my skirt between my legs, draw it up in front, and tuck it into my waistband.

I grow colder and colder. My teeth start chattering. Every so often the judas opens. The guard looks at me. Around noon, I guess, he cracks the door and hands me a thin slice of bread.

For those first few hours I suffer only from the cold. Suddenly I feel tired. I have been standing for hours. Almost without moving, for want of space. Leaning now against one wall, now against the other. My feet ache. My ankles swell. I am dreadfully cold. I am chilled to the bone. Tired. I am tired. I am tired unto death. I begin to mumble: I'm tired to death . . . tired . . . tired . . . so tired. To forget the feeling, I concentrate on the idea of tiredness. This litany lulls me to sleep. I manage to sleep a few seconds. Standing up. Without swaying. A fist raps on the door. Jolts me awake.

I don't know how many hours I've been here. I don't know whether it's night or day. That first evening, in the corridor, I'd seen a telephone on the head guard's table. It rings at all hours of the day and night. It's the summons to the interrogation room. Then one of the seventeen cells opens. Muffled footsteps pass in the corridor. Go up the stairs . . . I abhor this telephone. Out of a dread of the interrogation room. As soon as I hear its shrillness, I cease feeling cold or fatigue or sleepiness. Nothing. I wait anxiously for the guard's footsteps. I feel only my fear.

Words take time. They can't tell it all at once. How can this anxiety be expressed? I would need a single word. A word that creates a synthesis. A crushing blow of a word. A thunderclap word. A blood-soaked word. Shrieked from a throat choking with anxiety. The waiting in the hollow of my stomach. My heart squeezed by horror. The dread that tugs in my chest, high up, a place, a point on the left, where usually there is nothing. My heart. A flesh word. A blood word. This word does not exist.

So many words that so far say nothing. How can I express the despair? The revolt? The physical pain in my heart? The pain obliterates everything. Nothing further goes on in my mind. Nothing in that strange place that I find hard to locate. High up. No. In back of my eyes. Higher yet. So much higher it is almost outside this other disgusting self, my body. No. Nothing in the head. Everything happens only in that lump of insentient flesh, mute and as a rule nonexistent. Suddenly in the hurt, the pain, the fear, I feel assailed by my heart. I knew it was there. Theoretically. Now it is all that exists. It hurts. To the point of wanting to scream. And my belly and my bowels clench, clench harder, and harder yet, without stopping . . .

. . . toward me? No. A door opens. Not mine. Again I am cold. So, so cold. I shiver. My teeth chatter. With a little noise. Pathetic. I am pathetic. Dirty, bristly, trembling from head to toe, hungry. Locked up in a cage, outside the law, outside time, I was truly pathetic. With such need for someone's, anyone's, pity. But I was alone, alone, all alone.

Nonetheless, I was the center of the world. This world existed all around me, *for* me, only because I was becoming aware of it. Accepting it, wasn't it I who made it real? To accept its reality was to accept my suffering. I had to disown it in order to live. To destroy it in order to survive it. In this dungeon of a cell for unending hours I became aware of my duality. I was two. For I was here and I saw myself here. I was two. For I couldn't go through this bolted door and yet I could be elsewhere.

The interrogator had ordered me to reflect and remember what I feigned—he said—not to know. On the contrary, I had to forget, forget everything, starting with him. No longer would I hear the click of the judas. Nor see the guard's eye. Nor "realize" the cold. Nor feel the hunger. I had to escape. Flee. Unable to get to the other side of the wall, escape from myself. To leave this body, now only a torment, behind. This miserable, hungry flesh. Repudiate my body's "me." No longer endure its pain. Nor tremble with its fear. My body could only be here. Me, I could be elsewhere. My body didn't have space to move its aching feet. But, *I* would grow wings. The wings of a bird. The wings of the wind. The wings of a star. And I would get away.

This was the beginning of a long apprenticeship. Escape is

no easy thing. Only gradually did I succeed in learning. By going through distinct stages.

I couldn't bear the fatigue any longer. I allowed myself to slide along the wall. I flexed my knees. I hunkered down, crouched into a ball. I faintly hear the sound of the judas. It opened. It closed. The guard said nothing. He went away. Crouched on the floor, curled over with my forehead against my knees, my arms hugging my legs, I fall asleep. Like a dog. Worse than a dog. A dog can drag itself off in search of shelter. Be lucky enough to find a garbage can. Get a crust of bread, a bone. Dogs are to be envied. Humans pitied.

I am awakened by the cold. The cement floor is ice. I laboriously stand up. I rub on the cement with my right sole. Fatigue. I shift from one foot to the other. I warm my place. Again I crouch down. From time to time, I repeat the routine.

A knock at the door. "Get up!" I get up. It's the next morning. A guard takes me to the toilet. There it is warm. The wooden seat is warm. I would like to stay there. Sitting. Not leave. He raps on the door. Back to the cell. Through the half-opened door, someone hands me a thin slice of bread. A bowl of water.

The telephone . . . This time it is for me. The office again. The hangman. And he asks me if I have done some reflecting. I can't answer. My teeth are chattering. I can't stop them from chattering. I can't stop trembling. A guard brings me a cup of tea. He orders me to drink it. I raise the cup. My hands are shaking. Drops fall on the table at which he has me sitting. I finally manage to get the tea down. It has warmed me up a little. Not much, but I have stopped trembling.

He speaks. Of his rights. Of his power. Of the force he represents. Of his own patience. Of the infinite patience of this force. He says that everything depends on me. On my good will. On my sincerity. He knows about my "criminal" doings. All my offenses are known to him. They've got hold of all the proof. They can convict me and sentence me. If I persist in my denials, I will be judged and sentenced along with the other defendants. Sentenced to death. If, however, I agreed to help them by telling the whole "truth" about the others accused, he would release me from prison. He cannot free me right away but he promises me excellent living conditions. They would satisfy all my desires. They would provide me with a house, clothing, food, books. Until the trial. Witness for the prosecution.

I would be a witness for the prosecution. Then, freedom. The choice was mine. Either the overlooking of my crimes, or my death. He gives me more time to think. And space. The cell.

I am cold again. Ice cold. Aching. Escape is far away. I try to think. To comprehend. Witness for the prosecution . . . what does it mean?

What is the accusation? They can know nothing about my "crimes," for the crimes are nonexistent. I have never "worked" for anyone. Not before and not after the war. And not during the war. At the very most, I had helped the wife of one of the defendants. Out of pity. Out of a horror of fascism. Despite all the risks. I had hidden her. Twice. For a few days in my apartment. The fascist police were looking for her. Her photograph had appeared in the newspapers. With a falsified caption. Saying the body had been recovered, lifeless. Drowned, as I recall. The police asked for anyone who recognized her to come identify her. That was all I had done, nothing else. Neither for good nor for bad, and I was of sound mind.

So this man was lying. I had the proof. The investigation was fishy. An investigation is an attempt to discover something. Deeds and the motives behind them. Arresting someone demands more than suspicions. But was this man really trying to find out anything? No. From the start he knew there was nothing to find out. His attitude proved it. And his threats. He wanted to intimidate me. Why?

Shivering from the cold, I weighed another possibility. Perhaps he had received a false denunciation about me. Even so, what should his attitude have been? To make inquiries. To discover the truth by asking precise questions. No. This investigation had been faked. Leaving the limits of any law out of consideration.

The truth, he had only to create it. His aim was to create a wholly different truth. How? Through the force of words. For words can say something or they can say its opposite. Join or separate. Express or conceal. Create or destroy. Words can deceive. Betray. Kill. Words can do anything.

At noon, the guard gives me a little hot liquid and a slice of bread. The heat from this make-believe soup, from this doubtful-tasting water, is pleasant. Friendly.

The minutes continue to creep by. Heavy, ice-cold. Now and then the phone rings. I hear steps. Muffled voices reach me through the door. The judas opens. The judas shuts. Prison life.

I am sleepy. I even manage to fall back asleep. Standing. Struck down by fatigue. Mainly, however, I make an effort to think logically. To dispel the fog that takes possession of my mind. To reflect. To understand.

Witness for the prosecution . . . witness for the prosecution . . .

These were frightening words, and I was mortally frightened by them. In plain language this meant accusing one or all of the other defendants. Accuse them how? Accuse them of what? Why accuse them?

But who were these accused? All I was sure of was three arrests. Had they arrested still others? How could I manage to convince this man that I knew nothing incriminating about anyone? For I was still giving him the benefit of the doubt.

What must I do? Or say? It is possible to provide evidence of a perpetrated act. But what evidence is left by an act never done, never even contemplated?

Only four-and-a-half years later, at the first session of the trial in court and hence after about 1,650 days, did I see that there were eleven of us defendants. Only then did I also learn what we were accused of. Of the eleven defendants, I knew only four. The six others were completely unknown to me. Five men and a woman.

One of the four was my best friend, Harry Brauner. We were married after leaving prison. I knew his life, all the way back to childhood. Almost twenty years. I knew he was as innocent as I was.

The second, H. Torosian, had become close to the Party toward the end of the war. Out of friendship for Lucreţiu Pătrăşcanu. To combat fascism. He had made many sacrifices. Risking his life.

The third, Herbert Zilber, a longtime member of the Party, had never prompted any great fondness in me, but I admired his intelligence. In my youth I had a mania for intelligence. The snobbery of intellectuals. I prized them above all. I have recovered from that since then.

Pătrăşcanu, the number-one defendant at the trial, was one of the most important members in the Party. Secretary of the Political Bureau. I had worked with his wife for four years. Both of them had been Party members since they were young. For a long time illegally. Both she and I had worked hard to launch a marionette theater. The first in our country. She was a set designer; I, a painter; my companion, a musician. He had helped us. The three of us were together most of the time. During the weekends and vacations, it was all four of us. I had admiration, respect, and great affection for this man. I saw the Party only through his eyes. I knew about the underground work he had done to get the country out of the war against the Soviet Union before it was too late. The important role he had played in the first months of the change of alliance and regime. I knew that since then he had had more and more ideological problems with other Party members. That he had been gradually shouldered aside. I knew that his intellectual lineage was doing him harm. Even more harmful was the trust he had inspired in a whole people. Or nearly. He was the sole person to be received anywhere in the country with unequivocal good will.

I knew something of his views. I guessed that he disagreed with certain of the Party's decisions. Overhasty. That he wanted a pluralist government for these early postwar years, which were made harder yet by the country's partial destruction and Hitler's pillaging, and appreciably worsened by the huge war reparations demanded by the Soviet Union. He did not approve of the excessive purges or the unbridled acts of revenge. It was a long way from this to believing him a traitor to his Party and his country, and I could not believe it. At the interrogator's request, however, I was supposed to accuse him. Me. Why? Simply because this man was asking me to?

But who was this man? What did he represent? Despite my lack of political experience, I could answer this question. We were no longer a free country. I knew on whose behalf he was acting.

This is now clear to everyone. We had been only marionettes in the classic government trials. Didn't every country in Eastern Europe have one of its own?

All the marionettes had been simultaneously manipulated with long, long strings, tugged from afar by very nimble hands using the most masterly techniques. The only imperfection was that the strings were plainly visible.

By the end of the investigation, I had reached some understanding of this technique. Moreover, before my arrest I had read a book, Arthur Koestler's *Darkness at Noon*. This was in fact one of the interrogator's complaints. I had committed the capital offense of reading a book. That book. This view has had its precedents in the course of history.

Once I was freed, I read Arthur London's *The Confession*. A book about a trial. About a technique. Only then did I finally grasp what was puzzling me. Everything had been the same. Down to the tiniest details. No new stroke of imagination. No attempt at modification. A lesson well learned and recited by heart. In fact, with enthusiasm. Why, even furiously.

And yet, although the technique was the same, the result only appeared to be so. This perfect organism tripped over a hurdle that it could not altogether overcome. The defendants.

Our trial differed from the other governmental trials in two important respects.

The first difference. Two of the eleven defendants were not Party members. Three of the others had joined the Party only after it had come to power. Thus, only six were long-standing Party members, clandestine ones. Thus, concerning the first five defendants, nothing could be alleged about their belief, their fidelity, their devotion to their earlier commitment to their party. These arguments could be used only against the other six. We hadn't struggled for the cause of the other six. We hadn't conspired in its coming to power. For us, the only argument was torture. Physical or mental.

The second difference. All the defendants in the trials analogous to ours had "agreed" to cooperate. They had all acknowledged "their crimes." They professed to be guilty. Asked to be punished. Nearly all were condemned. To death. Every one of them was innocent. Only one of us all, the man whom I had been asked to accuse, the number-one at our trial, did not knuckle under. He answered "no" to the wretched arguments. "No" to torture. At the trial, he branded the judges with infamy. Branded the number-three man with infamy, accused him of knowingly agreeing to lie. These were his only words, moreover, for he met all the judge's questions with stony silence.

None of the survivors of the corresponding trials in the other eastern countries speaks of the Pătrăşcanu trial. Yet they knew about it. They are the only ones who could know what heroism it took this man—made of flesh, like them—to find the strength to choose an honorable death over a desecrated life. He alone managed to put the flawless arrangement of the trials in check. Thanks to him, our country's trial was the only one that failed. Though the other defendants did not totally resist to the end, I must say in their defense that the investigation went on for five years. It took five years to break down our resistance. Even at the trial there were attempts to deny, which were brutally quashed by the presiding judge.

Pătrăşcanu was of course sentenced to death. His sentence had obviously been decided far in advance of the trial. At the trial a second defendant condemned to death tried in vain to declare his innocence. The others received either life sentences or long prison terms.

I hesitated for a long time before beginning to write all this down. I am not a writer. Why write? What good would it do? Others, far more adept than I, have done it already. I could say nothing more, nor say it better. *The Confession* has already been written. It says it all. About our trial too. From the standpoint of its essence.

As for me, I played only a minor role. A bit part. An extra. To insist on the reality of a putative conspiracy, it was absolutely necessary for the investigation to exhibit liaison agents between the number-one man and the Party's "enemies." There had been no conspiracy. No liaison. No agents. So these things had to be fabricated. To give body to the fictions. My husband and I appeared to be ideally suited for these roles. Enjoying an intimate friendship with the chief defendant and his wife. Also, having many friends abroad. Who, in addition, were artists, and therefore daydreamers, and therefore gullible fools. These were the needed traits of character. What "they" didn't know, however, was that artists reason more with the heart than the mind.

So why write about it? So that I, too, may bear witness. Human witness. To pass over in silence, as much as possible, the political element of my detention. It is the detention itself that I will address. In full possession of the facts. Of life in a cell from one day to the next. I lived through an experience that is unique, I think. A woman, alone, for many long years. Years made up of hours, minutes, seconds. I would like to tell of those seconds, those 3,600 seconds an hour, those 86,400 seconds a day, that slowly twist all over your body, slimy serpents coiling from your feet to your throat, relentlessly, pitilessly, from morning to evening and in the too-frequent nights of insomnia, continuing to wind round you without end and beyond remedy.

Because I wish to speak of human dignity, as well. To talk of all those women, later my companions at the penitentiary, who despite everything and everyone remained deeply human.

To speak also of hope. The hope that on some distant day humanity will conquer nature. Not by changing the course of the waters, the deserts, nor by conquering outer space, but by changing the nature of humanity. Of its heart and mind. Because my conviction is that nature is imperfect and unjust. What a waste to enable a species to perpetuate itself! And what murders. I have often asked myself how humans, "nature's most perfect creatures," happened to rebel against its laws. How they invented the ideas of goodness, justice, perfection. Religion supplies its answer. Ideas created in the image of God. Best not to speak, however, of divine goodness and justice.

For me, this seems more plausibly explained by the degeneration of the human brain. Degenerate or not, however, man has promulgated the concepts of justice and equality. If men are not equal by nature, let them be so at least under human laws. A doctrine was erected on these principles. A political party. This party's goal and justification was to correct nature. To place itself at the service of all men. To furnish them with justice, equality. What happened . . . It did succeed in making them a promise. Give us your labor, your well-being, your dreams, even your life. Give everything and one day the children of your children's children will be happy . . . perhaps . . .

Hope? Yes. The doctrine of equality and justice lingers on. In principle. There also exist, I wish to believe, men of good will. Not all has been said . . . yet.

Finally, to write in protest.

Against absolute power.

Against thought control.

Against arbitrary detention.

Against detention as a means of doing away with freedom of thought.

Against the absolute power of the interrogator and the interrogations.

Against detention as an instrument of punishment prior to sentencing.

Against torture.

Against total isolation.

To ask for men's justice for men.

To ask for men's pity for men.

I am still, forever, in the prison cell. This time, after nightfall, a mattress is shoved into the cell. A canvas sack, more or less stuffed with straw. The cell is so tiny that part of the mattress turns up against the wall and forms a pillow. At last I lie down. Curled up. A fetus. With no blanket. I'm very cold. Even so, I'm stunned by fatigue. With sleep comes the anguish of my first prison dream.

. . . I am wandering through a labyrinth of unfamiliar streets . . . desperately looking for a certain house . . . they have given me only a few hours' leave . . . I must hurry . . . soon I must go back . . . go back through the dark door . . . street after street, I get lost in this maze of streets . . . deserted streets, black streets . . . no passersby . . . no noise . . . A gloomy silence hanging over this lifeless city . . . it is time . . . I know . . . time for prison.

This dream was typical. A dream had by every prison inmate. With a few variants. Sometimes I happened to find the house. To go inside. To find my family. To kiss my mother. But in fear. The inevitability of parting. The powerlessness. That was my inexorable fate, even in dreams.

I wake up closed in by the cement walls. Paralyzed by the cold. Aching all over. With the obsessional idea of death. To die. I'd like to die. To escape? What a mockery. Reality holds me in its grip. A pincers. Breaking my bones. Crushing my brain. No way out. Apart from my will. My will, which is also disintegrating. For, the hardest part is keeping alive the willpower to will. Resisting the urge to give way. To give up. To give up even oneself. The urge to wish nothing more. To let oneself go. Adrift. To lose everything. To lose oneself. To sink into mental vacancy. The most difficult struggle. Against the most treacherous enemy. And the subtlest. Oneself.

This time, the cold comes to my aid. I stand up. The misery of this cold is stronger than anything. My entrails are cold. My chest is cold. I am racked by a coughing fit. Then I'm warm. Too warm. My body catches fire. I've got the chills. I regain consciousness. I am ill. I have a fever.

They must have realized this, for the judas opened several times in a row. There was whispering on the other side of the door. The key turned. A guard tells me to come out. To follow him. Yet the telephone hadn't rung. This couldn't be an interrogation. Besides, he motioned me to follow him not toward the stairs, but toward the cells. He opened a door. Nodded in the direction of the bed.

This was my second cell. A bed, a table, a chair, a wooden floor, a window with whitewashed panes, a heater, warmth. Finally a steaming cup of herbal tea.

Days 9, 10, 11, 12, 13 of detention—January 30, 1950

Five days in this cell. Lying on a bed. Being warm. Too warm. Submersed in an almost-enjoyable torpor. My eyes closed. Losing consciousness. Going outside time. No delirium. Utter mental exhaustion.

Occasional rushes of fever. Then, a voice made itself heard. A familiar voice but one I couldn't quite identify. This voice cried out a lament, a murmur that floated around my ears. Under my eyelids, coming out from a central point, a black line uncoiled in a spiral. This spiral revolved, widening as it turned. The black thread slowly uncoiled. The spiral unwound, grew wider and wider, calm and beautiful. Suddenly, the pure line of this perfect spiral snarled up. A tangle of lines. A lunatic black morass? The throbbing lament bore into my ears. Anxiety infiltrated. Dread.

I have only a hazy memory of those five days. The fever abated. I recall only that my period was due. I asked the guard for some cotton. To no avail. One morning I wake to a blood-soaked bed. I look with horror at the large red stains on the sheet. What should I do? How can I wash them out? How can I bathe? Where? With what? What should I say to the guard? This is all I recall. My anxiety and embarrassment. I will speak more about this serious problem for women in prison.

Day 14 of detention—January 31, 1950

First thing in the morning comes a summons to the interrogation room. At my refusal to accept the deal he's offered, the interrogator states he has full proof of my guilt. He picks up a notebook, opens it to a marked page, and shows me a passage of a few lines to read. It is a statement made by one of the defendants. Having to do with me as well. A certain meeting with Pătrăşcanu at which it seems my friend Harry and I had also been present. This was in fact partly true. Without taking part in it, we had vaguely known about this get-together.

Unfortunately for me, I'd made so little of it that I'd altogether forgotten it. Was this forgetfulness due to an unconscious defense mechanism? I couldn't say. But the fact is that it took me many long days and much distress to unearth it from memory. That day, however, after reading this excerpt, I protested vehemently. I stated that this was untrue. Entirely. That I knew nothing about it. That nothing could get me to say otherwise.

This time, the interrogator was within his rights. Whether or not it was of any importance, the fact was real. By denying it, I was putting a wrench in the works. He was forced to get me to confess. He sends me back to my cell. The cold awaits me. I spend the day searching for a reason for this untrue charge. Asking myself if it really was false. The handwriting was that of "number one." He couldn't have been lying. Slightly mistaken, of course. Four years had gone by, he'd written. How could I find out whether it had really happened? What could I do to remember?

I'm cold. I'm frightened. Too many unknowns. Too many dangers.

The notebook from which I'd read only a few lines was fairly thick. What else was in there?

The footsteps in the corridor die down. Vainly I wait for the mattress. The time must be around eleven at night. A door opens. I hear some halting steps go past my door. And those of the guard as well. The door to the toilet. A few moments of silence. Then the slow, unsteady gait again. The guard's voice. "Why haven't you drunk your tea? You should drink it." Saying this in a kindly tone. Then a low, somewhat quavery voice answering: "I'll drink it . . . I'll drink it. Later." I feel all my blood rushing to my heart. I press my ear to the door. To hear! To hear that voice again. But a door opens, then closes. The key turns. The guard goes off. I weep. I thought I was miserable? Unhappy? Desperate? I had used these grand words much too lightly. Only that voice bore the weight of despair. That voice, the unrelenting pain. That seventy-three-year-old voice. That voice that I had never heard meek and shaky. The voice of my father.

Why had they arrested him? What did they want from him? He lived in near-seclusion. Retired. With my mother and one of my two sisters. He knew hardly any of my friends. I didn't even live with my parents. True, to me their house was "home." The place where I had spent a portion of my youth. It was their house that I'd have dreams about. Not my own. I went there every day. I always had the midday meal there. The five of us were very close. This was known to everyone, so how could "they" not know it? He is here. Close by. In a cell. In prison, because of me. My door opens. I am taken to another office. There are three of them there. One of them does the talking. He asks me whether I will take full responsibility for any criminal offense that my father may have committed and that the investigation had just uncovered. If I sign a statement to this effect, he will be released immediately. They have me write out a statement. I wrote it out. Are they in earnest? Is this a trap?

Back in the cell, I keep an ear out for sounds in the corridor. I prick up my ears—nothing. I hear nothing.

Twelve years later, I learned that they had indeed let my father go home the next day.

Days 15, 16, 17 of detention—February 3, 1950

Two more days go by. Every time a guard opens my door, I plead with him to tell me if my father is still there. Under his breath, one of the two says that the old man has left. I am overjoyed. I accept the cold. I accept everything. Just let them leave my family in peace.

I am taken to the interrogator several more times. I continued to deny the charge. But, I was racking my brains. Everything appeared to be true. But I recalled nothing. Nothing. Not the least image emerged. I had to do something. On my thrice-daily trips to the toilet, I always walked past several cells. In the cell next to the toilet, I had heard a man cough. I thought I recognized Harry's voice. I had to do whatever I could to make sure. The guard always walked ahead of me. On the second trip, I held my breath, darted at the door, and peeked for an instant through the peephole. He was reclining on the bed reading. So they had given him a book. That was a good sign. So they hadn't punished him. He can surely tell me if this meeting really did take place. How can I communicate with him? All night long I wrench my mind to come up with an answer. Write to him. Throw a note into his cell through the opening over the door. Through which the cells get some air.

Write to him? On the first trip in the morning, I tear and hide the blank margin from an old newspaper that is used for toilet paper. But I don't have a pencil or ink. What can I write with? I can use a sliver of wood for a pen. With my fingernails I extract one from the board blocking the window of my cell. Thus, I will write with this splinter of wood and my blood. The easiest way to get this blood? Bite my hand. I chose a place on my left hand. Between the thumb and the index finger. There where, by making a tight fist, the flesh plumps up. I sink my teeth in it. My mouth takes in too much flesh. It hurts but my teeth don't break the skin. After several painful but doubtless too faint-hearted tries, my teeth refuse to bite. This is infuriating. I will not have this miserable flesh prove stronger than my will. Stronger than I am. I bite again. Viciously. Several times. I bite farther into the flesh. I start tearing the skin. Finally, a small bead of blood forms. Too small. I bite deeper and deeper. Blood. A drop. Another drop. I begin writing. Cautiously, because of the judas. I write down a word. Another bite. Another word. I clench my teeth around the cut to squeeze out a few more drops. I write only a few words. They must certainly have asked him the same question. He had surely given the answer. He will understand. Yes or no. This was roughly the sentence: If the meeting took place, cough three times when I knock on the wall. If not, then just once.

On touching the boards covering the window, I had felt some mortar deep in the wall. I scratch some out about the size of a pea. I roll up my paper over it. This maneuver takes me several hours. The time for the "program" approaches. That is the name given in our prisons for going to the toilet. The guard was already coming down the corridor, rapping on the doors and shouting: "Get ready for the program!"

I clasp my letter in the palm of my hand. I am tremendously scared. In prison I was always scared. Finally, it was my turn. On the heels of the guard, my eyes glancing for a second in the direction of Harry's cell, I tossed my paper straight through the opening. I didn't hear it land.

The night went badly. I was anxious about the next day. Tortured by the cold. But the night passed even so. Finally, the morning's "program." The door to the toilet closes behind me. I wait a few seconds before rapping on the common wall. Silence. Harry doesn't respond. He doesn't cough. He hadn't found my letter. Or didn't understand it. Or possibly he was not in his cell at that moment.

Days 18, 19 of detention—February 5, 1950

I move out of the cell. A third one. Smaller. But with a bed, a sheet, a blanket. I'm in luck. On one of the squares of newspaper in the toilets, that day, I find a fragment of poetry. For me, it's a treasure. The beginning of one of our greatest classics. I learn it by heart. Too quickly. Then, line after line, I endeavor to translate it into French.

At last I had an escape. The first. I still recall the first two lines of the translation:

> Beyond the mountains of copper I see it, so distant, so
> white
> And hear the sweet hushed language of great woods with
> silver leaves.

And for the first time I departed from my cell and strolled into the woods.

Day 20 of detention—February 6, 1950

The interrogator has me brought in. Asks me if I will finally agree to speak up. I reply that I cannot. I recall nothing. How can I speak to him about something I remember nothing of? In a hostile tone he announces that he will make me see the light by using more energetic means.

I spend several hours waiting. Wondering what is going to happen to me. Trying to forget this wait. Wishing to get back into my poem. But they come for me. The head guard and his assistant. The boss himself is still surly. His other, older coworker is still sitting by the telephone. As he passed by a few times, I thought I saw some encouragement in his eyes. They hustle me to the end of the corridor. They open a door. The room is fairly large. Bare. In the middle, a table. That's it. Only a table. The boss orders me to hike up the back of my skirt. To bend over so my chest touches the table. I don't understand. Glancing from one man to the other, I am petrified.

In a deep voice the boss explains. He had had an order to act firmly. At the first cry, at the slightest hint of resistance, the penalty will be doubled.

I raise my skirt. I bend over the table. I spread my hand and grip the edges of the table. I clench my teeth. I mustn't cry out. I concentrate on this thought. Don't cry out. Don't even moan. Not because of his threat. No. For my sake. Against them.

At the first swat, my body tenses up. Constricts. The pain stings. Second swat. Third swat. My body writhes. Cry out! I must cry out! No. Groan. No. Fourth, fifth blow. I hear them snapping on my buttocks. It stings. It cuts. Brutes! Brutes! Scream. I must howl like an animal. Howl! No. Howl!!! No. They whack me ten times.

I am lying on the bed. On my stomach. I touch my skin. On the places where the cracks fell. I want to know if they left perceptible marks. I can feel slight swellings. It hurts. Really hurts. Bad compared to the normal state. Compared to the time before the blows when I had little sense of having buttocks. But this didn't really hurt compared to the pain I'd felt during the whipping. Now it was bearable. I thought I was tough. I thought I had conquered through the experience my fear of being whipped. On my skin I learned that they could do worse.

Days 21, 22, 23, 24 of detention—February 10, 1950

It was strange, this new cell. Low-ceilinged. One of the walls bow-shaped. The bed scarcely fit. Virtually no sounds reached it. Except, several times a day, the powerful hum of a ventilation unit close by at the end of the corridor. For two days they let me be. The guard took me on the three "programs." I washed my hands and face at the faucet in the corridor. Nothing was provided for my other hygienic needs.

The pain subsided. I passed the time working on the translation of the poem. The translation was difficult for me. For the first time, the problem of verbal rhythm.

In the morning I was given some herbal tea. At noon, a meat dish. Of poor quality, but passable. A slice of bread. In the evening, noodles or polenta. On the third day, they had me change cells once again. I went back to my original one. It was there that I heard the voice of my elder sister. She who lived with my parents. I couldn't tell what she was saying, but her voice was calm. I set about coughing very hard. A brief silence . . . then she, too, coughed. Long, long afterward she told me that they had held her there for a whole month. She was interrogated several times, then released. She hadn't had any contacts with the defendants. There was absolutely no credibility in their implicating her. No thread connecting her with them. On being released, however, she had lost her post as an instructor in social work. For many months she was without work or the means of subsistence.

My father's voice had been painful for me. Heartrending. Despite my anguish at learning she was there, my sister's voice soothed me like a balm. Because her case was of so little interest, she was not treated harshly. The guards chatted with her. Moreover, the guards had to be reliable and well-trained agents. At night I heard them having long exchanges with some of the detainees.

My sister had been given the "privilege" of sweeping the hallways. Consequently I heard her more than once softly humming just in front of my door. She had never sung at home, as she was tone deaf. I was touched at hearing her sour notes and the noise of the broom she slammed up against my door. A guard caught on to her game, called her names and roughly hustled her back to her cell.

Days 25, 26, 27, 28, 29, 30, 31, 32, 33, 34, 35, 36, 37, 38, 39, 40, 41, 42, 43, 44 of detention—March 1, 1950

Twenty days. Identical. Hard to single out. Prolonged, sadistic torture. With a few crescendos. Twenty days of compulsory and nearly continuous walking. In their lingo, it was the "drill ring." Only someone who has been in the countryside and seen an emaciated nag at the end of a ten-foot tether endlessly circling its stake would be able to comprehend.

On the twenty-third day, a young interrogator entered my cell. Amiably, he advised me to get smart. To accept the reality of that get-together. Then tell everything I might know about it. Everyone else had done this. His boss had demanded a new punishment for me. His boss couldn't believe in a memory lapse. His boss was certain that everything ever known, seen, and forgotten remains hidden away in the folds of memory and is retrievable through willpower. For my own good he, personally, asked me to concentrate on this problem with all my strength. I then asked him to help me out of this impasse. That he give me some precise details. A sign. Something to jog my memory.

After he leaves, the head guard comes in. Right away, this is a bad sign. He takes me to the shower room and closes the door behind the two of us. He's wearing civilian clothes. No strap. So I won't be whipped.

He takes a chair, sits down, and tells me to walk. In front of him. From one end of the room to the other. To walk continuously. Without stopping. I will be under constant surveillance. Every pause I make will mean additional punishment. He goes out. Locks the door. His eye is glued to the judas. So I walk. He keeps his eye on me for several minutes, then I hear him stride off. He leaves the judas open.

This prison consisted of a long corridor that started at the bottom of the stairs. There were the toilet, the washroom, then four cells. Two on each side. The corridor made a turn. In this angle, the small cell. The corridor continued along to the little low-ceilinged cell. Before this last cell, to the right, the room with the table. To the left, the guards' room. I had spotted another door at the end of the cloakroom. I had understood that it was a luxury cell. In the middle of the corridor there opened a second, shorter hallway. Four cells. At the far end, the shower room. At the junction of these two hallways, the telephone table and the head guard's chair. From there he could keep an eye on his entire hell.

So I began walking. In this cement-floored room with damp sooty walls. Laundry was piled up in a large tub. In the darkest corner, a heap of old iron cots, broken chairs, boards. The prison's scrap. On the other side, a bed with a straw mattress, an ironing board, two chairs. Along a wall, some showers.

I walked for a while before feeling tired. First, my feet began to ache. Then my back. I was afraid to stop, however, because from time to time the judas went dark. After two or three hours, fatigue made me slacken my pace.

Abruptly the door opens. The boss enters. He sits on a chair. Watches me. After five minutes, he has me halt. He seems displeased. He tells me that I am not doing my about-face properly. He'll teach me how. Military-style. In front of me he takes a few steps, then turns in two strides. Repeats the movement several times, counting: one, two, one, two. . . . Finally he tells me to go on walking, turning in just that way.

I resume walking. Eight steps, then the attempt at his military turn. Two steps instead of three. When I manage to do this, he finally leaves. But not for long. He's had an idea. He wants me to make believe I'm going up a hillside. Wearing a backpack. To be halfway up the mountain. So I must be bent from the weight of this imaginary pack. Flex my knees sharply. Keep my head down. Look at the ground.

I grow more and more tired. This way of walking is exhausting. All this is ridiculous. Pitiful. I can't take any more of it. I tell him so. He then orders me to run. I am out of breath. My heart beats faster and faster. Faster, faster, it begins beating in my throat. I can't get enough air. I am on the verge of suffocation. He constantly yells: "Faster, faster!" This man must be out of his mind. I've fallen into the clutches of a lunatic.

But the door swings open. Led by a guard, a man comes in. A civilian. Slender. Well-dressed. Distinguished-looking. I realize he's the prison doctor. He sees me running. Signals me to stop. He takes the boss man out. Gradually I recover my breath. But this race to the death has worn me out. I'd already done nearly five hours' walking, for the doors are now opening one after another. Lunch is being distributed. My feet hurt badly. My back, my head, my insides. My whole body hurts.

A guard comes in. He says I have the right to two hours' rest. I can even sleep. He has me enter a waiting cell. It is absolutely empty. A wooden floor. It is fairly warm there. I sat on the floor. I took off my shoes. My stockings. Stretched out my legs. I receive my rations. I get only a few mouthfuls down. I don't have the strength to chew. The meat is too tough. Life is too tough. I give up. I lie down on the floor. The minutes go by. I sense them going by. Quickly. Much too quickly. I'm frightened. I'm sleepy. I can't fall asleep.

I was much too tired. Too many questions got stuck in my mind. What did they want from me? Why had I fallen into this pit of crazies? How long would this nightmare last? How long would I have the strength to bear it?

I was just nodding off when the guard came to fetch me. I stood up like a chump. I went back to the wash house. I resumed walking.

I went back and forth in front of the open judas. I cast a quick glance through it. I saw the head guard. He was stationed at his post. Seated on his chair. His head was turned away from me. Fortunately. Then I realized that without going to any trouble, he could keep an eye on me through the open judas merely by turning his head. Each time I crossed the room, he saw this little too-bright hole go dim. For my part, I saw it black out where an eye was on the lookout. What could I do to spy on them myself? Without the judas giving me away? From a distance, I couldn't make out anything through the tiny opening. I had to glue my eye to it. That way wouldn't work at all. Find something else.

I am congenitally nearsighted. I've worn glasses since the age of ten, and they had been taken away. Without glasses, my field of vision was limited. At four or five yards, the outlines of things became indistinct. A face was blurry. Without glasses I was somewhat unsure of myself. Lost. Apprehensive. Threatened. Defenseless. I had to see through the door at any cost. How could I "see through this door"?

Walking, turning, still walking, I turned this problem over and over in my mind. Then I had an idea. Count the number of steps I made from one end of the room to the other. The number of steps I took between two passes by the judas. From a distance the only surveillance possible was my body blocking the little opening. As long as he remained seated on the chair, he could monitor only my passing by the door. My regular transit. He would notice any pause. Any unanticipated halt. I was, however, going to anticipate my pauses. So I had to calculate the precise length of my rhythmic pauses. Take only the two steps needed for him to observe my passing by that darkened judas.

Two steps right, two steps left, pause, and so on and so on. Between the two pauses, count up to eight. So, two steps, then I count: one, two, three, four, five, six, seven, eight, another two steps in the opposite direction and one, two, three, four, five, six, seven, eight and so on and so on.

Those eight seconds' rest were a great help. Not walking.

Not making an effort to move my legs. Catching my breath. Fooling them. This trick had a weakness, however. A dangerous one, even. From time to time the head guard or one of his men came by to look in on me. I couldn't be sure of hearing their steps. An eye could suddenly be stuck to the judas just as I was resting. I had to prick up my ears. To manage, despite everything, to see through that door.

My stubborn search for a solution was helpful in two ways. Focused on this problem, I was less sensitive to the fatigue, to the pain. I resumed the regular walking, but occasionally trusted my luck and risked taking a brief pause for rest, the resumed walking. Waiting for sundown. Waiting for the night. Sleep.

In the middle of the room a cover for the sewer outlet had been set down. Since the cover fit loosely, the sewer occasionally gave off a sickening putrid odor. I became suddenly aware of a stench that I had only vaguely apprehended earlier. It then grew unbearable.

Still walking, I try to focus my thoughts on the fatal get-together. To call it up from memory. To conjure up from the void a word, a single word, an image, the least sign that would lead me to this unknown. To have done with it. To bring this senseless hiking to an end. I had little success. I was prevented by the unflagging attention needed to hear the guard's potential steps, and the concern to count regularly up to eight.

Again, the head guard enters. Informs me of the doctor's decision. They may continue to apply their scientific treatment to cure my forgetfulness. It seems that my health could withstand it. He had only forbidden them to make me run.

I can't bear my shoes a second longer. I slip them off. The cement is cold. At first, this cold is salutary. But very soon my feet are freezing. I put my shoes back on. With some difficulty. My feet have swollen. The walking becomes increasingly painful.

. . . I've nearly reached the end of a steep path. A very long path. A few steps, only a few more steps and "home" would rise up before me. I must walk, keep on walking. I must get home. A few steps, a few more steps . . .

And I go on walking. Dragging along, half-asleep, my eyes all but closed to the dim light of the cramped space, my body, my despair, my obsession.

Six more hours passed in this way. With the help of luck and chance. They always found me walking when they stopped by to check. Most often I could hear them coming. Despite their precautions. But that couldn't last forever. At the end of these six hours they once again let me return to the resting cell. Supper was brought in. I stretched out on the bare wooden floor. I had a whole night before me . . .

Turning over and over on the floor, I managed to find a position that I could remain in. I dropped off. The entry of the guard startled me awake. It seemed as if I had just dozed off. I went back to the laundry. There was a faucet there. The guard let me wash my hands and face. But . . . be careful! He had me under surveillance.

Bit by bit, the silence weighing down on the prison became palpably oppressive. Yet it was time for the wake-up. This total silence hung over me like a threat. I would no longer risk pausing too often. The danger was there. My whole body sensed it. What was the explanation for this silence? Now and then I looked up at a small window set high in one of the walls of this cellar. It was as black as the silence. As black as my heart. As black as my fear. My anxiety was becoming more pronounced. What was the explanation for this silence? Had everyone left? Were they all dead? But the guard at the judas was very much alive. I waited for the first glimmer of early light in the window. Intently. So I reckoned the approximate time from my to-and-fros. Giving each step a second, I took twenty seconds to make a round trip. Sixty seconds, that is to say a minute, for three full trips. In the end, 180 trips an hour.

I made these 180 treks with a few pauses for rest, and the silence still reigned. The window was black as ever. Daylight was still far off and I finally understood that I had been allowed only two hours' sleep. No more than two hours.

Thus they coerced me into doing three periods of walking a day. Twenty-four hours divided by three. Each of these eight-hour segments involved six hours of walking and two for rest. I had begun at eight in the morning. First rest from two to four in the afternoon. Second period from four in the afternoon to ten at night. Rest for two hours. Midnight. He had woken me up at midnight. At night. In the silence, in this concentration-camp space, nothing but me. Me and the guard.

I was sleepy. A need for sleep. A vital need for sleep. Passing by the faucet, which I had left turned on slightly, I refreshed my eyes with a few drops of water that I'd catch as I walked.

I walked, asking myself: why? Why not stop? Why not dare to stretch out on the bed? Why not fall asleep?

Drunk with sleep, stumbling with each step, I finally sat on the edge of the bed. Perhaps I forgot to count to eight, perhaps I passed out . . .

The guard bursts into the room, club in hand. He rushes over to me—I'm already on my feet—and he begins hammering with his club on my ankles and calves, shouting: "Walk, you piece of shit, or I'll break your legs! Walk, unless you want to go home as an official notification!"

Under these brutish blows, my muscles tense up, my whole body rebels. As though jerked by an electrical discharge, my feet hurriedly resume the pace.

It was nighttime. He has nothing to do. Perhaps he too is sleepy. He has found a way to take his mind off sleep. Seated on a chair, his stick in his hand, he intently watches me make the transit, laughing at the jumps I make to evade him. He pounds hard. On my anklebones, on my calves, but no higher than my knees. I cannot hold back my tears. They run down my face. Mingle with the mucus streaming from my nostrils.

This guard was young. He couldn't be over twenty. But he was short. He was ugly. They had made him a jailer. Given him a club. And the right to use it. Good wages. A privileged situation. All this didn't fit him very well.

He finally began yawning. He stretched out on the bed, still watching me. But at last he closed his eyes. The club slipped to the floor. He began snoring. I went to the faucet. I drank a little water. I washed my face. The pain was bearable. Close enough to him to be able to make sure that his eyes were closed, I remained motionless for some time. Struggling against the fascination of the club and his head . . .

Several days go by. All alike. Each day the doctor gives me an injection. To strengthen me? To weaken me? I shall never know. He gives me a piece of sugar before injecting me.

I'm afraid of their threats. I'm afraid to stop. I'm afraid. What new punishment will they invent to punish some possible resistance? Soon . . .

It is after eight in the morning. I have just begun the walking period. A guard comes in. He looks furious. He swears at me. He is going to be punished because of me, because of his lack of vigilance. I too will be punished. Just wait.

Ten minutes later, three guards come in followed by the boss. Tell me to take off my shoes. Get on my knees on the bed. Not along the bed. Crosswise. My feet hanging over the side. My face to the wall. I take off my shoes. I kneel. I can't see them. My heart is pounding. From fear. Behind me they are hatching a plan. Against me. They're going to do something to me. What are they going to do?

I hear some cloth crumple. A metallic sound. The boss's voice. Don't cry out. He has told me not to cry out. Are they going to beat me again? I don't understand. I hear some noises. Cutting the air. One snap, two, three. Pain. Pain.

One of the guards is whipping me. The soles of my feet. With all his might. With his leather belt. His heavy leather belt. With its heavy metal buckle. With his belt be whips the soles of my feet. Shocks of pain. Waves of pain. My body writhes. The other two guards grip my shoulders. One on the right. The other, the left. They hold me with all their strength. It's over.

They have me sit on the bed. I can now see them. All four of them. See one of them rebuckling his belt. With the metal buckle. See his sweaty face. Red. His drunken face. Hear his rapid breathing. The guards leave. The boss speaks:

I must obey. He had ordered me to walk without stopping. I had stopped. He had warned me that any pause would be punished. I was punished. They are stronger than I. They know everything. They can do anything. I must resume walking. How long this walk will last will depend on me. They do not know the word pity. I should decide once and for all to confess everything. So as to end the agony. To remain peacefully in a cell. Lying on a bed. Like the others. At last, I resume walking. "Like the others?" The little cell was now occupied by Harry.

I got up. I resumed walking. Without even trying to put on my shoes. I was in too much pain. The soles of my feet were too swollen. The blows had caused me searing pains. Now the pain stretched out in time. I was in pain all the time. I was in pain every second. How can I describe the pain? The soles of my feet developed large blisters filled with water. Like those left by a burn. But I still had to walk on them. I tried walking on my heels. To walk on the sides of my feet. Nothing worked. I was in pain.

The doctor came in for the injection. I wanted to speak to him. To protest. Tell him I couldn't go on this way. The guard made me keep silent. When the rest period came, I was not even given the room with the wooden floor. I was handed a bucket, two bandages, and an anti-inflammatory solution. I filled the bucket with water. I sat on the chair with my feet in the water, the mess tin on my knees. The coolness of the water.

I sat down on the floor. I rolled the two wet compresses around my feet. I slowly stretched out on the cement. The pain gradually lessened. I wasn't too cold. I wasn't hungry. I wasn't in as much pain. I went to sleep.

I began the new period with a single idea in mind. To see through the door. I took two steps in front of the judas, then, instead of staying in place for eight seconds, I poked about in the junk piled up in the corner of the room. I found a short length of iron wire. About four inches long. Slender but sturdy. Then I inspected the door. It was a standard sort of door. A wide wooden frame. Two long vertical boards, two short horizontal ones. The two vertical boards were connected by a third horizontal board about three feet from the floor. These five boards formed the frame for two thinner wooden slabs. The lower slab, which may have been too dry, did not fit properly into the crack of the frame on the right-hand side. This was where I could insert the iron wire. This operation took a long time, for I couldn't forget to keep on counting, then get up and go by the judas. After several tries, the wire broke through to the other side.

I don't know how I managed to overcome my fear all this while. For I had no way of knowing what the guard was doing. My eyes did no good. I could use them only in the corridors, the offices, and for a quick inspection when the guard opened the door. But prisoners are a species that has yet to be studied. Their adaptation to the environment in which they are compelled to live is as rapid as it is surprising. Their five senses change their function. Sight can no longer see. It is replaced by hearing and smell. Taste quickly atrophies because of hunger.

My ears had instinctively adapted to their new role. I relied only on their extreme attentiveness to "see" the guard sitting on his chair. See him turn the pages of a book, read the newspaper. See him change position or push back his chair. See him finally walk stealthily over to me. He couldn't do this without making a minimal amount of noise. In the total silence hanging over the hallways at this early-morning hour, I had no trouble sensing him. But that certainty did not suffice to neutralize my fear. The danger was always at hand. But the despair was permanent. I had to go on. Little by little, pushing down on the wire, I managed to create a very narrow crack about an inch long between the board and the slab. This enabled me to keep an eye on the corridor.

I continued to take the two steps. I got on my knees and looked through the crack. If the guard was there, I went back to doing my "drill ring." But if he wasn't, I did not get up but stayed there, motionless until he came back. It is true that my knees hurt. That the muscles in my back and shoulders ached. But these were easier to endure than the exhausting walk.

This system seemed to be helpful. It helped me bear for long days what I could normally have stood for only a short while. I was not prepared for prison life. I was not prepared for physical suffering. I managed. Badly. But I did my best. I didn't have time to think. Today, I realize that what I did was the opposite of what I should have done. After being beaten, I should have refused to walk. Stretched out on the bed and stopped agreeing to obey them. Overcome my fear not by bits but totally. Not to be a coward at the prospect of suffering. They would have beaten me again. Twice. Three times. What more could they do? Kill me? No. They needed me at the trial. Now I know that one should always protest. But I know this only because of the experience of living through twelve years of detention and penitentiary.

To repeat day after day, hour after hour, that prison life is impossible. Perhaps even tiresome for the reader. Ten pages for twenty days of torture may already be too much. Twelve years later, I was free. I saw all kinds of people. These people knew I had just been freed from prison. Not a single one had the patience or courage to listen to me for any length of time. They all used the same gimmick for interrupting me. Their pity. Their hypocritical pity. To keep me quiet, they each in turn claimed that these memories were bad for me. "You must forget" was one of their typical statements. Nobody wished to shoulder the least of my memories. It might disturb the important process of their digestion.

Their second typical statement was of an undisguised egocentrism. "You were on one side of the bars, we on the other, so we were all in prison." To this, no retort is possible.

Nevertheless, I would like to tell it all. But I know that this mass of words says almost nothing. Nothing but some piercing moments from those days and nights in a cell. Between those moments of crisis came all the periods of walking. I experienced them all. In twenty days, I went through sixty of them. Sixty times six hours of walking. Sixty times two hours of rest. This says almost nothing. In this world of numbers, perhaps the figures will be more suggestive.

So I shall translate these twenty days of the "drill ring" into numbers. If I assume that one step took a second and two steps covered just over a yard, walking back and forth for twenty seconds covered thirty-three feet. That made ninety-nine feet a minute and 5,940 feet or just over a mile an hour. So my reckoning is based on a very low hourly speed. Three periods every twenty-four hours make over nineteen miles and sixty periods in twenty days equal 389 miles.

So in twenty days I was obliged to do sixty periods of walking equal to 390 miles and I was granted sixty pauses for rest, that is, 120 hours to eat, wash, go to the "program," and sleep. If I count thirty minutes for the first three activities, thirty hours in twenty days, this reckoning would leave ninety hours of sleep.

Ninety hours if sleep depended only on my eyelids being closed. If my body didn't take too long to find a less painful position on the cement floor or the wooden planks.

It is true that, thanks to my tricks, I actually walked fewer hours and did fewer miles than that. But this trick was a mere palliative. It wasn't a rest but merely a lesser evil. Remaining motionless, standing, on swollen legs, was not restful. Remaining on my knees on granular and cold cement was not restful. Endlessly counting attentively to eight was not restful.

In the days that followed, the guard used the club twice more. Then, something strange happened that hardly fit in with the guard's club.

It was about seven in the evening. A guard came in. Over his arm he carried a coat of long-haired golden lamb. My coat. He ordered me to put on my shoes and coat. Two men in civilian clothes were waiting for me in the corridor. Going through several other corridors, all three of us emerge into the prison courtyard. They have me get into a car. One of the two takes the wheel. The other sits in back next to me. We drive quickly through the suburban streets. I don't recognize them. They are poorly lit by a few streetlights. Without my glasses, I only confusedly make out the black mass of modest houses along some walls. Suddenly we reach the center of the city. A boulevard. A square. Many people. Free. Hurrying to their homes. Their warmth. Their rest. I see them pass by. I can't make out any faces. I don't know the purpose of this outing. I don't even want to think about it. My eyes drink in the images. Life. All around me. But here we are already on the other side of town. On a broad avenue lined with leafless trees. We go past the Arch of Triumph. A bit farther on, the car stops. They tell me to get out and we go into the park, the two men flanking me. It is cold. It is white. Everything is blanketed with snow. I am upset. I tell myself they mean to drown me. This doesn't scare me. I would even be happy to get everything over with. One of them tells me that I am permitted to take a walk all by myself. The only thing forbidden is to approach some passerby and speak to him. The park is, however completely deserted. I walk, slowly. Each step hurts. But there is the damp earth, the wind, even the stars. The men are walking some distance behind me. I can no longer hear their voices. I can believe I am truly alone. The lake has gone off to the right. Now, I wait for the bullet. I hope to die instantly. They will say I tried to escape.

There was no gunshot. After ten minutes the car took off again. For the prison. At the time all this seemed perfectly absurd. Later, their purpose became clear. They wished to present me with the temptations of freedom.

Days 45, 46, 47, 48, 49, 50, 51, 52, 53, 54, 55, 56, 57, 58, 59, 60, 61, 62, 63, 64, 65, 66, 67, 68, 69, 70, 71, 72, 73, 74, 75, 76, 77, 78, 79, 80, 81 of detention— April 7, 1950

I spent over a month more in that prison. With a few highs and a few lows. With the help of the young interrogator, I could finally sign a statement concerning the unfortunate meeting that in no case was worth such a to-do. I could finally rest in a cell. With a bed. Sleep. Not long. The interrogator, like all the others who succeeded him, pretended not to believe in the sincerity of this forgetfulness. He made the issue a weapon against me. He said that my claim to have forgotten was a lie. I was lying to and against everyone. Doggedly. Slowed down their work plan. Knowingly. So every time my answers went against his wishes, he accused me of lying. My arguments were worthless. Nevertheless, it would have been stupid of me not to confirm a statement by the main defendant.

This supposed lie would have done no good. To anyone. Least of all me. I finally understood that his attitude was deliberate. Very subtle. Perverse. Since I had come to recognize as true what I had said was false, owing to those days of torture, he insidiously urged me to accept straight off any accusation made against me and the others. To avoid new tortures.

Thus, this interrogation had another purpose. To put together the various pieces of a nonexistent plot. Following a scenario in which, as I later learned, the number-three man, Herbert Zilber, had collaborated. To make this plot credible through an accumulation of perjured testimonies. To muddle them up. To give them an illusory reality. By successive confessions extracted from the defendants themselves. From each defendant against the others.

The interrogator asked me still other questions. For a second time I was subjected to the "drill ring." Once again, the strap was used.

Day 82 of detention—April 8, 1950

I was in the midst of walking. The morning session. A guard brought me my coat. He tells me to wait to be fetched. I will be taken to a "real prison." While waiting I could rest. Even sit down on a chair.

They come. Have me go out. I'm in a courtyard. On a fine April day, warm and sunny. The light dazzles me. Hurts my eyes. I am told to get into a car. An officer takes a seat next to me. Another officer next to the driver. I am ordered to hunch down in the car. On the floor. They cover me with the fur coat. It's warm. I can't breathe under the coat. Since they are so afraid that I will be seen, our arrest must still be a secret. The car drives for some time. Stops. The coat is pulled off. I emerge from the car into a courtyard surrounded by walls. I don't have time to get a good look, for a guard hands me a pair of glasses. Special glasses. Prison glasses. Glasses that prevent you from seeing. I can see nothing. I feel the elastic band of the glasses around my head. A hand suddenly grips my arm. Pushes me. Pulls me. I stagger up two steps. I am yanked to the left, to the right, then down what is probably a long corridor. The sound of a key turning. I am shoved forward. My glasses are taken off. A cell. The door closes behind me. The key turns.

2 | Second Prison

Days 83, 84, 85, 86, 87, 88, 89, 90, 91, 92, 93, 94, 95, 96, 97, 98, 99, 100, 101, 102, 103, 104, 105, 106, 107, 108, 109, 110, 111 of detention—May 6, 1990

I couldn't see the prison. They always made me go through the corridors wearing opaque black-lensed glasses. A guard gripped my arm, nudging me right or left. Toward the offices, toward the cell.

The cell was about forty square feet. Filthy walls covered with graffiti. Some half erased, others still legible. Sometimes moving words. Attempts at a calendar. An iron cot, a straw mattress, a clean sheet, a coarse homespun blanket. A table, a chair. No window, a dim bulb diffusing a yellowish light through the room day and night. This light, combined with the pale reflection of the daylight coming through a square aperture above the door, gave me a vague nausea.

The surveillance was permanent and complete. For the whole year I spent there, for all those four hundred days and four hundred nights, the iron flap of the peephole in the door silently slid to the right. Every two minutes, an eye filled the round hole. The eye looked at me. Every two minutes. Then the shutter abruptly slid back with a metallic click. Every two minutes. Continually. For four hundred days and four hundred nights. For 576,000 minutes

I was subjected to this assault and this clicking about 288,000 times.

The regulations affixed to the wall were peremptory.

It was forbidden, under threat of punishment, to remain in bed after five o'clock in the morning.

It was forbidden, under threat of punishment, not to be in bed after ten o'clock at night.

It was forbidden to sit on the bed between five in the morning and ten at night.

In bed, it was forbidden to have one's hands underneath the blanket.

If, while sleeping, I was bothered by the cold and covered my arms and hands, a rap on the door woke me up with a start.

It was forbidden to sleep during the day.

It was forbidden to cry.

It was forbidden to shout.

It was forbidden to laugh.

It was forbidden to sing. On threat of punishment.

It was not forbidden to sit on the chair.

It was not forbidden to stand. It was not forbidden to walk in the cell.

I had lost a great deal of weight. I was tired. My feet hurt. Because I was unable to remain stretched out in bed, the chair produced sores in a few days. Painful sores. When they hurt too much, I was obliged to stand up and walk around in the cell. I took four steps up to the wall, made a U-turn, four steps to the door, U-turn, the peephole would open, four steps to the wall, the peephole would close, U-turn, door-wall, door-wall, four steps, four steps, peephole, door-wall, wall, wall.

The interrogation resumed with another interrogator. Young, handsome, self-important, cruel. His was a hard job. Without explicitly asking me to lie, he had to get me to state that I had been a spy. To do this, he skillfully supplied me with information. It concerned actions supposedly committed by me and denounced by the other defendants. All this was false. I grasped his tactics. His strategy. Pushed over the edge by threats, by punishment, by fear and suffering, I was to accuse myself. By taking in his information, I was to build the scaffold of a credible guilt. A fierce, unevenly matched struggle between the two of us.

At the time, the interrogator was the absolute master of the person accused. To achieve his collaboration, to force him to "re-call" or forget, make up, to lie, to frighten him or give him hope, finally to punish him, the interrogator could order whatever changes he pleased in the regimen. First of all in diet, of course. For the better, for the worse, or to the limit of survival. My first punishment was hunger. This punishment went on for four hundred days. I was hungry for four hundred days. A nagging hunger. Degrading. Bestial. A hunger that twisted my stomach. Piercing my belly with cramps. Flooding my face with tears.

I was given three cups of water a day. In the morning, the first cup was the only thing for breakfast. At midday, the second cup came with the single dish for lunch. On an enameled iron plate, two or three mouthfuls of meat surrounded by a little questionable liquid. Sometimes, the meat was replaced by some quarters of potatoes, seven or eight prunes, or three spoonfuls of noodles or polenta. I was also given a small slice of dark bread, wet and indigestible. At six o'clock, the same meal and a third cup of water. Between the evening meal and the next midday meal, nothing. Eighteen hours of starvation. It was forbidden to keep even a crust of bread to stave off one's hunger during these hours. Aromas of a roast of meat, cheese, and coffee wafted through the door. Exacerbating the hunger. For there were "rich" diets for those who had managed to satisfy their interrogators.

I was tormented by hunger day and night. Only in dreams did I get some feeling of satiety. After the dream of going home, the dream of food is the second kind of dream of the prison cell. Mainly I dreamed of eating cakes. The sugar of which I was totally deprived and my mouth kept the memory of it on awakening.

In the morning I barely moistened my lips in the first cup of water. I sacrificed my thirst to an even more pressing, more imperative need. To create the illusion of cleanliness. By pouring out this water drop by drop, I moistened a bit of rag. Each week I received a little piece of laundry soap. With the wet rag moistened with the black, evil-smelling soap, I rubbed the whole of my body as best as I could. Hiding myself in the blind spot of the cell, to the left of the door.

The wait for the interrogation session evoked a permanent fear. The guards walk with furtive steps. The steps of a spy. But the steps of those who fetch you for the interrogation make noise. I hear them resonating from a distance. The sound approaches.

Holding my breath, I listen for the sound of each step. I count them. The steps come closer and closer. Fear grips my throat. My heart stops. Ever closer. I am bathed in sweat.

Sometimes, the steps halt in front of one of the cells ahead of mine. Other times they continue to approach. My cell is the next to last along the corridor. One more step, yet another, closer, ever closer. I am just a mass of tense flesh. Of flesh oozing fear. They arrive. They are in front of my door. They go past my door. They go off. The corridor makes two turns, for there is a second row of cells after this one. My corridor leads to the courtyard, the other to the street. My body releases. Comes apart at the joints. My neck droops. My shoulders slump. I feel my arms fall to the floor. My sweat turns cold. My heart goes back to beating normally. Slowly everything goes back into place. Slowly I re-create myself. Not for long. The prison is packed. No leisure. Quite the contrary. Industriousness, much industriousness. And everything begins all over again.

It was the sour odor of these accumulated layers of sweat that I wanted to clean off with this now-gray rag. The sour odor of my sweat. The disgusting odor of my fear.

Sometimes, however, the footsteps don't go past my cell. The intervals between two interrogations are irregular. A few hours, a few days, weeks, months. The time of day? Never the same. Morning, evening, night. The key goes into the lock. The key turns. Turns in my bowels. The latch in the door goes down. The door opens. A hand presents me with the glasses. I put them on. I stretch the elastic around my head. I can't see anything. The hand grabs my arm. Hauls me out of the cell. Away from my shelter. Away from my safety. To the offices. To the interrogator. To terror.

An interrogation session could last five minutes or it could last an hour, or much more. I managed to conceal my fear. I could make my face a mask. Control my voice. I could even make my eyes vacant. But I couldn't keep the sweat from oozing from my armpits. I couldn't keep it from making rivulets that ran down my arms. In the crook of my elbow. Nor the palms of my hands from collecting the sweat from my armpits. And with its nauseating odor.

Only once a week could I take a shower. Quickly. Just enough time to get wet. To soap up. Fast. To have time to rinse, for suddenly the water was shut off. During this time the door was left ajar. A guard stood there. Always. I pretended not to see him. Still, certain gestures were hard to make in front of this voyeur. When I didn't have time to rinse away the remaining soap from my body, I wiped it off with one of the wet sheets lying on the floor. I was not the first to use it.

Every morning, after wake-up call, I was taken to the toilet. I suffered from constipation. Because of the lack of food. The food ingested was utterly insufficient. My digestive system held on to it as long as possible. Squeezing it. Evacuating only the completely indigestible bits. The evacuation of these nuggets, small hard black rocks, was slow and difficult. It sometimes happened that I was unable to do so for ten days in a row. Moreover, I didn't even have time for it. After a few seconds, the guard urged me, shouting, to leave.

The anteroom of the toilet had a small sink for washing up. Still in a rush, I washed my hands and face, but didn't always manage to rinse out my rag. A sackcloth towel hung from a nail. A single towel for the whole prison. Over fifty cells.

Soon I had pimples filled with pus on my forehead. Then all over my face. I couldn't see them. There wasn't a single mirror in the prison. But I could scratch them. My fingers always came back to them. I couldn't keep from touching them. They spread to my shoulders. Then my arms became covered with them. The interrogator used them as an occasion for obscene sarcasm.

The pimples made me even more depressed. I couldn't stop squeezing them with my fingernails to lance them of their pus. This became a habit. A kind of morbid source of relish. And each time I was demoralized by it.

I was forbidden to retire before ten at night. When an old rusty gong sounded down the corridor. For a long while I was kept awake by the anxiety, hunger, and physical pain. The straw in the mattress was brittle and full of twigs. I was scrawny. Lying on my back, the sores on my buttocks hurt. Lying on my side, my hips began to hurt.

The endless murky glow of the light bulb continued to nauseate me. The mournful stillness weighing on the prison at night oppressed me from all sides. From time to time a train went by on the edge of town. Its whistle, piercing the night, made sleep impossible. Made nostalgia more poignant.

There were also the crickets. Usually, they were small and black. They could be heard chirping in the corridor, in the cell. Under the bed. The monotonous chirping tickled my brain. Lent a dull voice to the silence of the prison night.

I still remember the monster cricket with the same dread. It was loathsome. A huge green and yellow bug clinging to the wall. As repulsive as vomit. The time was around 4:30 in the afternoon. Suddenly I see it near me, on the wall. It is an outgrowth of the prison. Horror makes me lose my head. What if it leaps on me? I am being ridiculous and know it. But I can't stand to have this thing near me. I scurry over to the door. The peephole immediately opens. In a jerky voice I beg the guard to open up and take the awful thing away. I can see it on the wall. He doesn't even answer. He closes the peephole. Goes off. I knock again. He comes back and says merely: "Wait!"

I often heard this word. It was their only response. "Wait!" I had to address the guards formally. They always answered as though I were a dog: "Wait!" when I asked for water. "Wait!" if I asked to go out to the toilet between "programs." "Wait!" It was always, "Wait!"

I wait. He doesn't open the door. The animal begins to move. I feel I am on the verge of a nervous breakdown. I feel I am on the verge of madness. The animal moved. On the wall it slowly moved the three angular segments of its oily, greenish legs.

In the cell I had an enameled metal chamber pot. Without a lid. The inside was coated with a thick chalky crust. Giving off a strong smell of urine. I was allowed to use it when I couldn't wait for the "program." I held off doing so because of the stench I would have to put up with until the "program." That was the only time I could go empty it and give it a quick rinse. I always brought it back with some water inside to hold down the odor.

I had the idea of drowning the bug. I picked up the chamber pot. I put the edge of it against the wall just beneath the monster. Suddenly raising the pot, I made the thing fall inside. Horror! It began wriggling about in the water. Hitting the sides of the pot. Jumping. Its carapace was hard. Loud thumping on the metal. Its movements faster and faster. The noise grew louder and I had nothing to cover the top. If it managed to jump out, I could never catch it. It would hide under the bed. During the night, it would leave its hiding place. Would leap up on the bed. Would leap on me. The only thing I had to cover the pot was my jacket. But the bug would jump up and touch it. I could never wear the jacket again. This animal caused me too much disgust.

I hurriedly rapped on the door. I would prefer any punishment to this presence. A guard rushes up. My face must look terrified and terrifying. He must let me out at any cost. At any cost he must let me empty the pot into the toilet. If he doesn't open the door immediately, I'll start shrieking. I'll call for help. I'll rouse the whole prison.

We were all there in great secrecy. Shouts were particularly forbidden. We always had to speak very softly. So as not to be recognized by our neighbors. The guard knew that it took practically nothing to create a disturbance in all the cells. So he opened the door.

Only one thing managed to amuse me. The electrical outages. When the guards went into a turmoil all over the prison. They then took up long poles. Attached to one end of the pole was a lantern. The cells let in air and and a little daylight through the openings set high above the doors. The guards patrolled the hallways two by two. One lit up the cell with his lantern while the other opened the peephole and looked at us. I saw the lantern dancing at the end of the pole. Even so, there were a few seconds of respite between two rounds. The darkness flowed around me. I plunged into this black water. Into this refreshing blackness. I stretched out for a moment on the bed. I made faces. The lantern bobbed again in front of the opening. It was funny.

Days 112, 113, 114, 115, 116, 117 of detention— May 12, 1950

The investigation was stalled. I had nothing to say. Concerning myself or the others. Once again he gave me time to reflect. It was up to me. Confess and go free or continue denying and be shut up in the rat pit.

With relish he described this garden of delights. In the subterranean depths of this building, he said, there is a narrow cell. Dark. In which there are many rats. Huge. They are accustomed to living on an abundance of raw meat. They are big. They are fat. They are voracious. Before someone is locked up in this pit, the rats are deprived of food. For several days in a row. The starving creatures become enraged. Bloodthirsty.

Three days later, a second interrogation session. No one can withstand an attack by these rats. They rush at you from all sides. They bite right into the flesh. The smell of blood intoxicates them. They screech. They crawl all over you. No way to fend them off. I had only a few days left. Already, they were withholding all food from the rats. They were being starved for me.

Cornered, I return to the cell. Wondering if this could be true. I wish at any cost not to believe it. I struggle with all my might. This has to be a bluff. But, what if it wasn't a bluff? The uncertainty alone was sufficient to keep me in a state of extreme tension.

Third session. A description of the last prisoner who left the pit alive. The interrogator says the man was there for twenty minutes. Screaming all the while. Resisting. Struggling to yank off these animals clinging to their prey. He had fallen, and the rats threw themselves at his face. Had devoured his ears. Attacked his eyes. Had scratched his eyes out. Eaten his eyes. Only two bloody wounds were left.

After the third session I believed those rats were real. Because of the way he looked. Because of his voice. Because of the zest with which he described the horror. He envied those rats. Their hunger whet his appetite. He couldn't get his fill of my fear. His existence was proof of their existence.

Back in my cell I sat transfixed in my chair for hours on end. Waiting. After three days, when he finally had me brought in, I had no strength left. No will left. Undermined by fear. By hunger. By the lack of sleep. For I could get some sleep only toward dawn and all day long I was keeling over from sleep. My eyes closed. My neck bent. A few minutes' sleep and the guard rapped at the door.

So I asked the interrogator what confession he expected of me. He had only to tell me straight out. I would sign anything. He uttered a sentence. Stated he would be content with that single sentence. With that short sentence. With those few words alone. All I had to do was write them down, sign them, date them, and the next day I would be free. Why not immediately? Because of the formalities of being released. As a guarantee, however, he pledged his word: the confession and freedom, or the rats.

I ask for another day to think it over. I return to the cell, but I cannot think anymore. I don't want to think anymore. I am scared of rats. I feel a gnawing anxiety. Will this lie implicate only me? But I no longer try to understand. Too bad. I'm scared of rats. But I also have an argument. "The meeting." Why did my name appear in that passage I'd read? I hadn't played any role in it. Why had the others mentioned me? No, I shall not mention any names. I shall lie only about myself.

Day 118 of detention—May 13, 1950

Eight in the morning. A woman guard comes into my cell. She's the first female guard I've seen. Her manner is friendly. She has been ordered to ask me if my underwear is clean. Yes. A smile full of innuendoes. If I would like to take a shower, she can take me there right away. "So you'll be ready . . ." Another smile. No. I want nothing. My nerves are on edge. My patience is at its end. The guard leaves. Is this performance a trap? I don't want to believe it is. No. I will sign and they will let me go.

Around ten o'clock, the glasses, the office, the interrogator, the pen, the paper. I take up the pen. He repeats the sentence. I write it out. Just a few words. That's it. I have declared that I have committed espionage. He congratulates me. He is agitated. Repeats that this is the end of my interrogation. His investigation is over. Yes. I shall be free tomorrow.

I go back to the cell. On edge. Feverish. Defeated. I wait for the day to pass. The longest day. Seconds, still more seconds. I wait for the evening. The night. Tomorrow.

Day 119 of detention—May 14, 1950

Wake-up call at five in the morning. Two, three more hours of waiting. The breakfast cart comes along the corridor. As usual, not stopping at my door. I wait. For a long time. Nothing. I ask to see the interrogator. "Wait!" They serve the midday meal. My diet hasn't changed. I become more and more frightened. The interrogator? "Wait!" The hours go by. Supper is served. So it is now about six o'clock. Outside, the light is fading. I watch the window. Evening sets in. The noises die down. No door opens. The interrogators have left. Ten at night. The gong for bed. It's over. He's duped me.

Day 120 of detention—May 15, 1950

Around nine in the morning, the door opens. Blindfolded, I am once again led by a hand to the office. The interrogator receives me with the smile. Smiling, he motions for me to sit down. Smiling, he looks at me and, still smiling, speaks.

Two days ago, he says, I finally recognized my guilt in a signed statement. The statement amounts to a death sentence. Only one last resort. To win the court's leniency. How? By making full confessions. The investigation, the real one, is only beginning. He and I can at last work together seriously. No more prevarications now. When, how, with whom, why? I must divulge everything. Absolutely everything.

I ask for a sheet of paper. He hands it to me, along with the pen. I write a few lines. Three, perhaps four. Once again I sign. He reads. Turns scarlet. He showers me with a torrent of abuse.

I'd written that I was retracting my earlier statement, which had been coerced from me by threats and lies.

I go back to my cell relieved. I no longer wish to play hide and seek with myself. For two days I had wanted this freedom. Their freedom. I had cowardly paid for it. Alas, my salvation had come not from my heroism, but from his duplicity. But he had had a setback. He had failed his assignment. He had probably already boasted to his superiors about beating me down. So he will strong-arm me twice as hard. To win and get his revenge. A few days' respite, perhaps, and everything would start over. Except for the rats. In spite of his anger, he has not repeated his threats. I shouldn't have believed him. What would they do with a witness, a defendant, who was disfigured? They needed me. This certainty terrified me. So my relief was short-lived. The future looked bleak. Ahead of me was the unknown, a hateful unknown of which I was afraid.

Days 121, 122, 123, 124, 125, 126, 127, 128, 129, 130, 131, 132, 133, 134, 135, 136, 137, 138, 139, 140, 141, 142, 143, 144, 145, 146, 147, 148 of detention—June 13, 1950

They let me stagnate for many long days. Sink into anxiety. Escape? Flee? But I no longer had the energy to even wish it. I was like still water. Foul. The pimples burst on my arms, my face, my shoulders. These large white worms sprang from the foul bottom of the bog. They cleaned out the putrefaction. They helped me to emerge. Out of disgust. The effort lasted a long time. I finally managed to reach the shore of another world. Unfortunately, stupid, simple-minded.

I was the protagonist of an insipid novel. I had cast myself in the best role. I constructed its scenes meticulously. I polished up the landscape, the cities, the house, the furniture, the characters. The action was of no importance. I got lost in details. I made all the houses I had dreamed of into my ideal house. I eagerly furnished this house. In front of its wide French doors, I had laid down a lawn. I made it roll softly toward the brook. I remember the crimson tulips, the willow trees beside the water, the silence, and even the stones beneath the water.

I am seated on the chair of pain. I turn my back to the door. I hide the house behind my eyelids. The guard thinks I'm asleep. He taps on the door. With my right hand I make a few vague gestures. I am not asleep. I make these gestures out of habit. Automatically, like a machine. Around me stand trees. A path goes spiraling upward. Grass. Each blade of grass. Flowers. Each flower. Birds. Sun. I hear the crunching of pebbles underfoot. Below, bells are ringing. It is the church. Black. Torn apart, a spider's web. On it glisten drops from the rain shower. The moist earth. The smell of the damp earth. Between the twisting tree trunks, the roofs of the city. Red roofs. My land is beautiful. Joy. It is morning. No. I start over. Slanting shafts of sunlight. Golden light. A pink horizon. Fluttering leaves. The odor of fir.

Somewhere a noise. Indistinct. The peephole? Far away. In a dream. A nightmare. My hand moves through the air. It caresses the curved branches. It cradles the sound of the bells. I move slowly forward. In slow motion. Days to build my house. Days to furnish it. Each rug, the color of the curtains, the books. To get there I come across my second character. I speak to him. I spend several days seeing this encounter. Hearing our voices. Choosing our words. His tender words.

A week. Two. Three. Nothing. No interrogator. No investigation. No reprisals. The same starvation diet. The same hunger. My novelistic hallucinations could not feed it. Only make me forget, more or less. It was laughable to believe in the supremacy of the mind, to deny the reality of the flesh and be unable to overcome the hunger pangs. I didn't want to accept this degrading snub. I did not feel pity for my hunger, just hate. Only my nightly dreams were sympathetic to it. I submitted to them. In spite of myself. My will would not admit the humiliation of its presence in my waking dreams.

One of those days I experienced another kind of escape. It began vulgarly with intestinal spasms. Just after the early morning "program." A problem. Use the chamber pot? I couldn't empty it until the afternoon break. How could I breathe for six or seven hours the fetid fumes from this lidless receptacle? Up to that day, I had been able to avoid this.

The cramps became severe. When the guard goes by, I ask him to take me to the toilet. "Wait!" Slumped on my chair, I clasp my belly with both hands. In vain. I am transfixed by acute pain. This lasts a long time. The guard goes by, opens the peephole, looks at me, goes by again. Nothing. I don't recall the rest of the day. The too-brief afternoon outing was probably fruitless, for toward evening I was bent double on my chair. The pains were violent. I couldn't even talk anymore. Not even moan. I know that eventually the door opened. The boss enters. He asks me if I am ill. I don't even answer. He leaves. I am in greater and greater pain. The peephole clicks all the time. They watch me all the time. I hurt all the time. Once again, the peephole, the key, a guard, and behind him the doctor with a needle in hand. He gives me a shot. Gives me his permission to go to bed.

At last the pains subside. Still a little discomfort. Then no pain at all. A strange quieting down. I feel calm. Peaceful. No more pain. No more trouble. Fear? What had I to be afraid of? Why? The memory is not canceled out. I am conscious of the horror of all these months. But I no longer understand this horror. Why horror? Why suffering? Leave? Be free? Why? I wish only for the permanence of the present moment. Only this total reconciliation between me and the stained walls, the locked door, the straw of the pallet, the peephole. Only this total acceptance. This well-being . . . Without a past . . . Without a thought . . . Without desires. Floating in the void . . . In this unreal reality . . . Without end . . . I go to sleep.

The next day, the only thing that remained was the memory of a defeat, of this betrayal of the mind, and I felt the heartache and humiliation of it. I cannot go on with the game. My insipid novel comes to a sudden end. I am ashamed of its flatness. At least go back to being an adult. The floor of my cell provides me with my first opportunity.

White spots and black spots against a background of gray, it was pebbles and cement. Twice a week, the guard used his feet to nudge a pail into the cell through the partly opened door. The water inside was already muddy. A black, sticky piece of canvas immersed in it. Dip your hand in this filthy water, take out the slimy rag, imagine it had been soaked with the phlegm from all the nocturnal coughs, wring it out, smear my cell with this filth. Nauseating!

I had never taken a close look at the floor of my cell. Without my glasses on, the stains were blurred. Merged into each other. There was the cement. Cold. A drab gray. That was all. But that day, while moving the wet rag around the floor, I leaned closer down and saw the pebbles. The water made the cement glisten and livened up the colors. Lightened the white, darkened the black. Pebbles. A whole seedbed of little pebbles.

Abruptly, two pebbles look at me with a gaze of stone. Under these two eyes, a mouth grins sardonically. Nearby, another face emerges from the depths. One fused to another, the heads become organized, harmonized. To the left, to the right, above, below, large, small, impassive or grinning, beautiful or frightening, the heads swarm, proliferate everywhere. Here and there the animals worm their way in.

I can't drive them away. Those heads are there. Day after day. Under my feet. And they begin to crawl. Each spot on the wall is their sanctuary. The cell is filled with them. Heads all over. Everything causes them to be. The slice of black bread, the rag-handkerchief. Hundreds of times I throw this crumpled rag on the bed, each time to decipher there a new head, a new profile.

To finally escape this madness of heads, I had only one possible remedy, to express it. To give the illusion the reality of words. Without a pencil, without paper, without experience, I timorously slunk, step-by-step, into a world that did not belong to me, poetry.

I had read a great many verses, but remembered few of them. Bits of poems. A few scattered lines. Two or three strophes here and there. Mainly French poets. I had read Father Bremond. The notion of the ineffable remained with me. I now needed to understand. Analyze. Find out the rules. Learn.

What seemed paramount was to count the syllables, to find the rhymes. I was reaching for more. Thus, recalling all the lines I could, repeating them, and touching the mystery.

I knew by heart the first two lines of Baudelaire's "La Beauté":

I am beautiful, O mortals, like a dream of stone.
And my breast where each has in turn killed himself . . .

Scanning them over and over, I discovered the secret of rhythm. This showed me the importance of stressed syllables.

"And the fruit will pass on the promise of the flowers," with the repeated *f*'s, *p*'s, and *s*'s, taught me alliteration.

Mallarmé's "Those nymphs, I wish to perpetuate" taught me word inversion.

Valéry's "This roof where doves hover" taught me imagery.

"If the death of his basket had thingized my being" taught me freedom of expression.

Lines, other lines, taken from poems, in turn emerged. Snatches of Verlaine, Francis Jammes, other poets from my youth.

When, owing to so much repetition, these lines lost all meaning for me, I created my own lines. In French. Each new verse, added to the preceding ones, gave me great satisfaction. I managed four or five poems on the theme of the heads. I was pleased with them. My task was slowed down by a lack of paper. I could use only my memory. Because I couldn't see each line, I was obliged to murmur it many times, to hear it. To link it up to other, earlier lines. To learn the whole thing by heart. I chanced to forget a line. I made an effort to recover it. A line lost made me sad.

I had the idea of setting these poems to music. It was "The Songs of the Singing Madwoman." I recall only a few lines of it:

Sing to lull to sleep one's heart.
Poor heart that weeps and hurts . . .

Next, the song of the cricket, of the train, and still others. I was neither a poet nor a composer. But, even so, I made up poems, songs, and I was pleased with them. I absolutely lacked critical judgment. I felt only the advent of a miracle. I had finally found the key to escaping.

I was also finally rid of the guilty obsession with lost time. I went to a good deal of trouble. I worked. I abolished the prison. My fear. Myself. I really lived moments of utter plenitude there, in that cell as in many others over the years. In spite of everything. Hours of total forgetfulness. From time to time, I even managed to forget the terrible question of what they wanted from me.

But summer was there. In the cell. On my skin. Under my skin. In my skull. The mugginess of a summer without sun. The weather was hot. Hotter and hotter. My skirt, too flimsy in winter, now burned me. My blouse stuck to my body. But the worst was the slippers. They had taken away my shoes. In exchange they gave me slippers. In coarse cloth. Large, old, dirty, worn-down, giving off in the heat of the feet the fetid odor of so many other miserable feet. This stink stuck in my throat. But I couldn't leave my feet bare. With the filthy rag and dirty water, the floor seemed more soiled than washed. I couldn't keep from thinking of phlegm.

Day 149 of detention—June 14, 1950

That morning, the guard brought me five cigarettes and a box of matches. In the box, five matches. A little later, the door opens. The guard hands me a book. Gorky's *The Mother.*

Days 150, 151, 152, 153, 154, 155, 156, 157, 158, 159, 160, 161, 162, 163, 164, 165, 166, 167, 168, 169, 170, 171, 172, 173, 174, 175, 176, 177, 178 of detention— July 13, 1950

Cigarettes and a book. Unbelievable. Nevertheless, day after day, I reverently gazed at my open book and my cigarettes on the black wood of the table. Each morning, five cigarettes. From time to time, a new book, more Gorky: *Clim Samghin; The Family; Artamnov; My Universities.* Unfortunately, I detest Gorky. I find his universe of dark Slavic mysticism chilling even when mitigated by socialism. But I also received two or three other books. I wolfed down these books much too quickly, alas. Between forty and sixty pages an hour, even the thickest couldn't hold out for long. To make them last, I started translating them into French as I read. That slowed down my alacrity. I was forced to proceed more slowly. To stop and search for a word, a correct turn of phrase.

One day I had the good fortune to receive a short volume by Vladimir Mayakovsky. This treatise on prosody enchanted me. Brilliant, intelligent, witty, effective, it was a great help to me. It taught me the rudiments of the craft. First and foremost, how faithless inspiration is. He gives the example of a line reworked. Repeated some twenty times. Changes in word placement, the pursuit of an economy of expression. The search for the most concise, the fullest expression.

The intoxication of work. Pruning. Foregoing. Condensing. Compressing two or three lines into one. Finally the rhyme that clicks.

I'll say it again. This wasn't my line of work. The reason I speak time and again of poetry is that my whole life in prison was infused with it. I had nothing. No paper or ink. The books lasted only a short while. But in this vacuum I had struck a rich vein. Words. The force of words. I had the words and I had the time. A huge amount of time. Enough time not to know what to do with it. Time lost. But lost or not, this time was mine. To allow it to become lost in vain was to lose a part of my life and I wanted to live my life. With this joining of words and time I lived. Survived. I even managed to be happy. Sometimes.

I owe Mayakovsky a great debt of gratitude.

The weather grew increasingly hot. I felt dirty. Sticky. My blouse had torn. I wore a coarse canvas military shirt. Having no nightgown, I kept the shirt on when I slept. The light bulb in the cell glowed day and night. The shirt came down almost to my knees. Because of the judas, I was obliged to cover myself with the sheet. Had I uncovered myself that night as I slept? That might explain the sexual crisis of one of my guards.

In any case I was awakened by some whispering. A voice mutters some words at the peephole. These words seem totally nonsensical. Perhaps I wasn't hearing properly. This time, there is no mistaking it. The guard wants to play the voyeur. He asks me to pull down the sheet. I pretend to be asleep. Each time he goes by he hurls an obscenity at me.

Now, every time he is on duty at night, I am afraid to go to sleep. For he keeps it up. I wrap myself up in the sheet. I play the mummy. But how can I stop up my ears? Shut out his panting harangue? His imagination is unbounded. His vocabulary precise. He scares me. He sickens me. One night, I am awakened by a little plop on the bed. Sugar. He tossed in some sugar for me. A quarter of a piece of sugar. A quarter. For a strip tease? Annoying.

The guards alternated night duty and day duty. I managed to identify him. It was one of the older guards. Short, sickly, an unhealthy look about him. I could have denounced him. I should have done this. But for him that would have been extremely serious. How could I decide to make so much trouble for him? A pathetic type.

This lasted about a month. Then he vanished. But it was hard to bear the lack of sleep, which couldn't be made up for during the day.

Days 179, 180, 181, 182, 183, 184, 185, 186, 187, 188, 189, 190, 191, 192, 193, 194, 195, 196, 197, 198, 199, 200, 201, 202, 203, 204, 205, 206, 207, 208, 209, 210 of detention—August 14, 1950

The cigarettes. I received just five of them a day. The first time, I smoked two in a row. My head swam. Intoxication. Strange visions. Once the craving died down, I realized that the tobacco, as bad as it was strong, dulled my hunger. To smoke only half a cigarette at a time was to secure ten minutes of relief instead of five. But how could I light these ten halves with only five matches? Extremely carefully, I managed to split each stick in two with a fingernail. I sometimes failed. Sometimes because of the wood, sometimes because the layer of phosphorus was too thin. The match broke crosswise, the phosphorus came unstuck. The loss of a match that day deprived me of the two sections of my last cigarette.

A month went by this way. Another month. At work. The

seeming calm of a stagnant pond. In the silt, the swarming of shapeless creatures. Above, a blinding flash of dragonflies.

During this period, I switched from French to Romanian. Romanian doesn't lend itself to minor poetry. To affectedness, to sentimentalism, to rose water, to empty pleasantries. In Romanian I tried in vain to make up some verses for a love song, and I understood why all our popular music is so banal. The genius of the Romanian language demands the epic, heroic ballads, depth, the cries of love, blood, and hate. It is a language like no other for expressing suffering, struggle, injustice. Poverty, too, and love. The men and women of this country have always "sung" their numerous pains and lack of joy. For centuries, they have forged a musical and poetic language of great nobility.

I analyzed everything I could recall from Romanian poetry. Popular and literary verses. It took some time before I realized that it is the rhythm that creates the incantatory, not the rhymes or equal number of syllables. To understand that the rhythm comes from the syllabic stress of the words. By the symmetry of the odd or even rhythm chosen, and all the possible variations on it. Every day, hours went by in this demanding pursuit. Without paper or pencil. Escape into a dream that I found more real than reality.

That is, as long as they leave me alone. Suddenly, however, they remembered my existence. I then fell rudely back into the lower depths. I was once again in prison. Did I mention the horror of the lack of freedom in itself? Of being locked up. In complete isolation. To be forbidden to send or receive letters. To know nothing of what is going on in the world. Outside those walls. In my family. Had my father, my sister really returned home? A question without an answer. But a gnawing anxiety, day and night.

Days 211, 212, 213, 214, 215, 216, 217, 218, 219, 220, 221, 222, 223, 224, 225, 226, 227, 228, 229, 230, 231, 232, 233, 234, 235, 236, 237, 238, 239, 240, 241, 242, 243, 244, 245, 246, 247, 248, 249, 250 of detention— September 23, 1950

The investigation resumes. New questions. I realize that the interrogator is groping. Indeed the whole investigation must be, most likely. They try to bait us randomly. We are making their job hard. Very hard, for we are too innocent. And generally honest. They have finally uncovered an outing in a fishing boat. Had I taken part in it? I have no reason to deny it. In all good faith I try to give him some account of it. But I get various names mixed up and transform others. Now I have an urge to laugh when I think of the bomb I inadvertently exploded. He has me brought to him every two or three days. Makes me repeat the same explanations ad nauseam. He tries to trip me up. Makes me repeat the names. Write them out over and over. I don't understand, I lose patience. He too, but even more so. He becomes aggravated. I too. During this time, surely the machine is running at full steam. Once again, they have to check out all the statements. The result is that he is forced to take account of my mistake. To claim that it was deliberate. Hence a guard bursts into my cell. He tears the book out of my hands. Grabs the cigarettes. Slams the door. Once again my hands are empty. They are not to touch another book for eleven years.

In connection with I don't remember what, a new punishment. A hell of a punishment. Stupid. Exhausting. I must stand on one foot. Keeping this position, constantly repeat a certain sentence. Repeat it aloud. A sentence lifted from one of my statements. This sentence did not have the good fortune to please him. It runs counter to the scenario. So I play the stork. For an hour. For two hours. For a long while. And I say my sentence. I repeat my sentence. I stammer out the sentence. For a very long time, for a guard is there. His stick and his shouting are a real support for me when, staggering, I lose my balance.

A few days later, the interrogator becomes angry once again. He orders me to get to my knees. In a corner. I kneel down. I begin feeling pins and needles in my legs. Then my knees hurt. Kneeling for a long time hurts very much. My back hurts, my shoulders, the nape of my neck. Then I close my eyes. He cannot see my eyes shut, for I have my back turned to him. He looks at me and imagines that I am searching for answers to his questions. How could he know I have slowly taken my leave, that I am already far away, very far, in search of an effective rhyme? This probably lasts a long time. What do I know? At his desk, he shuffles some papers. I hold him and his papers in contempt. In reality, however, it is he who holds me in contempt.

Sadism? Infantilism? Perhaps just revenge. Bitterness at his own humiliations. Can he, in his line of work, avoid an inferiority complex? To suppress it, there is nothing better than cruelty and the abuse of power.

Three days later. The same farce. Black glasses. Hustled along the corridors. The open door. Halt. Probably the office. Yes. The guard lets go of my arm. Is he there? Is he not there? My arms dangling, I wait standing. Finally, his voice. Take off my glasses. Take a seat. In front of the little table. The guard is still there. He asks him to bring some coffee, bread, butter, and ham. The guard goes out. The interrogator asks if I am hungry. Yes, of course. The food is inadequate. I am hungry. Silence. I have the time to reflect. Does he think he is buying me at the cost of some breakfast? He is mistaken. I don't need his breakfast. Too bad.

The guard comes back. With a tray. On the tray, a steaming cup, plates. All I can see is the bread. The crust is yellow. No. Golden. The bread is white. Moves me. There are several slices of it. The guard hesitates. Where to set down the platter? The interrogator raises his hand and points. The tray is now on his desk. Right in front of him. He takes a slice of bread. He spreads it with butter. Carefully spreads the surface with this thick layer of butter. Places a slice of ham on it. Covers it with a second slice of bread. He brings the sandwich to his mouth, opens his mouth, bites into it and chews. He drinks a mouthful of coffee. He bites again. He chews again. He drinks. He bites. He chews. He drinks again, bites again, chews again. He disgusts me. His bread disgusts me. Pig-hog-swine, pig-hog-swine, pig-hog-swine. These words give me a measure of satisfaction.

Another idea. I adopt a new gimmick. Cursing. We Romanians are great experts with swear words. Our language, with its opportunities for contractions, lends itself to swearing. "Go to hell" is a juvenile phrase, simplistic. Common. Almost friendly. Swearing, real swearing, combines God, Jesus, the Virgin Mary, every saint in the calendar, the church, and the genitals in expressions that are lapidary, savory, picturesque. In the countryside, I chanced to hear all kinds. I had retained a few of them. The classic ones. The foundation for all the variants circulating in the suburbs, in the countryside, on the lips of peasants as in the most snobbish salons, but particularly on the lips of the interrogators. From that point onward, the swearing I did at him during our encounters—

in my mind, of course—were of great help in allaying my fear and rage.

Occasionally, he employed charm. Compliments, double entendres, innuendoes, questions about my dreams. Erotic dreams? Did he figure in them? Loneliness? Was I suffering from "a certain loneliness"? And he made new allusions to my adolescent acne. But the swear words were there. Thanks to the swear words I remained impassive. With one regret. Not to have the courage or the recklessness to fling them in his face, aloud.

What was the use? My feet had slowly healed. I had found a remedy for the chair. I twisted my jacket. I made a cushion out of it. A leather hoop. I didn't want to be beaten again. The cigarettes had helped me stand the hunger. Unfortunately I no longer had them. I was hungry. All the time. From the moment I woke up. I had to wait seven or eight hours to swallow a few mouthfuls at lunchtime. They continued to give me nothing to eat in the morning. I heard the cart go by. The doors opening. Mine, never.

The hours go by. Finally, the squeaking of the cart. I am not the only one waiting for it. The announcement of lunch travels through the walls, from cell to cell. For some of us, it is good news. Through the half-opened door, I sometimes see the cart. It is large and loaded with covered dishes. Large and small. Different diets. For the good will of the accused is repaid primarily in food.

I finally receive my slice of bread. On an enameled plate, a small potato cut in two and a tiny piece of meat. With my eyes I calculate. I will cut each half of the potato into four pieces. The meat only into two. With the spoon (we are not allowed forks or knives) I shall cut a little of potato. I add a bit of sauce to it. I keep the tasteless mush in my mouth as long as possible. I shift it from left to right. For as long as possible I hold off from swallowing it. It isn't easy. My stomach asks, demands it. It's done, I've swallowed it. My mouth is empty. I run my tongue over my teeth. With my tongue I collect the last bits. Slowly I suck on them before taking a second mouthful. As long as I have something on the plate to fill my mouth again, as long as my teeth have something to bite into, as long as the saliva flows in my dry mouth, it is relaxation.

Very often, at the sight of this woebegone meal, the vision of an old woman comes back to me. I see Prague again, the cafeteria, and her, in front of me. We were eating standing up, almost face to face. She was very tidily clad. Even wearing a hat. An old woman.

Potato soup in her hollow plate. No believer would have received the Host with greater fervor than my darling old lady did her spoonful of soup. Without greediness. Slowly. She seemed to be performing a pious act of obligation. Nourishing her body. It was, I am sure, her only meal of the day. The cheapest dish. Perhaps she couldn't afford it every day. She ate it with dignity. This image stayed with me. It accompanied me to prison. It helped me accept my hunger with dignity. For me, it remained the very symbol of Prague 1947.

I remember a day . . . I don't know why the hunger became imperious that day. My belly was empty. Hollow. It hurt. Worse and worse. I felt my face screw up. Rigid. Whirlwinds in my stomach. A giant hand kneaded all this unknown in me. My intestines. My belly. The daytime guard, after several trips to the peephole, whispered to me: "Are you sick?"—"No, I don't think so. I'm hungry. I'm just hungry."

At lunchtime, I recognized him. It was he who handed me my rations. The plate, the bread. The daily slice of black bread, gummy, full of lumps. The dough it was made from was so soft that they must have cooked it in molds. On the plate, a zucchini. I had already had some before. Very small, very skinny, stuffed with a cigarette of meat. A few mouthfuls and a bit of liquid.

This time, in the plate sits a monster zucchini. The longest, fattest, the most stuffed of zucchinis. It fills the plate. Extending bounteously over the edges. He murmurs: "Eat quickly!" I understand. He's scared. He too. He has broken the rule for my diet, but I still feel the painful pleasure of that meal. I would like this pleasure to last. But I'm afraid for the guard and I put on speed. Nevertheless, the zucchini can't be eaten. By sitting crosswise, I hide the plate a little. I have finally fed my hunger. I feel replete. The blessing of satiety. I have never forgotten it.

Years, many years, have gone by since then.

Even today, my husband and I have a religion of bread. We have traveled. Visited various countries. Their works of art. But, for us, each time, in each of these countries, the bakeries are cherished along with the museums. We recall with as much pleasure the rye bread of Venice as the Ca d'Oro; the baguettes of Paris are associated with the quais of the Seine.

I never take food for granted. I give thanks to destiny or some divinity in whom I would like to believe.

Days 251, 252, 253, 254, 255, 256, 257, 258, 259, 260,
261, 262, 263, 264, 265, 266, 267, 268, 269, 270, 271,
272, 273, 274, 275, 276, 277, 278, 279, 280, 281, 282,
283, 284, 285, 286, 287, 288, 289, 290, 291, 292, 293,
294, 295, 296, 297, 298, 299, 300, 301, 302, 303, 304,
305, 306, 307, 308, 309, 310, 311, 312, 313, 314, 315,
316, 317, 318, 319, 320, 321, 322, 323, 324, 325, 326,
327, 328, 329, 330, 331, 332, 333, 334, 335, 336, 337,
338, 339, 340, 341, 342, 343, 344, 345, 346, 347, 348,
349 of detention—December 31, 1950

October, November, December. Three hard months. The attack had resumed. The details no longer matter. I have, moreover, largely forgotten them. For those three months, I was continually harassed. Pursued. Persecuted. Gasping for breath. Cornered. Attacked from all sides, with no escape. Driven to the brink of accusing myself, committing perjury. Against myself.

The interrogator is incensed. Probably cornered himself. Success or disaster. After a series of verbal battles, the threat of a confrontation? He says that one of my codefendants has denounced "my criminal activity," espionage. It appears that all my lies have been brought to light. The confrontation will overcome the stubbornness of my denials.

Something does come to light in all this. His own goal. And the lies of the denouncer. I have nothing to fear from this confrontation. In fact, I am quite curious about it. Who was the one who finally consented to lie? Pătrășcanu? Impossible. Harry? No. He is much too pure. He will be the last one to grasp the perversity of this investigation. Perhaps he will never realize that they want to drive us to lying as the only legitimate means of defense. That leaves two others. But which one?

My hair is disheveled, a wreck. I set one condition for the interrogator. That he give me a chance to present myself decently at the confrontation if he wants me to consent to answer even the most innocuous question. Since this no doubt goes along with one of his stratagems, he agrees.

The confrontation. I have bathed and my hair is done. I am wearing a clean skirt and blouse, requested from home. Thus my parents learned that I was still alive . . . somewhere, and I was pleased about that. When my black glasses are taken off, I see in front of me, behind a long table, my interrogator between two strangers. Two unfamiliar investigators, probably more important than he. At my right, rather far away, dreadfully thin and nervous, the number-three man. His habit of twirling a lock of his hair around his index finger has become a tic. I look at him speaking, declaring that during the war, in a port on the Black Sea, I frequently transmitted information to the captain of a Turkish caïque. He lies easily and volubly and, while avoiding looking at me, he twirls his lock with ever more obvious nervousness. My response was brief. "Let the investigation present a single piece of evidence for my presence even a single time in that city, during the whole duration of the war."

The number-three man had blown it. It is true that every summer before the war I had spent a month at one of the beaches on the shore, but the war had changed many things. Imposed many privations. Even pecuniary ones. His scenario left something to be desired. At least that was one scene that they had to give up. I did not hear another word on the subject. But . . .

A few days later, at ten at night, I had gone to bed as usual. From the moment I awoke in the morning, I waited for those seven hours of rest their regulations granted. Going to bed was, moreover, mandatory at the first sound of the gong. I went to sleep rather quickly. The violently clicking peephole wakes me. A voice orders me to get up and get dressed. Trembling with fear, I put my clothes on. Judging by my fatigue, I must have slept very little. It has to be around midnight. An interrogation in the middle of the night? What was the reason for this haste? What had happened? What do they still want from me? The judas opens. The voice orders me to sit on the chair. The judas stays open.

Seated on the chair, in front of the table, in the silence of the sleeping prison, I wait. I wait for the judas to close. I wait for the door to open so as to overcome my fear of the waiting. But time passes and my anxiety increases. Why is the peephole still open? Why is the eye framed in the round hole fixed on me for so long? Why have they awakened me? Why are they making me wait so long? I'm sleepy.

I put my elbows on the table. My head in my hands and go to sleep. A great banging on the door wakes me up with a start. The interrogation! I get up, take a step toward the door, but the voice orders me to sit down on the chair and "quit sleeping." The

judas is still open. Too bad! I'm sleepy. I go back to sleep. A new
bang. What on earth do they want from me? As soon as I close my
eyes a new bang on the door wakes me up. Why won't the guard
let me sleep? It's much too late for the interrogator to call for me.
I am growing sleepier and sleepier. My eyelids droop. He bangs!
My head nods. He bangs! They really don't want me to sleep? But
it's nighttime, the dark night, the night of men, the night of
animals. It is the night of the world . . . let me sleep . . . sleep . . .
die . . . don't bang anymore . . . forget . . . die . . . don't bang anymore . . . leave me alone . . . let me sleep, sleep, don't knock
anymore, bastard! Don't knock anymore, swine! Don't knock anymore, you fucker! Sleep, nothing, only sleep . . .

The window above the door turns gray. The night is ending.
A woman takes over the guard. She's a hateful, watchful shrew.
Through the judas, through the half-opened door, she has me un-
der nonstop surveillance.

The day has arrived. The wake-up gong sounds. The prison
awakes. Trucks pass by in the street. I hear the dull roar of their
motors. She has me go out for the "program." The breakfast cart
stops from door to door. Outside, the sun is shining. My cell is almost light. It seems easier to keep my eyes open. The need for
sleep lets up. From time to time I'm not even sleepy at all. Perhaps
the natural cycle of night and day makes it more bearable to be
kept awake during the day. I think of the coming night. Seventeen
more hours of torment and I shall sleep. Taking advantage of this
calm spell, I begin a new song. A song for the occasion: "Song for
the Sleeping Beauty."

Ten o'clock at night. When, at last, the creaking gong throws
this rotten day into the trash can, the guard orders: "Go to bed."
At last the nightmare is over.

No. Two hours later, a new wake-up. But this time the guard
takes me to the office. A nocturnal performance. Hoisted on a
high stool, feet dangling, I am lit by the beams of light from three
projectors. In the darkness, the interrogator. What do they want
from me? I rack my memory today in vain, futilely. I close my eyes
and I can feel my legs at the time. Heavy, heavier and heavier, en-
gorged with heavy blood. I feel my eyes go blind. The burning of
my eyelids. My body has a better memory than I do.

Twelve days, this torture lasted twelve days. Of those 288
hours, I slept for twenty-four. I now find this hard to believe
myself. How is it possible that one can, that I myself could endure

the vise, the pit, the void, the deliberate destruction of mind and body, fatigue driven to the limit, annihilating all will, that endless descent? How is it possible that one can, from such total despair, not die?

Being unable to work. Feeling all one's thoughts get muddled up, become lost. Vanish. Feeling one's mind go blank. Feeling that this void is heavy, that my head is heavier and heavier, that my eyelids are of lead, that they cannot remain open; with my elbows on the table, I hold my eyes open with my index fingers. My eyelids pulsate. Struggle. My finger cannot make the effort to keep them open. My eyelids droop. My neck bends . . . who's knocking? Who's shouting? My head is heavy. It falls forward. Who is shaking it? My neck twists. Hurts. Slowly I dislocate my vertebrae. I want to sleep! I must sleep! My head rocks, swings. They bang. They shout. They knock. I take my head between my hands, my fingers spread out to support it, stretch out my eyes to keep my eyelids from closing. And I ache . . . in my back, in my shoulders . . . my neck aches . . . and I am alone, so alone and no one takes pity on me, on my tears that drop one after the other on the table, on this small pool of tears, this pool so deep that no one can ever touch the bottom of it.

Each evening, when the gong sounds, I fall heavily into bed. A stone sinking in the black eddies, drowning in sleep. I sleep . . . two hours.

At the end of twelve days, I sign something. I don't even know what it is I've signed. My brain isn't working. Will? Principles? Dignity? Conscience? I was just a mass of drunken flesh. Nothing but rusty springs. A machine that is jammed, without lubrication. A hollow mold. They had assaulted my very nature. Violating a mysterious mechanism. Vital. To be allowed to sleep, if they had then asked me to sign that I had mugged, killed, murdered my parents, I would have signed. I would have signed anything, especially my death sentence.

Have pity on humankind.

I return to my cell. Seated on the chair, my head resting against the wall, I go to sleep. They let me sleep. Evening comes. I go to bed. I sleep the whole night. Seven hours of sleep. A sleep of stone. A sleep of death. An ivory tower. The consolation of the afflicted. Blessed sleep.

Two weeks of respite. Gradually I become myself again. I

wonder what it is that I could have signed. Definitely something very serious. What was this statement worth? Unfortunately, they knew as well as I did, not very much. Snatched from me by force. Recovering my spirits, I could, accepting the prospect of new suffering, disown my signature. I had done it before. That was precisely what worried me. They were forewarned. Having won this point, they weren't going to let themselves lose it once again. They had to find a way to force me to honor my signature. To add to it all the indispensable corollaries. By what trick? What torture would be so frightful that I couldn't bear the idea of it? I would find out soon enough.

Two weeks later.

Back in my cell, slumped on the chair, transfixed, I feel my head bang against all the walls of the cell, against all the walls in the world. Encircled. I am encircled. On all sides. Disarmed, utterly. And it is my fault. Thrown into a panic by my father's presence in prison, my sister's, I hadn't thought of hiding my sense of helplessness from them. Out of naivete, out of stupidity, I had shown them my weak spot. Now they were exploiting it. They had tortured my body. Clouded my mind. They were now after my heart. Trying to warp my conscience. After torture, blackmail. The interrogator had announced the arrest of my parents and sisters. They were in the process of assembling their files. All four of them will be convicted and sentenced to several years in prison. Futilely I protest their innocence. Response: no one is absolutely innocent. Rumor-mongering, criticisms of the regime, perjury, all you have to do is scratch beneath the surface. It all depends on me, however. On my good will. It appears that I have stated and signed that I transmitted information. He wants to know what information and to whom. He asks me to think long and hard. Have I decided to "collaborate"? No.

Second session. My mother has taken ill. She is in the prison infirmary. Not here. In a common-law prison. In preventive detention, for the time being. He says they had the goodness to allow my sisters not to leave her. To stay with her and take care of her. My mother is sixty.

Third session. He has been to see her. He has also seen my father, who is locked up in a large cell with some sixty thieves and criminals. There are too few beds for everyone. Being among the most recent arrivals, he is sleeping on the floor. He doesn't want to eat. He is very weak. My father is seventy.

Fourth session. He had left me enough time to reflect. To reach a decision. I could save them. Wasn't that my rightful filial duty? How could I still be hesitating? He was going to give me paper, a pen. They needed a complete statement. Unequivocal. Unambiguous. I refuse. I refuse again. I also refuse to believe that this can be true.

I am plagued by doubt. I hide behind this doubt. What should I do? Struggle for the truth to the end and lose them? Lie and save them? I am unable to make a decision. I cry all the time.

Fifth session. A letter from my father. I recognize his handwriting. He, my father, begs me, implores me to save my mother and sisters. He describes his situation for me. He asks me to do "anything" to save them. I read and reread his letter. I find a misspelled word. Does this prove the letter is phony? It is unlikely that if they had taken so much trouble to duplicate his handwriting so perfectly, they would have let a misspelling go by. More likely, this is a sign of my father's emotion, his fatigue. But how can I be sure of this? For me his arrest is uncertain, but more than probable. Do I still have the right to doubt it? To contend with such pointless qualms of conscience?

Session. Session. Session. The interrogator feigns outrage: I'm hesitating? and filial love? He has tears in his eyes over this. He is shocked. He tells me, and I quote: "One does not haggle over one lie more or less to save the life of one's parents." It is the first time that he bluntly mentions the word "lie." I don't have a handkerchief. I dab at my eyes with a corner of the sheet.

What to do? Sacrifice them? Why? For whom? For the sake of what truth? Of what good? For the egotistical pride of being an unsullied heroine? For politicians committed in their youth to a dangerous but freely chosen path? Pătrășcanu had once quoted his father, the historian and humorist: "Someone who does not agree to swallow a frog every morning for breakfast should not go into politics." This time the frog was a toad. They were so determined to have themselves a criminal that my resistance was almost foolish.

The scenario had been all worked out. The characters were forced to recite their role. Mine was not so important.

I had lived on ready-made ideas. Good—evil. Nothing simpler. Good was white, evil black. Conscience, an instrument of precision. Flawless. The good persons, like the angels, white. Satan, bad people, and traitors, black. Living for an ideal, very good. Dying for an ideal, even better. Overnight everything collapsed. Between black and white, too many shades of gray. My conscience no longer sees a clear line between good and evil. In my case, was the lie black or white, good or bad? Will the ideal for which one would even give one's life make it right to sacrifice the life of others? My conscience was blind.

The interrogator tells me that the trial has taken place. He has me read out the verdict. A judicial formula, a series of numbers of laws and articles, the names of my parents and sisters. They have all been given sentences of between five and ten years. Sentences suspended. The interrogator is waiting for my response tomorrow. If I answer "yes," starting tomorrow, all four of them will be set free. But the sentence remains in effect and can be applied if necessary.

I shall not be a heroine. I answered yes.

I must add that my parents had not been arrested. Nor my sisters. My father had never written that letter. They were neither tried nor sentenced. Finally, to close this sinister chapter, it appears that pressuring a witness is punished by law to the same degree as bearing false testimony.

A state of stupor. I no longer wish to ask myself whether I have acted well or badly. Whether all this is true or false. Have I not stupidly let myself be tricked? Better to be hoodwinked than run the risk of my family's condemnation. I didn't do it out of cowardice. Did I not lose myself by saving them?

Above all, don't think of the interrogator's last words. Since he had finally succeeded in cornering me, he could afford the luxury of sincerity. He no longer needed to conceal his game. What information and to whom? Realizing that I would never manage to make up answers, he had told me with his most triumphant smile that we would henceforth "collaborate." Especially, don't ask myself, "why?"

Much later, from one experience to another, I learned the two antagonistic codes governing the behavior of jailers and victims.

For achieving their ends, the former are permitted everything. For defending themselves, the latter are forbidden everything. They must at any cost get you to talk; to remain silent is the first law in the victim's code. They shamelessly offer you their assistance, their help, even their friendship to gain your trust, and then betray it; the victim's second law is never to trust in their good faith. I too often broke these laws. Every time I paid for it dearly. For woe to him who passes, innocent, over the threshold of this world without hope. He who premeditates has the obligation to foresee. He who hatches a plot surrounds himself in mystery. He who attacks must be armed. While the innocent person, sure of being right, delivers himself bound hand and feet.

After my arrest, they had seized all my papers. Three messages received during the war on official forms from the international Red Cross had already started them thinking. I had answered their numerous questions from the start. It was only one of the episodes in the story of friendship, perfectly simple and a bit grim. Because they didn't want to believe me, I had gone further than that. Provided many details. I had made a mistake and they took advantage of it. During the succeeding months, I was taken to the office only at infrequent intervals. This story was repeated every time. He was looking for signposts to erect agent-informant relations between Nicol Gross and me.

Thus:

I had met Nicol around 1937. Because he was rich, he became the pillar of a small group of friends. Frequent gatherings. A tennis club. Weekends in the mountains or by the sea. A small garden-restaurant with gypsy music. Sometimes a bar. Let's say no more about it.

Nicol!—He was Jewish. In 1938, called up as a second lieutenant in the reserves, he was removed from his post as army officer when the fascists came to power. Hazing. Racial persecution. On the horizon, the concentration camps. He is an engineer. Head of a construction company in oil. Very gifted. He is given an order to continue with his job. Work for the war on the Nazis' side? In 1940 he prefers to drop everything and goes abroad with his mother.

. . . this day doesn't end . . . it is still too soon . . . I am out for a walk . . . from the parapet I look down at the water . . . the waves . . . all along the jetty . . . go past the casino again and again

. . . a tall, wide, white ship . . . against the background of the sky, I reach the end of the cliff . . . down below, to the right, the port . . . the customs buildings . . . the pier. . . . A white ship . . . my white ship . . . the gangway . . . tiny people already going aboard. . . . I, too, in two hours I shall do so as well . . . I hope . . . on the water . . . a whole night . . . what a pleasure . . . despite everything . . .

. . . I get back to the hotel . . . my handbag . . . the passport . . . the money . . . my suitcase . . . don't forget the necklace . . . I take it out of the suitcase . . . Nicol gave it to me this morning . . . I had to promise to wear it . . . I look in the mirror . . . the little cross gleams . . . not visible enough? . . . I unbutton my blouse a little more . . . the suitcase isn't heavy . . . I leave on foot . . . go across the large square . . . go down the street to the port . . . cars go by . . . travelers, no doubt . . . others on foot . . . like me . . . but loaded with luggage . . . what odd people . . . fixed faces . . . haggard eyes . . . trembling lips . . . they are weeping . . . they are praying . . . this street oozes terror . . . it wets the round paving stones . . . runs along the cracked walls. . . . They are hurrying . . . terror is hot on their heels . . . runs after them . . . shadows overwhelm the street . . . give chase . . . surround them . . . grab them by the throat . . . the street goes down . . . faster . . . faster . . . the shadows emerge from all the porches . . . from every corner . . . from every wall . . . from closed windows . . . from bolted doors . . . and they stumble on the paving stones . . . get tangled up in their packages . . . to flee . . . faster . . . faster . . . toward the ship . . . toward the beyond-the-sea . . . beyond terror . . . men in uniforms . . . green shirts . . . bandoleers . . . revolvers . . . pogroms . . . torture . . . rapes . . . concentration camps . . . crematoria . . . beyond death. . . . They are Jews.

The former depart . . . but the others . . . those who remain . . . I saw . . . I saw them . . . behind the bars . . . picked up at random . . . penned behind those bars . . . awaiting the trucks . . . the death trains . . . old people . . . men . . . women . . . children . . . behind the bars . . .

Rachel . . . Rachel . . . my daughter . . . my daughter . . . where is my daughter? . . . call my daughter . . . good people . . . I am the mother . . . I am her mother . . . and she runs in the street . . . all along the bars . . . clinging to the bars . . . and the legionnaires shout . . . drive back the crowd . . . and the legionnaires hit . . . hit the gnarled hands that don't want to let go of the bars . . .

and they beat on them again . . . and the crowd collapses . . . little heaps of misery . . . the tide recedes . . . comes back . . . throws packages over the bars . . . bread . . . clothes . . . Rachel . . . Rachel . . . I am the mother . . . the mother . . .

 . . . I saw . . . I saw them . . . in winter, in the street . . . sweeping up the snow . . . pushing the carts . . . the reddened hands . . . frozen . . . and in the evening . . . shut up in their houses . . . turn off the lights . . . close the shutters . . . speak softly . . . don't go out, boys . . . don't go outside . . . they are watching for you . . . surround you . . . seize you . . . a dirty Jew . . . the pants . . . open the flies . . . lower your pants . . . look! . . . look . . . a kike, a dirty Jew . . . and they hit . . . and they hit . . . don't go out, children, don't go outside . . .

Customs . . . what a bustle . . . is my cross plainly visible? . . . what shame . . . they have put tables end to end . . . marked off a large square . . . open the suitcases . . . empty them . . . they search . . . throw everything over their shoulders into the square . . . why are you silent . . . protest . . . protest, good God . . . no . . . the trembling hands stuff what is left of their belongings back into the suitcases . . . go, go . . . faster . . . how to make them out . . . in this commotion . . . where can they be . . . I make the tour . . . I must wait for them . . . be sure that they were allowed on board . . . there he is . . . on the other side . . . his head stands above all the others . . . I see his mother . . . all red . . . he too . . . they are scared . . . he opens the suitcases . . . I am pleased to be able to help them . . . not leave them in the first days of their exile . . . he closes the suitcases . . . it's over . . . they head for the exit . . . toward the pier, the boat . . . it's my turn . . . my cross glitters . . . passport, tourism . . . yes, move on . . . thank you . . . pier . . . gangway . . . bridge . . . ticket . . . here's your cabin . . . I know they are next door . . . but the hallways are swarming with legionnaires . . . girls . . . boys . . . sinister-looking faces . . . clenched jaws . . . frowning brows . . . holding lists . . . revolvers at their sides . . . they knock on a door . . . force a couple out . . . the woman is sobbing . . . the man tries to protest . . . the coast is clear . . . I tap three times on the door . . . Nicol slowly opens it partway . . . here I am . . . things are going just fine . . . I enter my cabin . . . I don't have the patience to remain there . . . the corridor is deserted . . . everything is deserted . . . no passenger can be seen . . . but I sense them . . . tense . . . strained . . . short of breath . . . behind all the locked doors . . . in the exasperation of waiting for the departure . . . me . . . I don't give a damn. . . . I walk with my cross . . . my safe-conduct . . . I can go up on the bridge . . . and come down . . . I am alone . . . the ship is mine . . . only mine . . . I lean my elbows on the rails . . . out to sea . . . stern . . . prow . . . port side . . . starboard . . . elation . . . I light a cigarette . . . I have forgotten to be sad . . . I have forgotten why I am here . . . their departure . . . that really grieves me . . . but I'll be sad later . . . tomorrow . . . too bad . . . now I am happy . . .

. . . The motor begins to throb . . . a dull whirring . . . the floor of the bridge vibrates . . . the legionnaires disembark . . . the legionnaires leave the ship . . . the gangway is withdrawn . . . officers go by . . . it is after eleven at night . . . a whistle never stops blowing . . . the ship casts off . . . turns sharply . . . foaming of the wake . . . I go down . . . it's over . . . you can go to bed . . . sleep . . . your mother can sleep . . . good night . . . the umbilical cord has been cut . . .

The next morning. Istanbul. Thanks to my presence those first days of exile took on a holiday feeling. The city was packed with Jewish refugees. Train tickets for Palestine sold out long in advance. They had to wait ten days. I should have gone back with the returning ship. I was happy to put off my departure. Each day they were more dismayed at the idea of being separated. I had a friendly disposition. He was a devoted son. We looked after the elderly lady. To them I seemed indispensable. He asked me to go away with them. The war would last a long time, why split up? A mere "no" determined the course of my whole life and led me, after ten years, straight to prison. We said good-bye on October 4, 1940.

My return was even more solitary than my departure. I was the only passenger aboard the white ship.

Finally! The interrogator found the starting point. Enough of this sentimentality. Friendship? An alibi. The trip to Istanbul? To take a short course in espionage. From 1940 to 1944, Nicol sent me three telegrams through the Red Cross. Text: "We're doing well. Thinking of you. Affectionately. Stop." Coded messages. A gold bracelet sent by Nicol, thanks to the friendly offices of one of the first English officers to arrive in Bucharest after the armistice of

August 23. Engraved on the clasp: "Oct. 1940," a hyphen and a blank space. Easy to decode. The blank space was for the date of our reunion. The officer tells me he had worked with Nicol in Cairo. He seemed to have thought very highly of him. He conveyed to me that Nicol intended to settle in London and that he would wait for me there. Stop! The bracelet? The payment for the information passed on, it seems, during the war. Et cetera.

It didn't bother him in the least that all his wild imaginings were totally unproven. Information? Passed on by whom to whom? Unimportant. The bracelet, the pay? It weighed no more than half an ounce. Half an ounce or ten times that—no one at the trial will ask to see it.

So the interrogator was sitting pretty. Nicol hadn't returned to the country. The interrogator took advantage of this absence. Being unable to defend either himself or me, Nicol was a damned Anglo-American secret agent. His name appeared in a state trial. Served as a pretext for my conviction. Since the trial took place in closed session, he may never have learned about it. In 1964, a Romanian woman in London sent me a newspaper clipping. A touching obituary.

No one at the trial was bothered by the absurdity of a conviction of high treason for supposedly working for one or the other of the Allies in World War II. Moreover, every prison in the country was filled to bursting with real or putative spies in the pay of the "imperialists."

The interrogator took his time erecting this whole rickety structure of lies. Many sessions were needed. During the long intervals between sessions. I made up lines of poetry. I put my most beautiful memories into verse. I recounted cities, forests, mountain footpaths. The tree once again cast its shadow before me, over the silent medieval square. Doves pecked away at its smoky lacework. A footpath above the city. The raindrops on the spider's web, the black church and the sound of its bells. I told myself the story of the joy of a valley. Of its brook. Of the strawberries on its banks. I took great effort to describe the wind on the flowered meadow. The swinging of the bell. In another life Harry and I had roamed those country roads, hills, mountains. In pursuit of old tunes. Lost ballads. How young we were, just yesterday. Backpack on his back, the Edison recording apparatus with arc and wax cylinders in hand, he sang, all along the paths and at the top of his voice, folk songs from every region in the country.

Lines of poetry and nothing else all day long. I had nothing else to do. In the evening, I repeated the poetry I'd already made up. In order to recollect them and above all to keep from thinking of the present. I genuinely managed to do away with time. I concentrated totally on the search for the precise word, for the rhyme that clicked. It displeased me to reach the end of a poem. But, after a few days, despite the slowness of my work, the poem ended and I came back to earth. I had to find a new subject and this wasn't always easy. I then had the idea of doing a long-term work. A children's story. A month's untroubled work. My first tale, the story of bread. Sowing, green fields, golden fields, harvesting, flour, bread. I had already composed a poem in praise of daily bread.

Fall was coming to an end. Winter was at hand. In the cell one day, the wood-burning stove was hot. That Saturday morning I had received my weekly piece of soap. Better than usual. Creamy white. After my shower, I had to put it on the stove to dry it out. A little later, it was soft. Mechanically, I started to mold it. I made it into a ball. Cooled off, it rehardened. Heated up, it again became malleable. I took a piece about the size of a hazelnut. Sculpting it with a twig that had come out of the mattress through the weave of the rough-woven material, I made a tiny doll's head. Later, I made the doll's torso. A bit of thick straw served as a neck and connected the body to the torso. Lengths of straw for the arms and legs and still more soap for the little shoes. A little piece of frayed silk torn from the lining of my coat served as hair. The doll could even stand erect. She was between two and two-and-a-half inches tall and, despite her pallor, she was charming with her fine, fluffy brown hair. The guard of course reported us, my doll and me. The next day the interrogator asked to see the doll. Since my relations with him were looking up, I asked him to give me some paper and paints to dress the doll. To my surprise I received several sheets of paper, a pencil, a poor-quality brush and a little cardboard palette with six watercolor tablets glued to it. A child's kit. It took a lot of patience before I could make these watercolors, all hard as stone, work for me.

I didn't have any scissors. I drew the pattern of the dress and, after decorating it with flowerets, I folded the paper over the seams and carefully tore along the creases. I went on to make two more girls and three boys.

Out of one of the sheets of paper I constructed an oblong box and laid the dolls inside. Six little dolls in a cell. They moved me. Unfortunately, a few days later the interrogator confiscated them. On the pretext of taking better care of them. He let me keep the paper and paints.

Flowers, grass, birds, rabbits, a doe, illustrations for a second tale: "The Story of the Brook." I drew the spring. The interrogator wanted to see it. Demanded the written text. As an upshot of our "collaboration," he complimented me extravagantly. From him I acquired a tablet of better-quality paper and an eraser.

From time to time I was forced to ask the guard to sharpen my pencil. The customary response: "Wait!" That could mean a few hours or a few days. I had to attempt to be self-sufficient. After examining the pencil and seeing that the wood was made up of two pieces glued together lengthwise, I wrapped my wet rag around the pencil. The next day the wood had swollen and I could easily pull it apart. The pencil's lead slid along the groove. I got it to stick out just far enough to be able to write, and the two halves put back together facing each other were tightened with a length of hemp snitched from the mattress.

I sat drawing for hours on end. To escape being hunched over, I had to walk around my cell. While I walked, I worked on a new tale. The story of a little mouse. Leaving its mother to discover the world, only adversity befalls it. The little animal struggles in vain with grim reality, bad experiences, the flight into the night filled with terrifying visions, and its own spinelessness. Hounded, ridiculed, betrayed, ludicrous, the little mouse was me.

Hair stringy and dirty, a grubby body barely gotten clean by a hasty shower, hunger lurking in my belly, always equal to itself, judas that opened, judas that closed, finally I was pleased in the last line to have the mouse return home, safe and sound.

Happy? Is that the right word? I can find no other word for my complex feelings. The joy of work. The satisfaction of managing to go outside the walls, right from under their nose. To forget the hunger. The fear. To defy them. Despite everything, To tell the truth, I was less than proud of myself. The work bandaged the wound. Basically, being happy was, for me, for brief moments, being less unhappy.

Day 350 of detention—January 1, 1951

Winter. Christmas. The new year. I hadn't lost track of the days. I had acquired a reflex. Each morning I repeated to myself the date, the month, the year. In the early days I had scrawled a calendar on the wall of the cell. But they came in, inspected the walls, and destroyed my calendar. It was better to rely on my memory.

Days 351, 352, 353, 354, 355, 356, 357, 358, 359, 360, 361, 362, 363, 364, 365, 366, 367, 368, 369, 370, 371, 372, 373, 374, 375, 376, 377, 378, 379, 380, 381, 382, 383, 384, 385, 386, 387, 388, 389, 390, 391, 392, 393, 394, 395, 396, 397, 398, 399, 400, 401, 402, 403, 404, 405, 406, 407, 408, 409, 410, 411, 412, 413, 414, 415, 416, 417, 418, 419, 420, 421, 422, 423, 424, 425, 426, 427, 428, 429, 430, 431, 432, 433, 434, 435, 436, 437, 438, 439, 440, 441, 442, 443, 444, 445, 446, 447, 448, 449, 450, 451, 452, 453, 454, 455, 456, 457, 458, 459 of detention—April 20, 1951

January, February, March, April, I had a sense of being forgotten. No more interrogation. No more interrogator. I no longer even listened for the guards going by. Finally, one day, the interrogator called for me. Told me he was now working at the head office of the ministry. Once again he needed me. To have me nearby. He was going to have me brought to him there. Change prisons again? I had grown accustomed to this carapace. A familiar, lesser evil. Any change frightened me.

3 | Third Prison

Day 460 of detention—April 21, 1951

The glasses, the corridor. A breath of fresh air. The first in how many months? I am made to get into a car. Street noises. Stop. A metal door noisily opening. I am led down some steps. To the right. To the left. The guard nudges me into a cell. He removes my glasses. The guard closes the door. I am alone. Alone? No. Ahead of me, a few yards in front of me, a man in uniform. He looks at me. Takes four steps to the left. Disappears. How did he disappear? From this side I don't see the door. I am in a square hallway. Behind me, the guard has just closed the door. To my left opens another square space. No door between the two. I see a toilet and a small sink. In front of me, taking up the width of these two spaces, the cell. Rather large. A plain wall to the left. Another on the right. A full wall in the back. All dark gray. In the corner on the left, a large rectangle of cement: the bed. Straw mattress, sheet, blanket, pillow. In the middle of the right-hand wall, a cement cube: the table flanked by two little cubes: the chairs. A glance to take everything in and the man reappears. He takes three steps, stops, looks at me, continues his way to the right, disappears. I don't have my glasses. The cell is rather dark. As though hypnotized, I move forward step-by-step toward the back wall. Before reaching it, I collide with an unseen obstacle. There it is. The back

wall is a large plate of glass. On the other side, a narrow corridor.
Along this corridor the guard continually patrols. There must be
several cells like mine. Only four or five, for he has already come
back. In front of me. Close, near enough to touch me. On the
other side of the glass. I hurriedly move back. Bang myself on the
bed. I try to hide in the bathroom. Seated on the toilet seat,
I clearly see him. Therefore he can see me as well. At least when
he's coming from the right. Nothing can prevent him from stopping right there. Which he does. He stops. Looks at me. I go sit
on the bed.

This cell is not a cell. They have shut me up in a cage. An animal cage. I am the animal. I am the caged animal. The guard goes
by. Looks at me. Goes by again. Looks at me. This robot is driving
me mad. I can't stand the fact of him. His presence is insufferable.
I can't stand that look. He is there all the time. He goes by. Stops.
Looks at me. I am on the verge of hysteria. I'm going to scream. I
sense that I'm going to scream. I need to scream. Am I not an animal? An animal in a cage? The cries rush into my throat. Choke
me. But I do not want you to scream. I order you not to scream.
The shouts strangulate me. Grit your teeth. Make fists. I forbid
you to lose control! I'm going to scream! No! Sink your nails into
your palms! There he is! Don't look at him. Close your eyes.
Think of the little mouse. You are the little mouse. I am the little
mouse. Such a large cage for such a little mouse, it's really a waste.
I've made it through the crisis. But the tension keeps up. He is
there. He is there all the time. I furiously set about reciting the
first part of the tale. I shall never get used to this cell. Everything is
dead here. I would like to touch something living. Wood. Touch
wood. There is no wood in this cage. Cement. Nothing but cement. Here everything is dead.

I need to use the toilet. How to do it? Persuade myself that
this robot is not a man. Let's do it. I lift up the back of my skirt.
I sit down. I draw it over my knees as far as possible. I lower
the back of my panties. That is all I can do. But I have no paper.
The sink is there, within reach. I turn on the faucet. The water
runs. Abundantly. Cold water. Pure. Living. Quickly, I get up. Hug
the wall between me and the cell. I wash. Since I am up against
the wall, he doesn't see me. He raps on the glass. I go back out. I
go back to the bed. The mattress is thin. Filled with already broken straw. In the other cell the bed was made of iron. Under the

mattress was a metal grid. A certain elasticity. Here I'll be sleeping on cement. Sleeping in a crypt. I close my eyes. Not wondering what they can still want from me. I am suffocating. How can I manage to live here? But how can I die here? Never had I felt more vainly the need to escape.

The key. The door. A guard. Young. Smiling. Really smiling. A real smile. A good smile and he continues to smile as he hands me a mess tin and a piece of bread. A real mess tin. Deep, full. Pieces of meat, prunes, some sauce. Really full. For me? He has surely gotten the wrong cell. I am afraid of losing this mess tin. Still, I don't want to do him wrong, because of the smile. Is this really for me? I insist. You're sure this is for me? Has he understood? He looks at me. I look at him. His smile slowly fades. He understands. I sense that he understands. Gently, he tells me these are my rations. Really mine. He has been ordered to give me even double rations. He asks me if I want a second mess tin. I take the mess tin. It's very heavy. I place it on the cement cube. I pick up the bread. It's real bread. A great hunk of good brown bread with a brown crust. Crunchy. Tears slide down my face. I can barely mumble thank you. A ghost of a smile crosses his lips. A weak smile. He turns away. Closes the door.

I sit at the table. On one of the little cubes of cement. On the one to the left of the table. Thus I shall eat with my back turned to the guard. In front of me the mess tin and the bread. In the other prison I had had this dish several times. But in a flat plate and on the plate a single piece of meat. Nothing but six to eight prunes. I break off a piece of bread. It is fresh. It is soft. The wheat smells good. I bring the spoon to my mouth. I chew slowly. I don't want to hurry. The dread had wiped out everything in me. Now, I feel my hunger. I'm hungry and I eat. With the certainty of satisfying my hunger. I eat and the tears flow down my cheeks. They fall on the prunes. At the end I count forty-eight pits. I have never forgotten that number. I have never forgotten the guard's smile.

Days 461, 462 of detention—April 23, 1951

I spent two more days in that cell. In the same state of nerves, but receiving double portions at every meal. On the third day, a guard, another guard, handed me the glasses. Gripping me by the arm, he took me along a corridor, making me go into an elevator. Once again, corridors, a door, the interrogator. Because the threat of remaining mute had once been effective, I repeated it. If he still wanted me to answer his questions, he would have to change my cell, immediately. He seemed surprised at my vehemence. My cell was a luxury cell, he said. He had thought I would appreciate so much comfort. My nervousness didn't suit his plans and he promised me a change the next day.

Days 463, 464, 465, 466, 467, 468, 469, 470 of detention—May 1, 1951

Indeed, I was taken to a well-lit little room. Very white walls. An iron cot. A table. A wooden chair. A porcelain sink. But, most important, a high-set window admitting daylight. It looked out, I think, on an inner courtyard where they parked the cars. I heard the motors. The food remained plentiful. Even too plentiful, for me. For soon, the raging hunger appeased, half the mess tin would have been quite sufficient. But I didn't want the guard to know it. I realized that they reported every detail in the behavior of every prisoner under surveillance. I feared that the interrogator, learning that I couldn't manage to eat everything, would cut down on this reassuring diet.

This year of undernourishment had traumatized me. I needed, if not to eat everything, to at least see that full mess tin in front of me. It reassured me. Soothed my fear. My fear of hunger. So I had to empty the mess tin. I forced myself to eat everything, but this gorging risked becoming a remedy worse than the evil it was supposed to cure. And just as humiliating. The sink saved me. I emptied the excess into it. But the outlets were narrow. I had to break up the food, knead it, and force it through. And keep an eye on the judas. Afraid of being seen. Of being heard. Fear of clogging the drains.

Days 471, 472, 473, 474, 475, 476, 477, 478, 479, 480, 481, 482, 483, 484, 485, 486, 487, 488, 489, 490, 491, 492, 493, 494, 495, 496, 497, 498, 499, 500, 501, 502, 503, 504, 505, 506, 507, 508, 509, 510, 511, 512, 513,

514, 515, 516, 517, 518, 519, 520, 521, 522, 523, 524,
525, 526, 527, 528, 529, 530, 531, 532, 533, 534, 535,
536, 537, 538, 539, 540, 541, 542, 543, 544, 545, 546,
547, 548, 549, 550, 551, 552, 553, 554, 555, 556, 557
of detention—July 27, 1951

The interrogation resumes. The money. The money. Where is the money? What money? The money that's hidden. He says they have torn down the walls of my apartment looking for this stash of money. But what money? The foreign currency that Pătrăşcanu must have left in my keeping. Where is that money? Why did he entrust me with it? What was it to be used for? Stupefying questions. Repeated day after day. Hammering my skull. The money, the money. Where is the money? I never received any money. I had never heard about any money. Furthermore, I was already convinced that this was just a new deceptive tactic introduced into the investigation. Why did he want at all costs to get me to admit the existence of this money? Did he want to accuse me of theft? I was absolutely resolved. Nothing would get me to capitulate to this lie. He was unrelenting. This was to last a long time. After two months he had to give up implicating me in this story. Besides, they'd found a better one.

At the trial the prosecutor mentioned a large quantity of foreign currency in an airplane. Pătrăşcanu was accused of having tried to flee in this plane. Of buying off the pilot with this money. In any case I was not implicated.

But during this time I had still other worries. The weather was hot again. This was already my second summer in a cell. In this prison, no change of clothes. I had to wear my rags. My tattered blouse, my threadbare skirt. In the cell I remained in my slip and skirt. The hem of my slip was completely in shreds. To go to the interrogation I was forced to wear the fur coat along the corridors. I walked in the dark under a shower of jeers. The heat and the weight of the coat made the interrogation even more exhausting. I returned to the cell weak and sopping wet. The coat had a lining of light brown silk. Unstitched from the coat, this made a kind of long dressing gown, wide and loose-fitting. Ludicrous. I needed at least a hem and a belt. A little piece of metal attached to one of the skins of the coat served as a needle. Fringed at two ends, pierced with a slot, it was less than half an inch long. This makeshift needle tore the cloth, but I could forego the coat.

Seeing me thus attired, the interrogator announced that he had decided to send for some clothes from my parents. But he insinuated that he was doing so because I would soon be needing very warm clothes. He hinted that I was facing a trip to Siberia.

Later Harry told me that they had used the same threat against him. The terror of this deportation took my breath away and for some time prevented me from sleeping. I finally received a skirt and blouse.

At the time of my arrest I was wearing one of my first pairs of nylons. This newly introduced article cost a great deal on the black market. Probably trade with the American GIs. I took the greatest possible care of them, washing them as often as possible. In the previous cell I washed them on the table, dampening them drop by drop. I gently soaped the wet stockings. Finally I gave them a quick rinse during one of the "programs." But to make them last longer, I spent most of the time bare-legged. So they had held up very well for more than a year. Now they began to develop runs. I had hidden in one of the seams of my skirt the iron wire with which I had widened the slit in the door during the "drill rings." From it I made a miniature crochet needle. I used it to make my stockings last almost three years. Of course I could use it only in secret, pressing myself to the door so the guard couldn't see my hands.

The money problem. The prospect of exile. The ignorance of the world outside. The thought of my family. The severe suffering of my mother. The undoubted repercussions of my arrest on their lives. The inactivity. The solitude. The powerlessness. The loss of time from my personal work. My physical misery. I had trouble falling asleep, and slept only in fits.

It was in the middle of the night. . . . The prison had been drowned in silence for hours when I was finally overcome by fatigue. I go to sleep. I go to sleep and I dream. In my dream some loathsome thing crawls insidiously over me. Moves sinuously over my thigh. With horror I feel it slither over my skin. Suffuse me with panic. A man is leaning over me. On my thigh, the clammy touch of his hand. Mute, paralyzed, I look at him. Then, in a start, my body tenses up. The man straightens up. The light falls on his face. It is the guard. He sees my staring eyes. Dilated with terror. The silence of the prison is profound. If I cry out, he is lost. I threaten to scream. He takes fright, steps back. Steals out. I hear him slowly turning the key. I am afraid to fall back to sleep.

The guards stand watch for twelve hours at a stretch. Thus, the next day it is he who takes me to the "program." The toilet is at the end of a long, deserted corridor. He walks behind me, enters and wants to come into the toilet with me. I push him back with all my strength. The door to the toilet opens outward. Seated on the toilet, I must pull hard on the doorknob to keep him from opening it. The same contest at each "program." I am truly frightened by him. He is far stronger than I. A few days later he manages to force the door open. The fly of his pants is open. I threaten to denounce him. He backs off, but the minute he is the only person on duty (here the vigilance appears more lax), he opens the judas and treats me to his love talk. He feels sorry for my solitude. It is unhealthy for a woman to be so long alone. I can fall ill from it. Go crazy, even. He only wants to be helpful to me. Give me the remedy that, it seems, I absolutely need.

All this seems laughable now, but at the time it turned more and more unpleasant. With a sink in my cell, I could now wash all over each morning. I could do so, however, only by standing in front of the sink, half-visible from the judas, and in positions that clearly were of the greatest possible interest to him. He doubtless was on the lookout and when he heard the water running, his eye would be glued to the judas.

I could of course have denounced him. I should have done so. I didn't. Denouncing him would have been to use one of their ploys. Then, once my initial fright had passed, I realized I could easily defend myself. Finally, the disgust he provoked in me was accompanied by a bitter pity. A poor specimen of human misery. Denouncing him would amount to destroying him. But it was also to attack a brotherhood, an all-powerful caste. My life was hard enough already. What was the use of making it worse? It was a relief not to see any more of him when they had me change cells. Unfortunately, through my own error, I saw him again a year later and I regret it.

Day 558 of detention—July 28, 1951

The interrogator tells me that his boss wants to speak with me. His boss the general. He wants me to undergo an examination. He, my interrogator, hopes that I have finally understood what is expected of me. I have twenty-four hours to get ready.

Day 559 of detention—July 29, 1951

Twenty-four hours. A whole afternoon, a whole evening, a long night, and still more hours the next morning. Get ready? How? I prefer oblivion. The void. I don't want to live these hours, these minutes. I had begun a play. In prose. A romantic comedy, very old hat. Two lovers separated by their different ideas about life, love, marriage, and freedom.

The plot determined, the framework set, I had become acquainted with the characters. I had only to let them live and to listen to them. But it took great concentration to record dialogue without writing it, to memorize it without the help of the rhythm and rhyme of verse. The comic roles were giving me a lot of trouble. I don't know if they were truly funny, but they often made me laugh. I thus did away with the present and immersed myself in the play.

Day 560 of detention—July 30, 1951

A bad night. A worse morning. At ten o'clock, I am seated on a chair placed almost at the center of a large council room. A desk sits several yards in front of me. Seated behind the desk, a man of about fifty, in civilian clothes. He gets up, walks about, declaiming, treats me to some vaguely sarcastic discourse. All around him everything is red, curtains, rugs, armchairs. I understand that my interrogator is satisfied with this stage of the investigation. He wants to ask me but one question. I don't have to answer his question until the next day when several other very important persons will be present. His question? Were my declarations sincere? Have I told the truth? The whole truth? Yes or no.

I don't know whether I'm coming or going. I have to think. What does he want? The interrogator got me to lie. Forced me to lie. He couldn't have done this without his superiors' approval. Without orders from them. So? What does this general want from me? Is it a test? Do they want to know whether I have really learned their lesson? If I recite it without a mistake? If I have finally understood that the word *truth* means their "truth" and not mine.

But what if I am wrong? This general may belong to a group that has recently come to power. Why wouldn't he be honest? Perhaps he merely wants to foil the plot. The likelihood of this is minimal at best but shouldn't I try to make the most of it? It's a great risk. Will I have the courage to take it? The strength to tell my truth? Despite the threat of new punishments? New tortures?

The day drags woefully by. I don't know what to do. What decision to make. Evening sets in. I've decided nothing. Night comes on. I'm allowed to go to bed. I go to bed and sleep. In my dreams I talk with my friend Harry. I ask his advice. What should I do? What should I say? And in my dream Harry answers: "Tell the truth." My decision is finally made.

Day 561 of detention—July 31, 1951

The same office. On the right, very far away from me, three men. I cannot make out their faces. In the blurry halo of my near-sighted eyes, they appear to be unknown to me. I take my place on the chair. The general speaks. I am terribly frightened. I try not to tremble. I think I manage not to tremble.

"Have you stated the truth?"

In the heavy, petrified silence, I hear myself answer: "No! My statement was false. I lied. I was completely worn down. I still am. But you have asked me a question. Perhaps this question conceals a trap. I repeat: I am completely worn down. I cannot go on. I lied. I have never engaged in espionage. I have nothing more to say. Nothing to hide. Come what may . . ."

Days 562, 563, 564, 565, 566, 567, 568, 569, 570, 571, 572, 573 of detention—August 12, 1951

Because they were so heavy, the earliest days that followed do not come to the surface. I lean over the edge of a well. I sound out the still water. I search the black reflections of those lost days. I only vaguely make out the interrogator's face. Without threats, without fuss. Discouraged. Defenseless. Overpowered. Vulnerable. His final reflection is without distinction.

At the time I had no way of knowing that the investigation was really at an impasse. The defendants were defiant. Only much later did the investigation start moving again, after many changes at the top and bottom of the hierarchy. I, however, had no source of information. Nothing but indiscernible signs. Real or spurious. I picked up on them. Analyzed them. I drew conclusions. The mania for signs and inferences is endemic in prison. To construct a world of invalid syllogisms from a grain of sand. To live on illusions.

Some signs were odd. Others absurd. Most, hermetic. Hence, the episode of the tray.

Day 574 of detention—August 13, 1951

It was about two weeks later. The bread had already been handed out. Still the same fine bread. The best of all foods. I had a hard time holding off from biting into it. But I had made it a rule to wait for the mess tins to be doled out. This was one of the items in my personal code. Yet the wheels of the meal cart were already squeaking in the corridor. The doors opened. Mine did not. The cart went off. It was a sign. How should it be interpreted? Were they putting me on a bread diet? Was this the beginning of the punishment? I sat down on the bed. I picked up my bread. Lovingly. I had just broken off a bit when I heard the key turn in the lock. My heart gave a tug. Were they coming to take my bread away? A guard opened the door. He was empty-handed, but already stood aside to let another guard in. Carrying a tray.

The tray was set down on the table. My gaze leapt from the tray to the guards. A hint of a smile, a gleam in their eyes would have given me trust. But, nothing. Their faces were impassive. The door closed. The key turned. I was alone. Alone in front of the tray.

It was just a large wooden tray. A serving tray darkened with use. No mess tins on this tray. Nothing but plates. White plates. Large and small, many plates. The soup bowl was filled with broth. On the clear liquid shone flakes of gold. On a plate lay a leg and thigh of roast chicken surrounded by fried potatoes. Next to that some kind of meat dish. Salad in a bowl. Cream cheese. Finally, fruit, a cake, and a glass of milk.

I was no longer starving, but the usual diet was of the meanest kind. Before me I had a free man's more-than-plentiful meal and still I looked at it suspiciously. To tell the truth, this meal frightened me. What was the explanation for it? What shameful deal did it portend?

Days 575, 576, 577, 578, 579, 580, 581, 582, 583 of detention—August 22, 1951

The next day the chicken was replaced by some turkey and the potatoes by peas. But the cup of milk was not there. The third day, the meat dish was omitted. On the fourth day the cream cheese evaporated. On the fifth day the salad disappeared. On the sixth, the fruit. On the seventh day there was no more broth. On the eighth, no more cake. On the ninth the large tray held only a single dish. On the tenth . . .

Day 584 of detention—August 23, 1951

On the tenth day, alas, they sent me to the lower dungeon. Early in the morning a guard handed me the glasses. For the first time pushed me to the right all along a corridor. I stumbled down some twenty steps. Below, another corridor, with a musty smell. A right angle. The key. A second key and, taking off the glasses, I look despairingly at the wall of my new cell. The black cell.

A permanent twilight filled the cell. The air was saturated with the damp cold of the rainy days of autumn. The feeble rays from the light bulb only vaguely pierced the darkness. There too, the bed, the table, the two stools were just blocks of cement. Above the bed, barely three feet above, a cement slab served as a second bed. The cell really had two doors. A first full door and a second, lower door that was just a grillwork with thick iron bars. This was in fact just a deep cellar. For me, a subterranean living space to inhabit for eight months.

Days 585, 586, 587, 588, 589, 590, 591, 592, 593, 594, 595, 596, 597, 598, 599, 600, 601, 602, 603, 604, 605, 606, 607, 608, 609, 610, 611, 612, 613, 614, 615, 616, 617, 618, 619, 620, 621, 622, 623, 624, 625, 626, 627, 628, 629, 630, 631, 632, 633, 634, 635, 636, 637, 638,

*639, 640, 641, 642, 643, 644, 645, 646, 647, 648, 649,
650, 651, 652, 653, 654, 655, 656, 657, 658, 659, 660,
661, 662, 663, 664, 665, 666, 667, 668, 669, 670, 671,
672, 673, 674, 675, 676, 677, 678, 679, 680, 681, 682,
683, 684, 685, 686, 687, 688, 689, 690, 691, 692, 693,
694, 695, 696, 697, 698, 699, 700, 701, 702, 703, 704,
705, 706, 707, 708, 709, 710, 711, 712, 713, 714, 715,
716, 717, 718, 719, 720, 721, 722, 723, 724, 725, 726,
727, 728, 729, 730, 731, 732, 733, 734, 735, 736, 737,
738, 739, 740, 741, 742, 743, 744, 745, 746, 747, 748,
749, 750, 751, 752, 753, 754, 755, 756, 757, 758, 759,
760, 761, 762, 763, 764, 765, 766, 767, 768, 769, 770,
771, 772, 773, 774, 775, 776, 777, 778, 779, 780, 781,
782, 783, 784, 785, 786, 787, 788, 789, 790, 791, 792,
793, 794, 795, 796, 797, 798, 799, 800, 801, 802, 803,
804, 805, 806, 807, 808, 809, 810, 811, 812, 813, 814,
815, 816, 817, 818, 819, 820, 821, 822, 823, 824, 825,
826, 827, 828, 829, 830, 831, 832, 833, 834, 835, 836,
837, 838, 839, 840, 841, 842, 843, 844, 845, 846, 847,
848, 849, 850, 851, 852, 853 of detention—May 21,
1952*

Those eight months, as well, I drag them out from their stagnant gray mists. No point of reference. Nothing happened to break up the hideous monotony of days, all alike from one to the next. Here and there some pale halos pierce the fog. In this primordial twilight, it seems to me that I was merely the ghost of some creature who lived long ago, very far off, somewhere in I didn't know what shattered and forever-annihilated world.

. . . the tenth day . . . A metal plate with a little of something unidentifiable on it. A slice of black bread. After a few days I was hungry. By the end of the month I was starving. Once again, seventeen hours of hunger to keep in check. To endure. At midday and in the evening I forced myself to chew slowly the two tiny portions, for in facing the empty plate, my hunger became even more acute. I got into the habit of keeping a crust of bread for the torment of the next morning. I broke it into fourteen very small pieces, more like large crumbs. During the night, the crumbs dried. Became hard. I had seven hours to deceive my hunger while waiting for lunch. Around every half-hour I took one of these nuggets of bread in my mouth. I couldn't bite, suck, or swallow it. Just let it become soaked in saliva, as slowly as possible. Melt in my mouth.

Thus, going dazedly round in the cell and deluding my hunger with crumbs, I worked on a new play. A fairy tale. The story of a little princess who cannot smile. To fulfill a wish of her mother the queen, three fairies, at her birth, had dried up the source of tears in her heart and in her eyes. Unacquainted with woe, how could she know joy? At the age of thirteen, the princess loses her parents, castle, and fortune. The hard life, friendship, love, and work in turn teach her suffering, tears, hope, and finally the smile of joy.

This play had a pretentious and difficult subject. I had to walk the princess and her friend, a good little peasant boy, through cities and countryside. Invent a good many adventures, sad or merry, with numerous characters. I had to get this cast of thirty-five characters to speak. To speak in verse. Finally, to learn these verses by heart. The extreme difficulty of this project eclipsed the cell, the prison, and myself. My eyes nearly always closed, the hand of the little princess in mine, I went from cottage to castle, pricking up my ears, my eyes, on the lookout. In chance encounters, children sometimes came to us, sometimes lords, peasants, merchants, or servants. I worked slowly. Barely a few verses a day. Repeated the next morning. Muttering them over and over, I analyzed the sound, the rhythm, and above all the need for each word. I was pleased when I managed to merge two or three verses into one, with no loss of meaning. I would spend several days on three or four verses. Continuously recasting them. Waiting for the mental click. I never managed to understand how or why or at what moment the click happened. But it was a verdict with no appeal. As if I had done my best to copy an ideal model. I could forge ahead.

As a child, I searched through the grass for a four-leaf clover. In the sand, and among the broken shells, the perfect polished pebble. In the grass, in the sand. With infinite patience. Now, with a desperate patience, I searched the grass of death and the sand of time for words, alliterations, rhymes.

I stumbled from fatigue, hunger. I rested on the stool. I couldn't stay there for long. The cold of the stone soon pervaded me. Toward the end of the day I could only mechanically repeat the beginning of the play. Finally, everything got mixed up. I felt the night squeezing against the walls. No more escape possible. It was the hour of the trap. I was caught. I could no longer struggle against myself. The hour of solitude and sadness. The hour of despair.

At ten o'clock I was finally allowed to collapse on the block of cement. I was barely separated from it by the few inches of straw. Because of the upper bunk I had a sense of lying in a niche of a mausoleum. There, the darkness became denser, almost black. Sleep eluded me. Words, scraps of verse swirled in my head. Sometimes the solution vainly sought all day came to me in a flash. I would even wake up in the middle of the night, trying to remember a fugitive verse, heard in a dream, and whose loss I regretted. Also, weird images often appeared behind my closed eyelids. Faces formed and were transmuted into other faces. Surreal cavalcades cantered by, unfolding like images in films, fantastic images in black and white.

The tapping on the wall of the cell one day did not please me. I realized that a next-door neighbor wanted to communicate with me and that made me afraid. Why did he come to draw me out of my madness? What did he want? But the taps continued and despite myself my ears registered them. Someone was softly making irregular series of short taps. Three seconds and a new series thumped on my brain. The next morning, the game began again. I started counting the taps: seventeen—twenty-one—nineteen, five—nineteen, twenty—twenty-one. This sequence was repeated several times. Soon I was on to it. Instead of counting, I had to go through the alphabet. One tap *a*, two taps *b*, and so forth. The neighbor was asking a question: "Who are you?" I tapped my name in the same way. A surprise. He knew my name, about my arrest, the trial in which I was implicated. But he couldn't give me news of my family. He advised me not to despair. We would soon be free. But when I asked how, his answer was disappointing. Even silly. The Americans were about to intervene and save us. Fool! Despite my two years in prison, I could not cling to such a flimsy prop. In 1950, the date of my arrest, five years had already passed since the end of the war. We had finally understood it, their agreement. The Iron Curtain, and we were behind it. Sphere of influence. . . . A war? Impossible. Was my neighbor that naive? Or was he merely trying to offer me a ray of hope?

On the third day, one of the guards surprised us. The interrogator proved calm enough. With whom had I been speaking?

Speaking? But I am alone. And the tapping on the wall? I acknowledged the tapping on the wall. I was too lonely. From time to time
I had tapped to feel a presence. He pressed me. What message had
I received? Eventually, incensed, he exploded. If your neighbor
didn't communicate anything to you, why are you looking at the
place of the portrait? I was dumbfounded. It is true that in order
not to meet the interrogator's gaze, I had determinedly kept my
eyes on the wall just over his head. It was the exact place where, in
every office, their minister's portrait hung, but I hadn't noticed
that the wall was now bare. The portrait had been taken away. Thus
the minister had been dismissed and the photo of his successor was
not yet in place. I was saved by my open astonishment. The interrogator appeared so disconcerted by his gaffe that I took advantage of it to complain. Solitude. Inactivity. Hunger. Lack of news
of my family, lack of books, of cigarettes. A constant torture.

The interrogation suddenly ended. I was led back to my cell.
No reprisals. On the contrary. Two cigarettes a day. This was in
fact our last encounter. I never saw him again. According to what I
could learn later, the discharge of the minister and probably the
change of interrogator were closely linked to our group. He had, it
seems, declared that despite two years of investigation, no serious
reason for the trial could be brought up against Pătrășcanu and
hence us.

No more taps on the wall. They had moved my neighbor. I
was happy about this. He had caused me to lose whatever spurious
calm I had contrived. It took me several days to recover it.

Two more months went by. With no interrogation. I was exhausted. I was hungry. By itself my mind could not fill the seventeen hours of the day. My body, my hand had to come to the rescue. Each morning I forced myself to do some calisthenics. I felt
its beneficial effects. My mind became clearer. Life became less onerous for a few moments. Struggling every day against my inertia, I
continued these exercises all during my subsequent years of imprisonment. Every day some effort was demanded to overcome despondency. To overcome the wish to die.

After the calisthenics, the smile. I began lifting the tensed
corners of my lips. This no doubt produced a grimace. But as I relaxed, the pressure, the grimace lingered on. I even felt a vague desire to laugh. It lasted several minutes and gave me courage.

My plate occasionally contained bits of bone. This gave me

the idea of doing some work with my hands. By rubbing the bones against the rough cement of the table, I got them slowly to assume the desired shapes. I thus made miniature tools just over an inch long. A tiny knife blade and a nail file. I made handles for them with two broom straws burned at both ends with a cigarette. I also put a handle on my crochet hook of iron wire, and with a tooth of a comb, similarly curved by the heat of a cigarette, I fashioned a second, thicker crochet hook.

The cigarettes were even more useful in making needles for sewing. Choosing the slenderest of broom straws, I stuck the two ends into the flame in order to round off the ends. A hair tied into a little loop and attached to one of the ends of the needles formed the eye through which I fitted the thread. Of course the hair slipped or broke after only two or three stitches. So I always prepared several ahead of time. But I needed thread. I ripped out all the seams of my clothes.

With my tiny knife, I sawed more than cut out a piece of the lining of my coat. After a month's work, I managed to finish a whole, very neatly made little kit. A sewing kit. It was closed by two hooks made from the teeth of a comb. I had not broken off those teeth on purpose. My unwashed hair was very hard to disentangle. One by one, every tooth in my comb broke off. In the sewing kit, there were also needles and three spools of thread as thin as matches.

This manual work demanded great patience. Even greater watchfulness. Naturally, I had to work in secret. With great mindfulness of noises in the corridor. My ear permanently on the alert. As soon as I sensed danger, I stuffed everything in my bosom. There were, naturally, unexpected searches. It even happened that I was frisked from head to toe. But this was cursory. They all knew that I had been locked up for a long time alone and kept under surveillance.

Later, I showed the new interrogator the kit, which I wore around my neck, attached by a string of my own making. He agreed to get it taken to the wardrobe room and returned it when I was freed.

The new interrogator was tall and thin. He had the sallow complexion of someone with an ulcer. I saw little of him. The interviews were peculiar. Two or three times he asked indiscreet questions about my private life. Obsessed by sexual problems? I couldn't see the connection between his questions and our trial. In any case it was a dead end for the investigation. For me. I think they were trying to develop a new strategy for a new offensive.

He motioned for me to sit and went on writing. I remained there, numb, looking at the rectangle of sky through the window. I knew that down below lay the central square of the city. But I was forbidden to go up to the window. After an hour he called the guard. Not a word had been spoken. One day he placed a large volume before me. Reproductions of French impressionists. In color. Another time he handed me a cigarette. Then, he said, scornfully, that I didn't even know how to smoke.

I continued to suffer from hunger. At noon one day I receive only half a potato. I rebel. I bang on the door. The guard runs up. Call the boss. "Wait!" The plate is there. On the table. In front of me. I bang again. Louder. Finally, the boss. I show him the plate. Let him take it to the interrogator. I don't want any. If I must starve to death, I might as well put on some speed. The next day I begin getting an additional slice of bread.

A boil, very awkwardly located between my legs, hurts a great deal. I cannot see it but I feel it with my fingers, a hard lump. Through the bars the male nurse passes me some cotton wool soaked in alcohol. The boil swells. One day, despite the pain, I in desperation squeeze it very hard with my fingers. The boil bursts. There issues a knob of hard white pus. No chance here of first aid.

The meal cart was sometimes pushed by an old man. All the time he hummed the *Marseillaise*, very softly. Like a message of hope. I hadn't made up any new songs. Sometimes I again sang "The Songs of the Singing Madwoman." They were laments, and it was good for me to lament. I would have liked to write them down but I had forgotten the little musical notation I had learned in school. Suddenly a series of notes came back to memory. *Sol, do, fa, re, la, mi, ti*. It would be tiresome to recount, from this mere sequence of notes and the little that I remembered about scales and rhythms, how I managed to write down my songs. This gave me great satisfaction. In fact, I was convinced that my songs were beautiful. I didn't want to lose them. Since a whole bundle of administrative papers of the old regime had been found, now good only for toilet paper, I stole some sheets of pink onionskin paper. Being unable to draw the staffs, I made folds in the paper for the five lines. For the notes, dots pricked with one of my needles. I had to do without bar lines. It was too difficult for me to make the separations into measures. I hid the paper in the shoulder padding of my coat. A week later the pink sheets were spread out on the interrogator's desk. An observant guard had ransacked the cell during a "program." The interrogator must have racked his brains for quite some time trying to decipher these "secret notes." Interrogators lack a sense of humor. My irrefutable explanation incurred their displeasure.

I spent around 240 days in that place. Which makes 5,760 hours. Yet this is just about all I can recall of them. Those hours, those days, so similar that I can't leaf through them. As though I had lived only a single endless day, slept a single too-short night. But I do remember the tiniest details of the little medieval square in the tale where the children slept under the stars. In the center was a stone fountain. I hear the water dripping on the greenish flagstones. The red rosebush with its arabesques clinging to a balcony. The first tears, the first smile of the little princess, these are my true memories. My life happened in another world of green villages, cities with narrow streets, castles girt with towers and ramparts.

That is all. Tomorrow I'll change prisons.

4 | Fourth Prison

Days 854, 855, 856, 857, 858, 859, 860, 861, 862, 863, 864, 865, 866, 867, 868, 869, 870, 871, 872, 873, 874, 875, 876, 877, 878, 879, 880, 881, 882, 883, 884, 885, 886, 887, 888, 889, 890, 891, 892, 893, 894, 895, 896, 897, 898, 899, 900, 901, 902, 903, 904, 905, 906, 907, 908, 909, 910, 911, 912, 913, 914, 915, 916, 917, 918, 919, 920, 921, 922, 923, 924, 925, 926, 927, 928, 929, 930, 931, 932, 933, 934, 935, 936, 937, 938, 939, 940, 941, 942, 943, 944, 945, 946, 947, 948, 949, 950 of detention—August 26, 1952

My third summer in prison was hard. The heat was a torment, kept me from oblivion. Every second, the appalling sweatiness of my dirty body made the summer months too present and yet so far away.

The year before, the month of June had possessed me. This year, it was merely compounded. I ardently wished for the end of those endless thirty days. To be delivered from my visions. To escape regrets. This "nevermore," never again, never again. . . . For I could not shake off the idea that the fine days of that fine summer would never again return. Lost days. Stolen days. Days killed. Murdered. Never again will the flower of that one and only 1952 blossom for my eyes. I will once again have lost you forever, the blessing of the earth, the trace of angels, the grace of the world, you, flowering grass.

I was haunted by memories, memories of fields and meadows in flower, of sweet-scented valleys, concealing the flute of brooks under their flowers. It sickened me not to inhale the fragrance of grass, the smell of hay. My pessimism and disgust for humankind were magnified. No law since the world has been the world has ever come to punish those who take from you the wind, the spring, the river. Those who take away your share of sun, clouds, and rain. Your right to the stars.

Yet this cell was better. They had taken me back to my second prison. The row of cells facing the courtyard was matched by a second row facing the street. Only a corridor barely three feet wide separated me from the street. Nothing but a wall, pierced high up by barred windows. Daylight came almost directly into the cell through the dormer window above the door. I heard women's heels clicking on the asphalt of the sidewalk. Indistinctly, the voices of passersby. Clearer were the laughter and cries of children.

Could Marianne live just across the way? The children in the street were no doubt calling her. Marianne! Marianne! I often heard her name. I could not manage to identify her voice. I also had to cope with the honking of the cars, the squeaking of the street sweepers' carts, the bells of the nearby church.

My new interrogator: a hard-eyed young man wearing glasses with heavy black frames. The interrogation began gently. Origin, studies, employment, relationships. He granted me permission to work. A drawing tablet, a pencil, an eraser, a brush, and watercolors. I finally had something to do. From morning to night, that made almost fifteen hours of work for me a day. No rest, no Sunday. I would have loved to continue even at night. I worked on illustrations for several of the tales in verse. The story of two little bears building their house. The story of a carpenter showing his rebellious tools that they all needed one another. Even he. I particularly took great pains with a story set in a forest. It dealt with the various misadventures of two rabbits, and I wanted to render the light and chiaroscuro of the underbrush. At the same time I worked on a new play for marionettes.

All these stories, of course, had to have uplifting passages. It was easier for me to put cheer into the lines of animals than into those of people. Similarly, I enjoyed illustrating my stories more than inventing them. I took infinite pains with these little images. Even the interrogator took an interest in them. At each interview, he wanted to see the new illustrations. When I complained of the difficulty of drawing the details of so many different animals, he brought me an illustrated children's book. A Soviet book, of course. I studied the text and the beautiful black and white images so carefully that I ended up able to translate it almost entirely.

I never could figure out what impelled the interrogator to pay so much attention to my illustrations. He even looked on the reverse side of the paper, and the least trace of the pencil displeased him. I had to go back to the cell and erase it. Unfortunately he locked up each completed series of illustrations in his safe.

Here, the food was somewhat more plentiful. I sometimes received a supplement. Between the two meals, some cream cheese or some small red apples. Like caresses.

It was clear to me that the interrogator was attempting to soften me up. To do this, he did even more. One morning at around ten o'clock, a guard came to fetch me. He handed me the glasses. Nudging me down the corridor. After only a few steps he stopped me. I heard him open a door. A gust of air envelops me. Where are we going? The guard tells me that the interrogator has granted me a daily outing. A seven-minute walk. I remain transfixed on the threshold. I refuse to go out. It is stronger than I. I refuse this fresh air.

Many years have passed. I try to explain my reaction to myself. That retreat. That fear. For a long time I was locked up not merely within the walls of a cell. Through my own will, I had woven a tough cocoon around myself, next to my skin. In this invisible shell, I guarded what little remained of my freedom. Of my spiritual freedom. Every thread broken, every opening threatened that fragile inner equilibrium. For nearly three years, nearly a thousand days, I had not crossed the threshold of any prison. The transfers from one prison to another did not count. Wasn't the sight of the sky, of the sun, going to overturn my frail defensive edifice? The guard does not insist. He presents his report. Two days later, he forces me to go out. The interrogator ordered it.

I finally leave the building. A few steps more. The glasses. I step off the sidewalk and my feet tread on the hard-packed ground. I leave the shade. Dazzle. Rays of pain. Sun. It takes me some time to get used to the sunlight. To see that I am not in a courtyard. I am in the center of a huge room without a ceiling. It is an enclosure surrounded by walls ten feet high. Overhead, the blue sky. The sun diagonally strikes a whole corner of the space. The guard has left. He has locked me in. I am alone. But of course every door in the prison has its peephole. This one as well.

Slowly I walk. In circles. Hugging the walls. I breathe in. I breathe out. To the fullest. The air is sweet, honeyed. I cannot walk for long. I lean against the warm wall. The heat from the sun on my face. On my closed eyelids. I play with the sun. I close my eyelids tight. The world is yellow, orange, red. I open my eyes. Spots of sun everywhere. I hold out my arms. My hands in the sun. My hands, so yellow. So dirty. A beggar's hands. I feel the urge to cry. The wish to cry. I do not cry.

They have me go outside every day. I get used to these excursions. I wait for the time for them. In the yard I try to exercise. The guard lets me be.

So the first months of the investigation go by fairly well. Only the first ones. The interrogator has probably received new instructions. Or perhaps he finds he has made enough overtures to me. I must talk. He takes up the crucial problem again. Espionage. He and his superiors have had enough of my lies. I had made confessions. I had retracted them. Twice. That would do. He will not let me play that game again. He needs a statement. Clear. Unambiguous. Yes or no. NO? With the greatest calm, he comes over to touch me. I am sitting, as usual, on a wooden chair in front of a little table. He gets behind me. He takes a long lock of my hair between his fingers. Twirls it several times around his index finger, for my hair is long. It had grown and now reached my shoulders. In the other prison I had managed to keep it fairly short. Thanks to the cigarette. Lock after lock, I singed the ends with the burning tip of the cigarette. The hair crackled. The cell smelled like smoked pork. Here, no more cigarettes. Only the occasional pair of scissors. So large, so rusty, so blunt—what could I do with them since they were taken from me after five minutes? I could not even get all my nails trimmed. I don't recall ever cutting my toenails. I think they broke off by themselves. So my hair was very long. Long and dirty. Sticky. The time allotted for a shower every Saturday was brief. Impossible to soap up my whole body, rinse it, and repeat the operation for my head. I had to choose. Hence, the turn for my hair rarely came. Even then, the quick rinse did not completely get rid of the laundry soap.

The interrogator enjoys pulling at my locks. With little tugs, then the movement speeds up. It begins to hurt a little. Yes or no? No. Then suddenly I hear myself scream. The pain was violent and unexpected. I cannot believe he is pulling my hair out. Yet the lock now lies in the wastepaper basket. Yes or no? No? He begins again. I grip the side of the table with both hands. Pain and scream. Another lock. Still another. I am weeping. More from shame than pain. For myself. For him. For both of us. My head joggles. Perhaps he's also tearing out the skin of my scalp with the roots.

I go back to the cell. No way to get a look at what he has done. I can only feel my scalp with my fingers. Gingerly, because of the pain. Above the left ear, on a round spot a little over an inch wide, the skin is bare. Slightly wet. I become enraged. The guard goes by with his pitcher of water to fill the mugs. I show him the hairless place. The next day the interrogator threatens me. If I dare to complain again, he will leave me totally bald. Still, he doesn't do it again. This torture left traces that were only too visible. Undesirable.

Never mind that. He will use his fists. He punches me in the face. On the left, on the right, on the chin. One of the blows is so violent that the chair falls over. I fall to the floor. I cannot get up. He comes to my aid with kicks. Another time his hand leaves a mark on my face. With so much force that I keep the swollen imprint of his fingers for several days.

I can't hold out any longer. I have no more strength. I have had enough. Come what may. He goes back to being friendly. Encourages me to work.

My paintbrush was bad. Thick, with no point, and losing its bristles. In the course of my walk one day, I spot a pigeon feather on the ground. I pick it up. In the next few days I am lucky enough to come across several more. Out of them I make a very fine brush that I attach with a thread to the end of my old one. With it, I manage to make the finest brush strokes.

Days 951, 952, 953, 954, 955, 956, 957, 958, 959, 960, 961, 962, 963, 964, 965, 966, 967, 968, 969, 970, 971, 972, 973, 974, 975, 976, 977, 978, 979, 980, 981, 982, 983, 984, 985, 986, 987, 988, 989, 990, 991, 992, 993, 994, 995, 996, 997, 998, 999, 1000 of detention—October 15, 1952

I have no particular memory of this thousandth day of detention.

Days 1001, 1002, 1003, 1004, 1005, 1006, 1007, 1008, 1009, 1010, 1011, 1012, 1013, 1014, 1015, 1016, 1017, 1018, 1019, 1020, 1021, 1022, 1023, 1024, 1025, 1026, 1027, 1028, 1029, 1030, 1031, 1032, 1033, 1034, 1035, 1036, 1037, 1038, 1039, 1040, 1041, 1042, 1043, 1044, 1045, 1046, 1047, 1048, 1049, 1050 of detention—December 4, 1952

At dawn I close my eyes to see the patches of vapor ripped apart by the branches. To see the sun of a spring morning on the trees, on the shrubbery, on the grass. I open my eyes to rest them on the white sheet of paper. To throw myself into my work like a hopeless beggar throws himself into the water. To escape. To escape them. To deliver me from everything and from myself. From my human appearance. A rag that will soon get used to its solitude, its misery, its filth.

With my watercolor tablets and pigeon-feather brush I attempt to render the depth of the woods. And the time goes by.

It was fall. Through the window, the increasingly gray light vainly competed with the light bulb. I heard the wind. I listened to the rain. The weather turned colder and colder. I often rubbed my icy hands on the brush. The outings became less frequent. One day, the sounds of the steps on the sidewalk died down. I saw snow.

Days 1051, 1052, 1053, 1054, 1055, 1056, 1057, 1058, 1059, 1060, 1061, 1062, 1063, 1064, 1065, 1066, 1067, 1068, 1069, 1070, 1071, 1072, 1073, 1074, 1075, 1076, 1077 of detention—December 31, 1952

Christmas Day went by. A day like all the others. In the previous prison, the evening of Christmas Day had been dramatic. I had to go to bed at ten o'clock as usual. I couldn't get to sleep. All of a sudden, I sit up with a start on my bed, banging my head on the upper bunk. In the total, mournful silence, a man screams. Screams wildly. Screams like a wild beast.

Here and there sobs burst out. Sobs and cries. The corridor is engulfed in a wave of madness. One after the other, the cells are carried away by this whirlwind of hysteria. The storm rouses the guards. Boots shatter the cement. Fists hammer on the doors. It is cold. It is dark. Hoarse voices spew up curses. The horror is here. Next to me. In my cell.

I cannot remain in bed. I get up. I go round and round. My head aches. Running from judas to judas, a guard sees me. It is forbidden to walk in the cell at night. It is forbidden to get out of bed. His fists bang on the door. I hurry over to the open judas. A cigarette. I want a cigarette. Bring me a cigarette or I'll scream. The voice of a woman screaming heard by all those wild men would have put the finishing touch on this madness. I had the cigarette. I went back to bed. The silence had returned, total, mournful. The smoke, inhaled in long drafts, deeply, acted like a drug. Strange visions and at last I sleep.

Here, the great calm. A prison night like all nights in prison. We are, after all, mature people. A low-key beginning to a new year.

Day 1078 of detention—January 1, 1953

I had spent three years in prison. The fourth year had just begun. It could bring nothing good. One lone hope, death. But it is quite hard to die in prison.

Days 1079, 1080, 1081, 1082, 1083, 1084, 1085, 1086, 1087, 1088, 1089, 1090, 1091, 1092, 1093, 1094, 1095, 1096, 1097, 1098, 1099, 1100, 1101, 1102, 1103, 1104, 1105, 1106, 1107, 1108, 1109, 1110, 1111, 1112, 1113, 1114, 1115, 1116, 1117, 1118, 1119, 1120, 1121, 1122, 1123, 1124, 1125, 1126, 1127, 1128, 1129, 1130, 1131, 1132, 1133, 1134, 1135, 1136, 1137, 1138, 1139, 1140, 1141, 1142, 1143, 1144, 1145, 1146, 1147, 1148, 1149, 1150, 1151, 1152, 1153, 1154, 1155, 1156, 1157,

1158, 1159, 1160, 1161, 1162, 1163, 1164, 1165,
1166, 1167, 1168, 1169, 1170, 1171, 1172, 1173,
1174, 1175, 1176, 1177, 1178, 1179 of detention—
April 11, 1953

Winter was long and hard. The interrogator summoned me only every so often. Without much enthusiasm he tried to get me to make some new statement. False, of course. He did this with restraint. I could pretend not to understand him. On my face a fixed mask of innocence. I ended up asking him for some paper for my drawings. I also had a feeling that the investigation was stalled.

There is nothing to say about those quite similar days. I had become sluggish. Apathetic. A resigned pessimism was strangely mingled with the desire for freedom. But it was only a desire that had lost its edge. I even happened to think of the pointlessness of that freedom among people. I was afraid of it. Fear of people. Fear of life. Fear and revulsion. Only nature still seemed to me desirable.

I sometimes had a pain in my chest. Cramps in my heart. I thought of my mother. Apprehension. Muscle spasms. I thought I was seriously ill. I hoped that soon, in a stronger spasm, my heart would stop beating. I thought I was saved. Unfortunately, one evening a male nurse in a charitable frame of mind gave me a few drops of valerian in a little water. The illusion of death left me. I lost that final hope.

Day 1180 of detention—April 12, 1953

That morning around nine o'clock I heard the doors opening. One after the other, all along the corridor. For a prisoner, anything out of the ordinary spells *danger*! His instinct never deceives him. Indeed there were protests at every open door. Something serious was afoot. I waited for my turn, at bay. The door finally opened. I had had time to imagine every possible disaster. The guard ordered me to take the chamber pot out into the corridor. Told me that starting now I was allowed only the three regulation trips a day. I protest as well. It would be hard to shake off the habit of at least being free to urinate at any time. It was one more major bother.

I was still wondering how I would manage this when my next-door neighbor called the guard. He must have done so several times. Finally, the guard's footsteps. The sound of the judas. I hold my breath. I listen. Some muttering, the guard's voice: "Wait!" I had gone back to work when an odd sound reached through the wall. A muffled wail. I stick an ear to the wall. The man is weeping.

A guard goes along the corridor, opening each judas. I have long been used to this. Very often I don't even hear it. This time, because of the weeping man, I am all ears. He opened my judas, then closed it. He goes on to the next one. I do not hear the metallic click of the judas closing. So the guard has stopped. This lasts for several seconds. I hear the sound of the key. Of the door opening. Finally the infuriated voice of the guard. He curses at the man. The weeping man. He who had asked to be taken to the toilet. Who had restrained himself with all his might. As much as he could. . . . The man who now wept. Out of shame. Out of impotence. Out of despair. Have pity on humankind.

My decision is made. At midday, I refuse the bread. I refused the plate. Much commotion. The head guard comes: "Why are you going on strike?"

"I'm not striking. I'm very hungry. I would love to eat. But I have a stomach. I have intestines."

I raise my voice. I want my neighbors to hear me. The head guard realizes this. He shoves me to the rear of the cell. Orders me to speak softly. I go on: "If I eat, my stomach fills up. The intestines must get rid of the waste. The guards won't take us to the toilet. It's better not to eat. I'm not going to eat anymore."

That evening, the same refusal. I go to bed ravenous. I am determined. The next morning, because I never get breakfast, nothing happens. Around ten o'clock a guard opens the door. In his hand I see the glasses. This is it. It is no use studying a guard's face. This one, however, looks especially surly. He tells me to collect my things, to put on my glasses and follow him. A change of cell is always disquieting. Each cell demands some habits. One clings to them. They help you to go on living. Sustain you. This time, which was it, a mere change of cell or the hole? In this uncertainty, each second takes on an unbearable intensity.

I gather up my papers, my watercolors, my two brushes, and the sliver of soap. That is all I have. My eyes sightless, I let myself be led. All my attention is engaged. The courtyard? A threshold, a few strides, then some steps. A corridor. Stop. A second guard comes up. I hear his key ring jangle. He opens a door. I'm nudged in. The glasses. I am in my new cell and I have come out ahead on this one.

Days 1181, 1182, 1183, 1184, 1185, 1186, 1187, 1188, 1189, 1190, 1191, 1192, 1193, 1194, 1195, 1196, 1197, 1198, 1199, 1200, 1201, 1202, 1203, 1204, 1205, 1206, 1207, 1208, 1209, 1210, 1211, 1212, 1213, 1214, 1215, 1216, 1217, 1218, 1219, 1220, 1221, 1222, 1223, 1224, 1225, 1226, 1227, 1228, 1229, 1230, 1231, 1232, 1233, 1234, 1235, 1236, 1237, 1238, 1239, 1240, 1241, 1242, 1243, 1244, 1245, 1246, 1247, 1248, 1249, 1250, 1251, 1252, 1253, 1254, 1255, 1256, 1257, 1258, 1259, 1260, 1261, 1262, 1263, 1264, 1265, 1266, 1267, 1268, 1269, 1270, 1271, 1272, 1273, 1274, 1275, 1276, 1277, 1278, 1279, 1280, 1281, 1282, 1283, 1284, 1285, 1286, 1287, 1288, 1289, 1290, 1291, 1292, 1293, 1294, 1295, 1296, 1297, 1298, 1299, 1300, 1301, 1302, 1303, 1304, 1305, 1306, 1307, 1308, 1309, 1310, 1311, 1312, 1313, 1314, 1315, 1316, 1317, 1318, 1319, 1320, 1321, 1322, 1323, 1324, 1325, 1326, 1327, 1328, 1329, 1330, 1331, 1332, 1333, 1334, 1335, 1336, 1337, 1338, 1339, 1340, 1341, 1342, 1343, 1344, 1345, 1346, 1347, 1348, 1349, 1350, 1351, 1352, 1353, 1354, 1355, 1356, 1357, 1358, 1359, 1360, 1361, 1362, 1363, 1364, 1365, 1366, 1367, 1368, 1369, 1370, 1371, 1372, 1373, 1374, 1375, 1376, 1377, 1378, 1379, 1380, 1381, 1382, 1383, 1384, 1385, 1386, 1387, 1388, 1389, 1390, 1391, 1392, 1393, 1394, 1395, 1396, 1397, 1398, 1399, 1400, 1401, 1402, 1403, 1404, 1405, 1406, 1407, 1408, 1409, 1410, 1411, 1412, 1413, 1414, 1415, 1416, 1417, 1418, 1419, 1420, 1421, 1422, 1423, 1424, 1425, 1426, 1427, 1428, 1429, 1430, 1431, 1432, 1433, 1434, 1435, 1436, 1437, 1438, 1439, 1440, 1441, 1442, 1443, 1444, 1445 of detention—December 31, 1953

So many empty days. But I go back to April 12.

It was what they called a studio apartment. A fairly large cell. In the blind spot, hidden from the judas, an angle formed by the wall with the door and the one on the left, separated from the rest of the cell by a length of wall, a Turkish toilet surmounted by a shower. Across, in the opposite angle, a cement table was placed on the diagonal. Two beds, also of cement, set along the rear wall and the one on the right. The foot of the beds served as chairs for the two sides of the table. The window, a larger one, above the door, made the cell bright. The white, clean wall and the cell's location on the second floor made the electric light unnecessary, and that was restful for my eyes.

In principle the shower could be used only on Saturdays. But I managed to run it every day and give myself a quick washdown. The water is most often cold, but always salutary. Finally, I was clean. I occupied this cell until the trial. For a whole year.

All I did was work stubbornly from morning to night. A play in verse for marionettes, a tale, romances, illustrations. With paper and pencil, I could have written out my texts. I much preferred, however, not to break the habit of composing strictly in my mind. Seated all day long, the forced sedentariness of so many years in a cell caused pains in my legs. From the ankle to the knee, they sometimes swelled almost visibly. The summer heat only aggravated these ails.

I suffered terribly from bad teeth. The cause was undoubtedly the anemia brought on by the lack of nourishment, the complete absence of fruit, green vegetables, and dairy products. I vainly asked the interrogator for medical care. At night the pain was excruciating. I had to give up stretching out in bed. For a whole month I could only sleep sitting up. My gums were purulent. One after another my teeth decayed. All it took was a crust of bread to break the walls of a bad tooth. The sharp points cut into my tongue and drew blood. My front teeth began to crumble. Sometimes a crumb penetrating deeply in the cavity made me sweat with pain. I had had a toothbrush. I didn't have it anymore. One day in the previous cell I was brushing my teeth with soap, spitting the water into the chamber pot. I could not be seen from the judas. A guard, unable to observe me, rapped violently on the door. Being unable to answer him, my mouth filled with the foul-tasting laundry soap, I had shown him the toothbrush through the judas. Seeing the handle of the brush an inch from his eyes, he took mortal fright and accused me of trying to put out his eye. I was hugely pleased at having terrorized him, but the toothbrush was confiscated. I cleaned my teeth with broom straws. I had to do this very carefully. But I still sometimes managed to touch a live nerve. The pain was agonizing. To calm it down, I had only cold water or the heat of my palms. Twice, the interrogator gave me two sedative tablets, claiming that in doing this he was breaking "regulations."

I spent the whole summer focused on the pain. I watched out for it. I felt it come on insidiously. It was a tide that gradually covered everything, a paroxysm that made a hole in my brain. Then just as slowly it receded. Allowing me a few hours' respite. Of sleep, when the lull occurred at night.

I could sometimes conquer the pain through work. In a poem, of which I recall only a few lines, I tried putting my sufferings into stories. I imagined a cockroach boring into my skull. Relentlessly gnawing away at my brain's gray matter, it gorged on my thoughts, my memories, transforming present and past into "white brain dust," and all my thoughts, even forgotten and lost, were just a torment.

I wasn't always alone in the cell. I sometimes had a visitor. Worrisome. The guard handed out slices of bread well before mealtimes. To put off starting in on it, I set it down far away from me on the floor on a blank sheet of paper. One day I was in the middle of drawing when I heard a sharp noise, very close by. I pricked up my ears. The noise was repeated. It was coming not from the corridor but from my Turkish toilet. The section of wall half-hid it from me. I leaned over a little and saw a filament, a sort of long, very thin worm hurriedly wiggling back and forth. Hardly daring to breathe, I leaned over a little farther. It was awful to see. My slice of bread had been stolen by a big fat rat. It was now trying to get it through the round hole of the toilet. The hard crust of bread hit against the sides. The rat's tail wiggled. I saw its claws clutching at the bread. It finally managed to get the bread through and together they vanished. Too bad about the bread, but having a cellmate of this kind filled me with fear and loathing. I called the guard. I complained. He began laughing and slammed the judas closed. I had several visits from the rat, but I had taken precautions. Finding nothing more to make off with, not even bread crumbs on the floor, he scurried away for good.

I have often spoken of the guards. I have said many bad things about them. Not enough bad things. All the same, in order not to be unjust, I must say that not all of them were sadists. Though they acted harshly, they were merely carrying out the orders of their superiors. For they were afraid of them. Moreover, they were just as afraid of their fellow guards as they were of the inmates. Both groups could denounce them to the bosses. Sometimes, when he could do so without risk, a guard would venture a word or gesture of encouragement, a larger slice of bread, a bit of soap, two or three additional minutes of walking, or a mere human smile.

It was high summer. A lack of air. Hot and humid. I felt like a beached whale. A guard opened the judas. He gazed at me for a few seconds, then murmured: "Let the water run, it will cool off the cell."

I turned on the shower. I let the water run over my face, my arms, my bare feet. The water was cool. The drops splattered on the cement. The air in the cell did indeed become easier to breathe. This lasted a good quarter of an hour, then he made a series of rapid little taps on the door. Danger! He was no longer alone. I hated certain guards. I detested most of them. I pitied others. A very few, a really very few, moved me. This one repeated this gesture several times, as often as he could.

I think that September had already arrived when the interrogator began talking of the "trial." I had managed to forget about it. To believe that there would never be a trial. That they would never get to it. That they would never succeed in transforming the innocent into the guilty. Nonetheless, the interrogator appeared very sure of himself. No more bluffing. For me, a disaster. I was seized with a mad panic. I was scared of the trial.

The interrogator realized this. My fear didn't suit him. He could tell himself that I had heard so many threats, I could go for broke. Deny at the trial the information supposedly given by me during the war, in order not to risk a serious sentence. He could not understand the real cause of my fear. How could he even vaguely suspect, he whose moral sense had been distorted by his profession and special training, how could he know that my fear was prompted by the lies I would be forced to utter, and not by the punishment that I knew was inescapable?

To gain my confidence, he tried to bribe me with the temptation of acquittal. Gradually, over the days, he turned this temptation into a certainty. By posing the worst case scenario, he said, the jury could condemn me. Even in this extreme case, however, the sentence could only be light "since I hadn't been completely intractable." It couldn't exceed the years already spent in custody. He could guarantee it. Thus, in any event, once the trial was over, freedom.

He treated me to small doses of these pills of hope. Cunningly. Throughout the fall and winter. He succeeded in getting me out of my stupor. Bit by bit, the confinement once again became unbearable. Each prison hour regained all its weight. Despite my skepticism about every allegation coming from the investigation, I now needed to believe it. A vital need.

The change of diet that occurred during this same period seemed to confirm his words. For the whole time, I had never seen myself in a mirror. More than three years. I ran my fingers over my face to feel the wrinkles. My face had always been too long and thin, my nose too long. Nearsighted, without glasses for so long, I had been obliged to force my eyes to see better. To squint. I imagined the crow's feet and the large dark circles under my eyes. Deprived of air and light, my dark complexion was surely yellow. My hair was dead. I must have looked like a corpse. A living mummy. Yet I didn't realize that this new diet was not to groom me for freedom, but to make me look less pitiable at the trial.

For the first time since my imprisonment, they gave me breakfast, tea, butter, cheese, bread. At noon, meat, vegetables, even salad. Milk, occasionally eggs.

No longer was I starving. No longer was I grubby. Though being perpetually ravenous is a torture, thought-destroying, to eat reasonably well is so normal and natural that one cannot delight in it for long. Satiety, doing away with hunger, freed up my demoralized mind. Freed from physical constraint, it became all the more receptive to mental tortures. To my solitude, my worries, and the prospect of the trial. To an entire miserable year sluggishly creeping to the void.

Days 1446, 1447, 1448, 1449, 1450, 1451, 1452, 1453, 1454, 1455, 1456, 1457, 1458, 1459, 1460, 1461, 1462, 1463, 1464, 1465, 1466, 1467, 1468,

1469, 1470, 1471, 1472, 1473, 1474, 1475, 1476,
1477, 1478, 1479, 1480, 1481, 1482, 1483, 1484,
1485, 1486, 1487, 1488, 1489, 1490, 1491, 1492,
1493, 1494, 1495, 1496, 1497, 1498, 1499, 1500,
1501, 1502, 1503, 1504, 1505, 1506, 1507, 1508,
1509, 1510, 1511, 1512, 1513, 1514, 1515, 1516,
1517, 1518, 1519, 1520, 1521, 1522, 1523, 1524,
1525, 1526, 1527, 1528, 1529, 1530, 1531, 1532,
1533, 1534, 1535, 1536, 1537, 1538 of detention—
April 3, 1954

In that same year of 1953 Stalin had died. I hadn't known it. As, indeed, I knew nothing about de-Stalinization. About the release of political prisoners in the USSR. The exonerations. How could I have understood our country's new political situation, which made the trial urgently necessary, without further delay. The Party secretary now rightly feared Pătrășcanu as a potential rival. To hold on to his position as the leading power—the only impregnable position in the Party—he now faced two major problems. Launching a semblance of de-Stalinization and eliminating Pătrășcanu.

Thus he put pressure on the agencies of repression. They were to bring this overlong investigation to a rapid close. He needed the trial. Pătrășcanu's total disappearance. A death sentence. The death of the one would ensure the survival of the other.

So what obstacles could trip up the undisputed boss?

The justice system? The constitution? The laws? Vacuities, mere paper.

Public opinion? Long ago silenced by fear.

The press? Under his thumb.

The West? Bah! One less communist.

The USSR? Much too preoccupied with its own problems, it took little heed of ours. Therefore, the secretary had carte blanche. The target date could be close. It was necessary to take the swiftest possible advantage of it.

The total absence of evidence? An impediment? No. Child's play. Phony confessions torn out with pincers, and not a shred of plausibility was demanded, a hundred perjuring witnesses—but none of them from our group—and legal murder was committed.

The date for the trial was set. A period a bit long for the impatient secretary, but essential for the minister (head of the investigation) who bore full responsibility for it. He needed to make certain of the judges, prosecutors, false witnesses, and to bind the defendants hand and foot. Finally, to nip any awkward pangs of conscience in the bud.

What did I know of all this at the time? Nothing. Absolutely nothing. All my inferences had rested on our innocence. But what innocence? Had I myself not signed a false statement? The trial, I thought, had to take place before long. To back it up, hadn't they forced each defendant to give other false statements? We had certainly been entangled in a giant spider's web. They had made up a time bomb from scratch. It had taken them five years to get it ticking. Nothing and no one would be allowed to stop it. Too many different interests were at stake. It was foolish to hope that at the trial I could repudiate what I had signed at the interrogation. During the trial, moreover, I saw the proof of this.

January. February. My memories are vague. I no longer remember exactly when the interrogator gave me several pages of typescript. To learn by heart.

Papers in hand, I returned to the cell. I read and reread the three pages. It was an interrogation session. About me. Parents, age, place of birth, education, political affiliation. Then questions about my friends. Their ideas. Their activities. Finally, the question of espionage. When and how.

But this questionnaire included a second part. Staggering. This second part was interspersed with the first. Regularly. Each question was followed by one or several lines of text. My alleged answers to the questions asked. The answers that I would be coerced into giving during the court's interrogation session. In that free court of law, this impartial court whose questions were determined far in advance by the investigating authorities and the answers to which were compulsory.

The answers? Yes to espionage. When and how? The old story. Informing Nicol in 1947 of the meetings with Pătrășcanu in 1945! Two years later. Meetings that were, moreover, inconsequential, and that he himself had spoken about and explained, but that the investigation had diverted to its own ends.

To the question regarding political connections, the required answer was not the correct one of "member of the Party since 1945" but "without political affiliation." Ideological questions intentionally confused. The answers, verbiage that was hard to memorize. From time to time the interrogator had me recite the lesson. I often got things mixed up.

I read and reread these answers. What judge could find them satisfactory? I reached a point where I told myself that the interrogator was right. No tribunal could condemn me simply on the basis of my confession. I was mistaken.

Day 1539 of detention—April 4, 1954

In the morning a guard brought me a pair of stockings and some new shoes. Also a blouse and a handkerchief.

Day 1540 of detention—April 5, 1954

The interrogator has me come in. He announces that this very afternoon I have the right to meet my lawyer. Appointed automatically. The trial will begin the next day, April 6, 1954.

I cannot conceal my astonishment.

"A lawyer? Why a lawyer?"

"Romanian law gives you the right to defend yourself. We are applying the law."

"But does this lawyer know me?"

"No. He will make your acquaintance this afternoon."

"But you just said that the trial is starting tomorrow."

"Yes."

"But in order to defend me, won't he need time to confirm what I say? To gather evidence? Witnesses?"

The interrogator is irked. Frowns.

"Confirm? Confirm what? I hope for your sake that you don't intend to change your attitude. Pay close attention. For us, your case is clear. Your earlier declarations are sufficient for us."

"Then what good is a lawyer? I refuse to see him."

He shrugs his shoulders and sends me back to the cell.

Day 1541 of detention—April 6, 1954

The guard tells me to get dressed and wait. I put on the stockings, shoes, and blouse. Another guard brings me a pill. He makes me take it in front of him. Has me open my mouth to make sure than I have actually swallowed it.

A bit later they come to fetch me. They have me get into a car. With the black glasses, of course. The car goes a short distance. I am ordered to get out. To go up some stairs. I find myself, without glasses, in an office. There is a guard there. He remains standing and looks at me. I wait. Long enough that I am forced to ask him to take me to the toilet. We go to a bathroom. He comes in with me. I wait. I wait for him to leave. He doesn't leave. I entreat him to leave. He answers that it is absolutely forbidden for me to be alone, even here. But pay no attention to him. I should just do what I have to do. It won't bother him. No? Then it won't bother me, either . . .

The interrogator appears. All smiles. He takes me downstairs. A very large hall. Guards everywhere. Particularly around a few of the men. Here and there, next to the walls, facing the wall. I don't have time to get a good look at them, for already they are dragging me. They place me in front of a wall. I, too, am facing a wall. I feel I am about to die of fear. Finally, flanked by two guards, nudged by them, I enter the courtroom. From the door I see a small gallery on my left. On my right, in front of the gallery, three rows of chairs. A certain distance behind the chairs, a droning throng of people.

The guards have me sit on a chair in the front row. I count nine chairs. I am seated on the eighth to the right. The guards are still flanking me. They are seated in chairs seven and nine. One of them tells me that I am absolutely forbidden to turn my head either to the left or to the right. He talks in an ill-mannered way. Looks at me malevolently.

Two men enter, each escorted by two guards. They look elderly. I don't know them. I've never seen them before. They are made to sit on chairs four and six. Herbert Zilber enters. Chair two. Chairs one, three, and five are occupied by their guards.

Two more strangers, then Herant Torossian. They are seated in the row behind me. My friend Harry enters. He occupies the second chair in this row. By turning my head I can see him. I would like to make some sign to him. I sense that he is as frightened as I am. I want to turn my head. Each time they stop me. Today this seems to me incomprehensible. Why obey those stupid orders? I can find only a single answer. By a reflex slowly instilled in me, in us—by fear. FEAR.

In the last row, a man and woman unknown to me, and finally Pătrășcanu enters. Since then I have often been asked whether Pătrășcanu had a wooden leg. At the time, it seems that this news was widespread in the city. It is true that at the time of his arrest he was treating a boil on one leg, but neither Harry nor I had noticed any limp in his gait. He is seated directly behind Harry and, to see him, I must turn my head around completely. I rarely manage this. Moreover, without my glasses, I see only the deep blue of his eyes.

The tribunal enters. A bunch of officers in dress uniform. The president of the court is fat and ugly. I even find him repulsive. The court clerk reads the list of the defendants. I hear the names of the strangers. I have never heard any of my friends mention any of them. Finally, a name I know. That of a person in the king's household. Finally the clerk reads a kind of statement: "In view of the fact that the defendant Lucrețiu Pătrășcanu declares that he will refuse to answer the court's questions, he will be judged on the basis of the declarations given by him in the course of the investigation."

In the box to the left of the gallery, a bunch of seemingly mummified men, young and old, in civilian clothes. Is my lawyer among them? Will he speak without even having seen me?

An officer stands up. It is the prosecutor beginning his indictment. The accusations rain down. The whipping boy is of course Pătrășcanu. He is spared nothing. He is accused of being "a traitor to the Party," "an agent of the General Securitate" (police agency of the previous government), "a spy for the English and Americans," "a counterrevolutionary," and the like. He is accused of arranging an attempted escape by communists in order to get them legally massacred by the prison guards who had been alerted to the escape by Pătrășcanu himself. An escape that fortunately fell through owing to the vigilance of the comrades who . . . et cetera. He is finally accused of trying to flee the country. The prosecutor speaks of a huge sum of money found in the airplane being readied for the getaway. I now understand why they went to such lengths to get me to state that Pătrășcanu had entrusted me with the hiding of money. Thus there would have been evidence that this money really existed and that the escape had been premeditated.

Right in the middle of the indictment, photographers show up loaded with cameras, all aimed at us, shooting each of us in turn. One of the cameras clings stubbornly to my face, comes up closer, steps back, comes back up. I don't hear the prosecutor's spite-filled voice. I freeze. I am terrified at the thought of this film being shown in the news. (But no one ever saw it.) I make an effort to erase any hint of life from my face. I don't even blink. I want people to realize that I am not really alive. Nothing but a puppet. A figure from a wax museum.

The prosecutor is still speaking. The prosecutor yells. The prosecutor barks. Several times, Pătrășcanu, despite himself, beside himself, cannot keep from interrupting. In a powerful voice he shouts: "Why don't you accuse me as well of murdering my own father?" or "So many words, so many lies!"

I once again attempt to turn my head. I see him yelling: "Lies! Lies typed out on a typewriter!" He turns around again. I look at Harry. He is very thin. He looks at me too and has just enough time to make a small familiar gesture from our youth. Pretending to fix the button on his shirt collar, he brings his pinkie finger to his mouth and flicks it in my direction. But the guards are there. One of them roughly clamps my arm.

I don't remember whether it was before or after the indictment that the clerk read the list of witnesses. An endless succession of names. Frequently the formula "unknown at this address" follows the name. All these "unknown at this address" are the witnesses called for by the defendants. A hundred witnesses are declared present. All of them witnesses for the prosecution.

The president calls for a recess. The trial will resume in a quarter of an hour. They have us go out. Cross the hall. I am led to another large room. The guard once again pushes me toward one of the walls, facing it, and orders me not to move. Behind me I hear footsteps, whispering. Finally, the interrogator. He seems very pleased. He says he has a surprise for me. He allows me to turn around. I turn around. A few steps in front of me is Harry. I hurry over to him. So quickly that they are caught unprepared. I embrace him and have only time to murmur in his ear: "Don't be sad," for the guards rush over, grab me and push me to the wall. Harry later told me that those three words were his only comfort during the worst hours of his imprisonment.

The trial resumes. The prosecutor goes on to the other defendants. To the five men unknown to me and to the woman. They are accused of various acts of treason. Perpetuated before the communists came to power. During the war and even before. Pătrășcanu acted as a go-between for their group and ours. I gather that three of them are old Party members accused of letting themselves be bought by the capitalists and the imperialists. One of them is accused of supplying information to the English and the Americans during the war. My head spins. Weren't these countries the allies of the USSR? Didn't this information concern their common enemies? Furthermore, won't I have the same fate in store for me? Even the old man behind hears himself accused of espionage in the pay of the English. He is also accused of having had secret rendezvous with Pătrășcanu. In a bleating, exasperated voice the man speaks to Pătrășcanu.

"I implore you, Mr. Pătrășcanu, I implore you, tell them that I have never met you. Never spoke with you. Tell them that you don't know me! Speak, sir, speak. I beg of you. Tell them that I don't know you!"

I hear Pătrășcanu's voice roar: "I don't know you. I've never met you!"

This shout surprises my guards. I quickly turn my head. I see his outstretched arm, the finger pointing at Herbert Zilber, roaring: "It's he! He's the guilty one! He's the monster who made all this up!"

Several times during the indictment, I'd heard murmuring in the room. But now it was a general uproar. Hearing the old man's desperate cries, the resolute voice of Pătrășcanu, the men and women who fill the room begin to laugh. I hear them laughing. Burst out laughing. I hear the coarse laughter of the men. I hear the hysterical tittering of the women. The verdict has already been given.

They had packed the hall with activists. Communists for hire. They had been ordered to produce an atmosphere that was unfavorable for the defendants. They had been ordered to laugh. They laughed. Blind, deaf, completely devoid of any human feeling, swollen with collective hysteria, with empty slogans; with hatred, rapacity, and fear, the mindless people laughed.

The guilty one, the only culprit behind the blood to flow, the Party secretary didn't have the guts to attend. Lurking in his den, awaiting his prey, he is not laughing. He is trembling.

The first of the trial's six days has just ended.

Day 1542 of detention—April 7, 1954

Nothing. At least for me. I am bored stiff in the cell and totally ignorant of what is happening in the courtroom. No doubt they are hearing the witnesses.

Day 1543 of detention—April 8, 1954

They brought me to the courtroom. All the lawyers are there. Motionless, frozen on their chairs. None of the other defendants is present. The president asks me the familiar questions, one after another. One after another, I recite the lessons I've learned. Without commas. Without periods. Without intonation. But quickly. The lawyers protest. They can't hear my answers. It is clear that I don't even take time to listen to the whole question. Not even time to think. I rush and blurt out the answers without taking time to breathe. My intent is too obvious. The president is annoyed. He asks me to speak more slowly. I am in such a hurry that I don't hear him. And then I get an answer mixed up. I've given the answer to the next question. The president pretends not to notice this. But I am trying to get this over with as quickly as possible. I would like to get away. Not be there.

I have finished. A man is called to the witness stand. All I know is his name. I know who he is. In 1937 Harry's brother the painter got a divorce. Then he went off to Paris. His wife had left him for this man. She married him. During the fascist period they both left for Israel, although he was not Jewish. I don't recall ever laying eyes on him. What is he here for?

His testimony is brief. He was living in Jerusalem, he says. It was in 1941. One day a friend of his had pointed out a passerby in the street. He did not know this man. His friend had said: "That's the engineer Nicol Gross from Bucharest. He works for the British propaganda agency." Period. That was it.

The court appeared to be satisfied with the testimony. No further question was asked of him. The president judged the proof had been given. Nicol was an important spy. Therefore, I was too. I was condemned on the basis of this testimony alone. (I recall once again that in 1941, the English and the Americans were allied with the USSR against fascism. The court took the viewpoint of the anti-Soviet policy of Marshal Antonescu. Logically, if I had really transmitted information that made possible an earlier victory of the *three* allies, I would have merited congratulations.)

It is true that they brought in a second witness, Pătrăşcanu's wife. She had been arrested with him in 1948. I myself was arrested for the first time that same day. After six months of detention, I was released but the Pătrăşcanus were placed under house arrest in the countryside, in a summer cottage that she had had built after the war. In January 1950, however, I had been arrested again and this time for good. The president asked her only a few insignificant questions about me. A mere pretext for having brought her before the court. Because the law forbade one spouse testifying against the other, having her come as a witness against another defendant was their means for circumventing the law. They thus had a chance to ask her all the insidious questions they wanted to about her husband's ideas and activities. Ideas and activities that were "Trotskyist and counterrevolutionary." Her answers, like mine, had been memorized. Two weeks later in a second trial, an adjunct to ours, she was found guilty.

Day 1544 of detention—April 9, 1954

Nothing. The cell and despair.

Day 1545 of detention—April 10, 1954

With the ceremonial of the first day, all the defendants were in the courtroom. The defense takes the floor. Our lawyers? Every one of them pathetic. Anxious, servile puppets. Their speeches for the defense? An amazing feat. They begin by admitting straight off all the charges brought against their so-called clients. They declare the charges not only real, but entirely proven. That is not enough

for them. They do even better. They show the profound indigna-
tion the defendants' crimes inspire in them. None of the lawyers
attempts to defend his client.

After describing my offenses, my lawyer nevertheless in-
vokes an extenuating circumstance: "It's her father's fault, it's her
mother's fault. Her only excuse lies in the petit-bourgeois education she's had . . ."

The final lawyer to take the floor is the dean of the Bar. He
must defend his former minister of justice. Even so he has a certain
opportunity. He does not succeed in making his shameful closing
statement for the defense. From the first word, the booming voice
of his "client" orders him to shut up. Forbids him to continue. He
forbids him to utter his name. He refuses to play a role in this
farce. After several abortive attempts to continue, the dean of the
Bar gives up.

The president announces that the defendants have the right
to take the floor to defend themselves if they can present some evidence on their behalf. The right? The interrogator had given me
the order to talk. To acknowledge my guilt. To ask for the bench's
clemency. I had thought that this was my chance now or never to
say "no." Not guilty. The whole investigation was merely a cruel
and macabre hoax. Would I have done it? If I had been the first to
take the floor, I would have at the very most the satisfaction of
having tried. Alas! I was not granted this opportunity, and what
happened before my turn shattered all my hopes.

Three of the six unknowns were longtime Party members.
Underground members. Elderly men. Serious. Desperate. Innocent. One after another, they tried to get a hearing for the truth.
To defend themselves. To explain. To prove. To accuse. The president prevented them from doing so. They could not speak of their
activity without constantly mentioning the "Party." Without using
the words "Party" or "communist." Abruptly, the president forbade them to utter the "sacred words." He could not allow them
to defile these words, and I quote, "defile" these words. Nevertheless, in their every phrase they came back to these words. They
had received "the order of the party." The president cries out. "I
sacrificed my life for the Party." Shouting. They are at the end of
their tether, trying vainly to stay clear of the taboo words. Struggling. Starting over again. And again. Banging with his fist, fuming, crimson-faced, just short of apoplectic, the president achieves

his ends. It wasn't by accident that his boss has made him president. The three shattered defendants, one after the other, give in. Any courage, any show of resistance is crushed, any remaining energy, destroyed. It is all over. I can do nothing more. They are the strongest. They will always be the strongest.

It is Herbert Zilber's turn. He begins talking volubly. With the self-assurance of an accomplished actor. He acknowledges his guilt. He can only regret the attitude of his friend Pătrăşcanu, who is just as guilty as he. But he has told the whole truth to the Party in order to prove his remorse. But he cannot get on with his evangelical speech, either. His words are cut off, drowned under a torrent of invectives uttered not by the president but by the furious voice of Pătrăşcanu: "Bastard, monster, swine! Have you no shame mentioning my name?" The president explodes. For a moment the courtroom is transfixed, then gasps. Zilber is forced to leave his friend to his grim fate. But he declares he expects a just punishment for his errors. A severe sentence that would allow for his atonement. When my turn comes, I murmur that Pătrăşcanu's past was unknown to me. I said nothing more. In the middle of the session, they could not force me to. The treatment they would accord me at the penitentiary allowed them a rather long revenge.

Everything has been said. Tomorrow at ten in the morning, the verdict.

I want only to return to my cell. To be alone. With my papers, my brush, and the colors that make this enclosed space inhabitable. But the cell has become a cell again. The table is bare. The cell is empty. They have taken everything from me . . . already.

Day 1546 of detention—April 11, 1954

I get out of bed. I get dressed and wait. I wait to be taken to the courtroom. I wait for the session and I am afraid. I know that the interrogator's promises were nothing but base deception. Haven't I always known it, moreover?

The morning cart rolls down the corridor. Doesn't stop at my door. No more breakfast? What difference does that make? I wait.

Tense. Feverish. I wait.

I keep an ear out for the guard's footsteps. For the first time, I want him to stop at my door. He's coming? No. He's only opening the judas. He only looks at me. He is only passing by. Passing by. Passing by. I wait.

Outside the sun is shining. The walls of the cell reflect its light. Become lighter and lighter. I wait.

Hours. Months. Years. A lifetime.

The sun must be at its zenith. The middle of the day, noon, and I wait.

At the end of the corridor, they are beginning to serve lunch. The cart comes closer. The creak of the wheels. The clinking of the mess tins. The door opens. The guard hands me a mess tin. In the mess tin a greenish liquid. In the greenish liquid some dried peas. A slice of black bread . . . and I know that there is nothing left to wait for.

It's the end. The end of everything. I have been convicted. Even so, one hope still remains. The only one. The last one. The death sentence.

PART TWO

Antecedents

5 April–October 1948

On that morning, I went as usual to the puppet theater workshop.

Before working with her, I had met Pătrăşcanu's wife only twice. By chance. The first time was before the war, in 1938, I believe, at an exhibition. The second time was during the war, in 1943. At a mountain resort. If I hadn't already learned that the communist Pătrăşcanu and his wife were living there under house arrest, I would certainly not have recognized her.

I recall the scene exactly. I saw them from a distance. Between us, a long stone bridge. Under the bridge, babbling water foamed over the boulders in the river. They were already partway across the bridge. To my right, a path followed the course of the water. I could pretend I didn't recognize her. I could still turn to the right. But the thought alone made me uneasy. So I made it a point of honor to greet them. They stopped, surprised. People generally tried to avoid them. On the roads, the local people looked only furtively at "the communists." Trailing them were the remnants of the old ancestral terror. The clanking of the leper's bell, the ball and chain. A whiff of brimstone in their wake. We exchanged a few words. She introduced her husband. When they wandered off, slowly, strolling nonchalantly, I didn't realize that these were the steps of destiny, of my destiny, that were fading away behind me. Then I, in turn, crossed the bridge. The water still coursed by and nothing could stop it.

Was it then that everything began?

It may be due to those few words, to the water babbling on the stones, that following the armistice she invited me to join the cultural department of a "progressive" organization (like several others, serving as camouflage for Party propaganda). She was its head. Her husband was now the minister of justice. A marionette theater. She had long dreamed of it. She spoke to us about it. Proposed that we collaborate to get her old plans back on their feet. Gave us a theme. Asked us to submit sketches for her. Mine had the good fortune—or misfortune—to please her. I became one of the set decorators of the first Romanian Puppet Theater. She designed the sets. I, mainly, the puppets.

Is that how it all began?

Now in that month of April 1948, three years later, we already had a hall and a public. But the beginnings had been difficult. With no experience, no tradition (there did exist a kind of game of puppets in Romanian folk art, but it was absolutely rudimentary). With no regular subsidies, no pay, some ten people had to do everything the best they could and with their own hands. Implementing the plan had required ingenuity, passion, and above all countless hours of work. Of course, we had at the same time to get on with our primary occupations.

Our drive to succeed brought us together. Spending a great deal of time together, often working late into the night, we were soon linked by a real camaraderie and, by the force of circumstances, my friend Harry joined in—as our musical adviser—and then Pătrăşcanu himself.

So, that morning, I had gone to the workshop as usual. I didn't stay long. My exhibition of book illustrations had had its opening a few days before, and around ten o'clock I left the workshop to go there. Around noon Pătrăşcanu's wife entered the gallery. She gripped my arm, took me to a corner and told me . . .

After I had left the workshop, Pătrăşcanu's bodyguard had phoned her. An hour earlier he had accompanied Pătrăşcanu, summoned to the Party headquarters. For two months now he had been blacklisted. He had, however, been allowed the use of the ministerial car, driver, and the police officer. They could thus more easily monitor all his activities and encounters. The summons to the Party headquarters was no cause for alarm. On the contrary. He himself had expressly urged it. To talk. To ask for some explanations. To understand what had happened.

The police officer went on with the story. The car was parked in front of the Central Committee. He and the driver had seen him leave an hour later, accompanied by two comrades. But without making any signal to them, without even looking at them, he and the others had gotten into a car belonging to the Central Committee. The car had started up in a hurry. The chauffeur had tried unsuccessfully to follow it. He had been shaken off at an intersection. This was odd, to say the least. Not to mention disquieting.

We both left the exhibition. I couldn't leave her alone, for she couldn't disguise her fright. We went to Harry's place. From there she phoned home several times. Nothing. Pătrășcanu still hadn't returned. He hadn't phoned. The situation looked serious. Around three o'clock I accompanied her back home. She begged me not to leave her alone. So I came up with her and we waited.

Not for long. At four o'clock, a comrade whom she appeared to know brought her a note. After reading it, her feverish face turned deathly pale. She let the paper fall on the desk, then led the man next door into the dining room. I heard her tell him she would be ready in five minutes. She and her husband lived in a three-room apartment. A study, the dining room, and a small bedroom. This overmodest apartment was part of the grievances gradually collected against Pătrășcanu and his wife. He was the Party's only popular figure in the country. The Party had now put down strong roots. As long as this popularity had served the Party's purposes, its first secretary had kept to himself his animosity toward the idealistic, honest, and genuinely patriotic intellectual comrade, Pătrășcanu. The time had come to eliminate him. To make him the victim of a Romanian trial, similar to the other trials instituted against important members of the Party in all the other "people's democracies," in order to denounce the machinations of the capitalist countries.

I had remained by myself in the study. I picked up the note. I read it. It asked her to come join him. That she bring along a change of clothes. That she bring him *The History of Diplomacy*, which he happened to be reading.

She reentered the study holding a small suitcase. Without saying a word, she embraced me. I stood at the door, watching her slowly go down two flights. They had a very devoted housekeeper. I saw tears running down her face. What could I say to her? I picked up my purse. I opened the door and left. Outside, the irony of a springtime sun, but also the car, the driver, and the police officer. Why were they still there? The officer offered to drive me. Where? To Harry's place. At the time I wasn't thinking that they had remained there for the purpose of checking up on my movements. I stayed with Harry only half an hour, for he was due for a radio broadcast. We had voiced all kinds of possibilities. Save for the one that we ourselves were implicated in this settling of scores. I went out in the street. By chance, our apartments were in two nearly adjacent buildings. He was the head of the Folklore Institute which he had founded after August 23 with Pătrășcanu's support, and he had a room at the institute. So I only had to take a few steps, cross the street, and I was home. I did not reach my front door until six months later.

Because a car was parked at the street corner. Because an old man wearing a cap opened the car door and motioned for me to get inside. Because the car started and after many turns entered a neighborhood of private houses and gardens and stopped in front of the gate of a two-story house. We crossed a small garden. An old woman opened the door for us. They had me go up to the second floor. There in a little hall two men were waiting for me. The old woman was Hungarian. The two men, Romanian.

Finally, they took me to a bedroom. Two beds. One for me, the other for my woman guard. I was strictly forbidden to go down to the ground floor. By crossing the hall, I could use the bathroom, but the door of my room was to be left ajar at all times. Next to it, one policeman during the day, another at night, could remain continually on watch.

The old woman brought me supper on a tray, really quite decent. But my throat was so constricted that I couldn't swallow a single mouthful. She seemed distressed by this and later she went to a great deal of trouble to stimulate my appetite, but in vain. I could get almost nothing down.

Every morning, a third policeman left all the day's newspapers and magazines on the table. Feverishly, I thumbed through them looking for a headline, an article, a word, or at the very least some reference to us. Nothing. Day after day, nothing.

Every evening around seven, two men came, gloomy and irate. They asked me one question. Every evening the same question: "What have you to declare?" Nothing. I really had nothing to declare. Absolutely nothing.

The two windows of the room looked out on the garden. A

few bushes, an iron gate, and, beyond, the street. Passersby were infrequent. It was a very quiet street. Adjacent to the house, an identical one. In front of the house, a little girl and boy often played in the courtyard with a big white rabbit. At midday, the father returned. With cries of joy, the children would cling to him. All three would go back in the house. I was very unhappy.

In one of the rooms on the first floor was a small library. The police officers randomly brought me only dull Romanian and French novels. It was all the same to me. But as I spent my days and nights reading, the house's library was soon exhausted. The magazines they brought me contained articles filled with dogma. It was the great period of socialist realism. Repudiate the past. Scorn the country's traditions, customs, culture, and values. Make up a new history. This literature was unreadable. But having nothing whatever to read was to go mad. I got along well enough with the old woman. After her housework was done, she took up some knitting and came to work in my company. We talked. She, about her daughter. I, about my mother. I read to her from a Hungarian newspaper. She had taught me to pronounce and read Hungarian, though I didn't understand a word of it. A friend of hers worked nearby in a house that was full of books. She promised to bring me some. Indeed, the next day she returned with two large volumes. On the flyleaf I was touched to read the name of the house's owner. I knew this book-filled house. I had painted a farming scene, "The Harvest of the Fruit," on one of the dining room walls. The books belonged to professor Dimitrie Gusti, the head of the Romanian school of sociology. My sister, Harry, and I had all been part of some research teams studying the sociology of the Romanian village. I had met Harry in one of the villages made famous by the monograph. Led by the professor, some fifty specialists and students swarmed down on the duly selected village, and during a too-short month of summer, the cards piled up in the files. Harry studied folk music. I, folk art, pottery, furniture, fabrics, the embroidery of costumes, and icons. Virtually everything that necessarily had some place in a peasant dwelling. The idea of an art object was unknown to the mentality of the village, where everything was functional. But the peasant man and woman unconsciously filled out the functional with their need for joy, escape, and beauty. Thus, for them, any decorated object had a precise function. For us it was an art object.

For the days devoted to enthusiastic research, for the nights of literary or musical discussion, of walking under the stars, the friendship and shy loves, for the rosy dawn that told us to get two or three hours of sleep, the sociological studies were the joy of our youth. We were grateful to the professor and loved him.

A name on a page of a book. . . . Why had all this past been condemned? The professor no longer lived in his house. His library no longer belonged to him. I had been the victim of an abduction, an official one. What had happened to Harry? All that was left was ashes.

The next day, out of idleness and especially out of the instinct of an animal pacing its cage, I opened the bedroom's armoire. It was empty, save for a few coat hangers. On the wood of each hanger were some words in blue ink: the name and address of the former tenant. My new address.

This was my first unconscious encounter with one of the dilemmas faced by prisoners. To follow or not to follow the rules set down by the jailers? But I didn't even consider this problem. The answer had imposed itself. This choice remained irrevocable during all my years in prison. To follow the rules is to respect the rules. I hadn't the least respect for my jailers nor for their so-called rules. I hadn't accepted them, and each time I had the courage to break them, I was deeply gratified.

Moreover, those days, I was subject to an idée fixe. This feeling was unbearable to me. I had to follow it through to the end in order to have done with it. I *had* to inform my family of my address. So I had an obligation to deceive my guards. In order to finally breathe easily.

I didn't even ask myself a second question. A fundamental one. For what purpose? Today I answer logically. None. They could not come rescue me. Nor come see me. Nor write me. So? But ask a caged animal for logic. It will obey only its instinct. Struggle and, if it can, bite.

The abuse of power leads to rebellion. Resistance is triggered by injustice, force, the prison system, the poor treatment, the lies. Resistance that, in the civilized being, takes the passive forms of dissimulation, guile, and the lie, for the restraints imposed on him by education, religion, and society remain in effect even in prison. For the primitive being, however, no inhibition prevents the savage outbursts prompted by any attack on his personal dignity and his conception of justice. The acts of violence that extend to crime will be no more than the spontaneous and inevitable expression of the instinct for freedom, for the defense of the intimate being, of the self in its uniqueness.

It is, so to speak, the explanation and justification for locks and shackles. Inverting this judgment, shackles are the "expected" penalty for the instinct for self-defense.

Years later, based on my own experience and that of Harry, I was able to separate the male and female prisoners into three categories. But the percentage of these categories varied according to gender and to the offense: political or common law.

I think of all the women I knew in prison. The vast majority of them belonged to the first category. The one that respects—as much as possible—the rules. Seventy-five percent of the female political prisoners were passive—owing to fear, despair, an edgy apathy, a lack of imagination, a desire to gain the good will of the authorities, or to preserve a minimum of physical health. They were probably right.

For the ones in the second category, the agitated ones, the insurgents, the revolutionaries, only made trouble for themselves. In the first place, a permanent state of anxiety. Their senses are ever alert. Their hands groping about, their eyes probing, their ears cocked. It is an obstinate search for the opponent's weak spot. And too often there comes the punishment. The punishment that will give a new and more forceful impetus to resistance and rebellion. Nearly all the legionnaires in my future penitentiary belonged to this second category.

Finally, the third category, insignificant among women, unveils the main difference between the sexes. For many of the male political prisoners "squealed." They were informers and betrayers. Always for some illusory gain, they betrayed their companions in adversity. Their brothers and sisters. The noble family of outcasts.

It is true that the vast majority of all women I knew were no more "political" than I was. The wives of former officials who were in prison, a woman who had sheltered a relative, a friend, or even a stranger (for financial gain), women who refused to denounce a father, husband, or son, peasant women whose husbands had resisted the collectivization of their land, peasant women who had collaborated in one way or another with the partisans hiding in the mountains and forests, all these women were small fry for the security agencies. It was different for the men. Politicians from the old system, members of various governments from the "historical" parties, great industrialists, high-ranking clergymen, senior military officers, civil servants from the former—mainly anticommunist—police, the information that they could still get from their associates in prison was or could be important for the "Securitate," the state police. The political officers in the prisons sought by every means to convince them or buy them—through promises or better food—to get them to talk or get others to talk.

I don't know if one can break the rules boldly. Perhaps. For my part, I have always broken them apprehensively. But it was stronger than I. So I looked for and found a solution.

They had let me keep my handbag. Without even checking its contents. I had my identity card, a comb, a tube of lipstick, keys, a hundred-*lei* bill, a five-*lei* bill, a few small coins, and, by some happy chance, an envelope with a blank sheet of paper and a pen. I took only half a sheet, to keep some paper in reserve, and I shut myself up in the bathroom. I wrote my mother's name and address, her phone number, and a few words asking the person who might find the note to phone her and inform her that I was in good health and that there was no need to worry. I had nothing of any weight within reach. I used the coins. I tied the whole thing with a thread taken from the old woman's ball of yarn and I stationed myself in front of the open window. The guard was dozing in his chair. The woman was downstairs preparing lunch. My heart pounding, I threw the note out the window. But it fell short of the fence, right in the hedge. I had missed my mark. I saw it, a little scrap of white. If it stayed there, the guards might discover it.

Children's shouts and laughter. The sound of a ball hitting the street. They ran in front of the house. The ball went up, came back down, and suddenly went over the railing and got lodged in the hedge, right next to my scrap of white. A little boy climbed over the railing, took a few steps, looking for the ball. He bent over. Picked up the ball. The scrap of white had disappeared. Had he picked up the note? Had he stepped on it? In any case it never reached its destination.

My second attempt was nearly intercepted by one of the officers. This time I wrote a real letter. My mother's name and address on the envelope. I had written only three sentences. "I'm in good health, I give you a big kiss," and I had added my address. I pinned the letter and the hundred-*lei* bill to a newspaper, folded over several times to give it some heft, and threw it over the fence into the children's yard. Fortunately it fell on their side and close enough to the fence not to be visible from my window. I had been leaning far out of the window to throw it and I was straightening back up when the guard burst into the room and ran to the window. Not sighting anything out of the ordinary, he asked me what I had done.

"Me? Nothing. I was watching a white rabbit."

"A rabbit? White?"

"Yes. In the yard next door."

Then he leaned out. The good white rabbit was indeed hopping about the yard. The guard forbade me to look at white rabbits or rabbits of any other color, or to lean out the window, and he went away rather crestfallen.

My parents received that letter. On Easter day. In turn, my father and my mother walked by the house. I never had the joy of seeing them. One day the old woman told me that that very morning two women, one short, the other tall, passing in front of the house and seeing her in the garden, had asked her for a glass of water. It is an old tradition in Romania to give someone water to drink. When a stranger asks you for something to drink, it is you who are grateful for the chance this person has thus given you to appease the thirst of someone—in the beyond—who was close to you. Even an elderly Hungarian communist could not disregard this custom. She brought them a glass of water. She told me this and in the end murmured: "One of those women looked like you." It was true. I could never console myself for not having seen them. She had given something to drink to my mother and my father's sister.

These "strolls" demanded a good deal of courage and emotion from them. It would have been better for them had I kept quiet. But I went on attempting to communicate with them by every means. In the end I dared to confide in the old woman. She accepted. Gave me paper and promised to mail the letter. She phoned Harry several times. Late in the evening. At a time when only he could answer the call. The old woman only listened to him say "Hello? Hello?" and came to tell me: "He's there." So I knew that he had not been arrested and that delighted me.

I dreamed I was ill. Seriously. Pneumonia. It might force

them to send me to the hospital. Several mornings in a row, I lay for some time in the bathtub filled with cold water. I didn't even catch a cold. I didn't understand until later why they had me change residences.

One evening, around ten, a car honked in front of the house. I was already in bed, reading by the glow of the night-light. The old woman was still downstairs. The horn sounded again. I got up, pricked up my ears. I heard the officer hurry down the stairs. The door opened, the sound of a voice, finally followed by a whole to-do. I waited for over ten minutes in a state of anxiety and apprehension. Finally the old woman came in:

"Quickly! Quickly! Get dressed. The car is waiting. We are moving."

She had already taken her stock of food to the car. We left the house. I had been there for some forty days. In the car, a towel over my face, I followed through the white cloth the diffuse light from the streetlamps. We drove through the district.

An ambiance of bourgeois wealth still clung to this second house. Downstairs, the large living room filled with gleaming furniture. At the rear of the room, behind large glass doors, the foliage of a garden. A staircase and upstairs, opening onto a wide hallway, several rooms including a boudoir and a large bedroom. I was to sleep in the huge green satin bed of the family who doubtlessly now slept in the bed of a hotel in Switzerland. The inordinate luxury of their house was well worth two passports against the bank account. The old woman was to sleep in the boudoir.

On the doorstep, I had already spotted the telephone on the night table. The guards settled in one of the bedrooms. The old woman had gone downstairs to put the food in the refrigerator. I was alone. I checked the telephone. It was plugged into the wall behind the night table next to the bed. The main receiver was surely on the ground floor. I was familiar with the setup. A similar extension phone had been installed for me when I still lived with my parents and had my studio on the second floor. Somewhere there had to be a little black box with a switch attached to a wall. When the switch was vertical, the bell rang on both phones. When the switch was horizontal, the circuit downstairs was cut. But could the phone conceivably be functional? I had only to make a single gesture. Pick up the receiver. A click sounded in the bedroom. Rather loud. I should have thought of it. Taken the precaution of

closing the bedroom door, for the click was picked up by the officer's experienced ear. I heard him going through the hallway, the
boudoir. But when he came in, when he picked up the receiver,
when he held it up to his ear, no click could be heard. The phone
was dead. By a lightning reflex, at which I am still surprised, I had
yanked on the cord, thus unplugging it. Vainly he banged several
times on the cradle. Nevertheless, he was very much convinced he
had heard something. Unable to clear up the mystery, he left annoyed, yet still very suspicious. The incident would certainly be
noted in his report, and the next day . . . I had to take advantage
of the telephone right away. That very night. The next day they
would understand and take the phone away.

It was already very late. I had to go to bed. Pretend to sleep.
I went first to the bathroom, at the end of the hallway. At floor
level, half-hidden by a chair, was the black box. All I had to do was
nudge the switch with my foot to disconnect the phone from the
ground floor. In case one of the officers wanted to use it during my
own call.

Toward midnight the old woman went to bed. She was soon
fast asleep. From my bed I could hear her deep, regular breathing.
I had decided not to phone until two in the morning. In the middle of the night. The time seemed to me interminable. I was beside
myself with emotion and dreadfully frightened. I asked myself, in-
cessantly, if I would succeed in conquering this fear, knowing at
the same time that I would not change my mind, yet, simultaneously, regretting this. What madness drove me? Why was I torturing myself this way? I was in bed. The bed was perfect. I could
have been sleeping. Sleeping and dreaming.

Two o'clock. In my bare feet I tiptoe past the sleeping woman's bed. I go out into the hallway. Everything is silent. I close the
circuit. I go back into the bedroom. I plug in the cord. I take the
phone and burrow under the bed's huge mattress with it so as to
muffle the sound of my voice. I hear the dial tone. I gropingly dial
the number. My sister is most likely sound asleep. Her phone rings
once, twice, three times. What if something has happened to them?
This thought is more terrifying than the fear. Finally, her voice, half-
asleep. Faltering. She wakes up in a start, frightened by this call in
the night. Bewildered, she doesn't realize that the voice she hears
is mine whispering at the other end of the world. She finally manages to answer me. Yes, they are all in good health. No, they have

not had any trouble. I am probably speaking too softly. She has difficulty making out my words. Have you received my letters? I'm not living there anymore. She keeps repeating: "Where are you? Where are you?" How can I tell her? How can I tell her that I am suffocating under the enormous mattress of a bed, in a bedroom, in some unfamiliar house? Moreover, I realize I have nothing more to tell her. Sadly I murmur "good night" and put the receiver back on the cradle. Once I am out, I go into the bathroom. In passing, I kick the switch. I remake the bed and get back in it.

I remained awake for a long while. Vaguely let down. I will call her again the next night. She was now alerted. She would answer me coherently. I awoke with a heavy heart. Before me I had all the hours of a difficult day. Waiting for the night. But at ten in the morning, the police officer came into the bedroom. He went straight to the phone. When I saw him leaving with the phone, I addressed him in all my cowardice with a mute "thank you."

Two days later I chanced to learn the house's address and the name of the former tenants. At the back of the bedroom was a large storeroom. There, under some empty boxes, three school exercise books. On each page, meticulously noted in grams and calories, the daily menu for some diet or other. On the first page of each notebook, a name. The same name. In the hallway, on a small pedestal table, a telephone directory. I had only to thumb through it to find my address. But the hasty nocturnal change of residence, a certain uncommunicativeness in the old woman, and especially my sister's incomprehension concerning my letters had gotten me thinking. Nevertheless, the old woman had agreed to mail two more letters for me. Still addressed to my mother. I thus kept the address to myself.

In front of the house, a pretty, round square. An indistinct statue in the center. Many fine trees. Infrequent passersby. Few cars. A great calm. I should have kept my capacity for suffering for later.

Ten days after that, another move. This time I was lodged in a little room in the attic. A bed, a table, a chair. A nailed-down window with whitewashed panes. The air up there was very hot and muggy. All day long the police officers played cards in front of my door. They allowed me to sit near them to take advantage of their open window. On condition that I didn't go up to it. From time to time a third officer paid a visit. In shirtsleeves and slippers. Through the floor came the sounds and wrong notes of a piano being played by hesitant fingers. I figured that the third officer must be the guard of someone sequestered on a floor below.

Each morning I was given a cup of tea, some bread, butter, and a rather large cube of solid marmalade. I barely touched them. Nevertheless, the next morning the cube had been cut into. With the tip of a knife I scratched my name on one face of the cube. Two days later I received a response. Since they had cut off my newspapers, I really had nothing to read. The guards, who were not malevolent, went down to the floor below and brought me up some books. Right in the middle of a novel published in the Fasquelle edition, on the blank margin, written in tiny letters, written in pencil, a first name. That of Pătrășcanu's wife. Not her real name. A nickname I had invented, one that was then adopted by all her friends. Thus she was there and alone since I heard no sound of voices and knew that it could not be Pătrășcanu who was playing, for he had taken piano lessons when he was young. I had even heard him play, rather well.

Around five o'clock one afternoon, the guards invited me to sit near them. All three were playing cards and seemed to be totally absorbed in the game. They snapped the cards down on the table, telling each other stories, breaking into raucous laughter. Listening without hearing their words, I kept my thoughts fixed on the square of blue sky framed in the window. Suddenly I felt a light touch on my left knee. It was impossible to be mistaken about this. It was only a sign and nothing else. A sign made carefully and discreetly. I turned my head slightly. For a brief instant my eyes caught the eyes of the third officer. He was seated to my left. He gave me a barely perceptible wink. What was he trying to tell me? A few minutes went by. Finally, I saw his hand move slowly under the table and set something on my knee. With the same slowness my hand slid under the table and I felt between my fingers a piece of fabric. I closed my hand around it.

I couldn't take a look at it until I got to the toilet. A little square of printed cloth. I recognized the cloth from a summer dress worn by Pătrășcanu's wife. On the cloth, in faint pencil markings, the names of two little characters from one of the plays that we had produced together at the puppet theater.

The message was a bad omen. Only two hours later, the

sweltering room under the attic was just a memory. And a regret. I had disdained my palace. My fourth residence? An unreal cell in the most real of prisons. Long. Narrow. An iron cot filling its width almost entirely left me only a narrow passage a foot-and-a-half wide between the bed and a wall. No table. The cell was in a basement and had a window set high up just under the ceiling. If I stood up on the bed, I could see through it, at eye level, a narrow strip of lawn. Beyond, a square courtyard. Surrounding it, the prison buildings. Along the corridor, to my right, a single cell. To my left two cells. To go to the toilet, I had to knock for some time on the door. No guard stood permanently in attendance. When I was eventually heard, the guard made me go through the door at the end of the corridor. Go through a little entrance hall. There was an iron washstand. The guard opened a second door in front of me. We crossed a rather large room that opened onto a long, wide corridor. The first door to the left opened to the shower room and the toilets. Farther on, both sides of the corridor were lined with cells. Many cells. Probably large. The doors were spaced from fifteen to twenty feet apart.

I had arrived at dusk. The darkness had already colored the corridors ash-gray. The cell was ominous. I stretched out, fully dressed, on the hard mattress. My eyes closed, devastated. When at last I could come back to life and look around me, it was already nighttime. Dimly lit by a weak bulb, enshrouded in silence, this pokey little hole was like a tomb.

It was also very hot. I took off my blouse and skirt and got back into bed. Too many questions ran through my mind. Then I sought in vain for the answers. I needed once again to enter the void and go to sleep. To sleep . . . I had almost gotten there. I began losing consciousness. Sleep was almost upon me. I was just about there when the silence exploded in horror. The horror of a voice. Of a desperate cry. Right close by. On the other side of the wall. From what maelstrom of suffering arose this woman's name, this harrowing plea for help? "Vali! . . . Vali!" A haunting "help me." "Vali! . . . Vali! . . . Vali! . . ." Cried unremittingly. Ten times, twenty times. Again and again. "Vali! . . . Vali! . . . Vali! . . ." Endlessly. I couldn't stand it anymore. Softly I knocked on the wall. The cry stopped. But at more or less long intervals, day and night, the man's voice hung on to this name, a life buoy, a shepherd's star. I didn't dare shut him up again, make his dream disappear.

In the morning, a quite young guard led me to the shower room. The water was cold but it was midsummer, and after a good washdown, I felt a bit more composed. They didn't give me anything to eat that morning. It was all the same to me. For three months I had eaten only a minimal amount of food and, even so, I had to force myself. At midday, I received a mess tin of clear dried-pea soup and a slice of bread. I found the soup revolting. Inedible. That evening, around six o'clock, the same soup.

The day had been never-ending. I didn't even have room to move around. Seated on the thin straw mattress, the edge of the iron cot cutting into my thighs, I remained motionless, my head bent over, I stared at the floor. I would have given anything for the gift of a book.

The next day was the same. No! Worse. The third day, I was taken to an office on the floor above. After having me sit in a chair in front of him, the man who was there, behind his desk, opened a file. He took out three sheets of paper. Set them before me on the desk. I recognized my handwriting. They were my letters. The letters sent to my mother. The old woman had duped me. She had white hair. She also had a daughter whom she loved. She had smiled at me. And betrayed me.

"What do you have to say?"

"Not much. These letters were sent to my mother. There are no grievances or messages in them. I was merely doing my duty. In my place, would you have done otherwise?"

The man took back the three letters. Put them back in the file. Closed the file. I heard nothing else about it. I shall not elaborate upon this interrogation or the ones that followed. Questions about me, my childhood, my studies. My friends. A detailed autobiography. I answered them honestly. I had nothing to hide. About myself, about my opinions. The opinions of others were not mine. This first interrogator always spoke to me politely. He neither threatened me nor called me names. He simply asked me questions. I asked him for a book. That very day, the guard brought me one, *Ann Vickers* by Sinclair Lewis. The life of a militant social-ist. Arrested at a meeting of feminists, she spends two weeks in jail. This determined her life. She would totally devote herself to

improving prisons for women. I would have preferred to read
something else. For two weeks, I had only that single book. I read
it. Reread it. Translated it into French. I had almost learned it
by heart.

I had to find a pastime. I was wearing shoes with crepe or
rubber soles. On the soles I drew countless designs for houses. I
thus discovered that the ideal apartment needs an entrance off to
the side. Then I decided that a country house should be laid out
around an inner courtyard. I already saw the great tree growing in
the center of the courtyard and the gate providing access to the garden by some broad steps. After completing my house, I set about
furnishing it. I don't recall what pseudo-pencil I used to draw all
this. I recall only the faintness of the line and how easy it was to
erase. All this was not terribly interesting but it brought forgetfulness. I spent hours in total concentration.

The book gave me an idea for another game. I chose a rather
long word, and with the letters of this word I tried to make other
words. As many words as possible.

At the end of two weeks I was given a new book. A very fine
novel by B. Traven, *The Death Ship*. The least advisable book to
read in prison. Austere and demoralizing. The life of a sailor. A distant port. A stopover. A night of debauchery. He misses the sailing
of his ship. Stuck on land with no money, no papers, he is arrested
for vagrancy. The police clandestinely take him across the country's
border just to get rid of him. A new country, another arrest, another border. With no identity papers there is no possible existence.
His perpetual flight clearly has only one possible outcome: death.
That book gave me a great deal of pain.

The interrogator was dissatisfied with my answers. No confession, no information. Even so, he had to display his authority. Two
weeks later, he stopped the daily shower. This was a hard blow.
Returning from the toilet, I had to wash myself at the sink in the
little anteroom. My hands, my face. But the rest? I begged the
guard to leave me alone for a few minutes. It was the young man
from the first day. I washed quickly without thinking to keep an
eye on the door. It is, moreover, not easy to wash oneself without
undressing. After some ten days, suddenly I saw the door ajar. I let
go of my skirt and quickly returned to the cell. He tried entering
the cell after me. I pushed him back and he didn't dare to touch

me. He closed the door, muttering that he would come "chat" with me the next night.

Because of him, I finally decided to answer the call of my neighbor on the left. About a foot-and-a-half from the floor, along the wall opposite the door, a heating pipe went from one cell to another. The hole by which it went through the wall was a bit wider than the pipe. Because the wall was fairly thin, a voice whispering on the other side of it, in this hole, was perfectly audible. Three days after my arrival, a question came to me distinctly through the wall. "Who are you?" I got up and immediately located this voice, which repeated its question. I had immediately recognized the voice. The voice of Herbert Zilber (the number-three man). I had known him for a long time. I had even done him some important favors. But I had never considered him a "friend." His brand of intelligence, his smugness, his headlong way of talking, his plumpness, the forelock that he constantly twirled around his index finger, all these things I found faintly repulsive. I tried to keep this feeling to myself because he was Jewish. Because of the implication of racism, it is sometimes hard to react naturally to certain Jews.

The message sent by Pătrăşcanu's wife, followed so closely by my imprisonment, had instilled me with a superstition. I was convinced that answering Zilber would create new troubles for me. So I had not answered his question. He then continued to pester me every evening.

The guard's threat drove me to the wall. I began by giving a phony name. But he in turn had recognized me as well. To insist was ridiculous. He had been the first one arrested. A few months before we were. He told me he had lost a great deal of weight and also that Pătrăşcanu had been far too naive. That I myself had nothing to fear. What could "they" hold me responsible for? Nothing. That I must above all not let myself be intimidated. They would take advantage of it to get me to say anything at all.

Five years later, "they" had partially succeeded in this, but only because this man had provided them with an imaginary scenario and had cast me in a role. The important role. That of the spy.

He gave another piece of advice. To cry. He had learned this from an old peasant man with whom he had shared the cell for a time. Crying brings relief. Speaking with him, however, brought me no relief at all. On the contrary. I told him the story about the guard and asked him to intervene by making some noise if he heard the guard entering my cell.

I stretched out on the bed without going to sleep. In the middle of the night I heard stealthy footsteps. The key went slowly into the lock. I waited. Tense, ready to scream. Too bad for him. Some noise, a call, or perhaps his own fear kept him from turning the key. Slowly he took it out and went away. I didn't see him again for six years, when he came into my cell one night. Even then I wouldn't have recognized him if he himself hadn't made some reference to the past.

I still recall one difficult moment. It was afternoon. I had knocked on the door to be taken to the toilet. No one heard me. I went on knocking. To no avail. Over an hour passed this way in a wait that was becoming ever more urgent and painful. What could I do? Unable to stand it anymore, I had a stupid idea. I took out the padding from the shoulders of my overcoat. I decided to urinate onto this padding in the belief that it would be sufficiently absorbent. It wasn't. A mishap occurred. A pool of urine on the floor. A closed-in space, oppressive. Granular and dusty cement. A puddle of urine and a woman on the verge of despair. Who could imagine a picture with greater Stalinist realism?

With both hands I picked up the soiled padding and, rising up on tiptoe to reach the window, wrang it out on the grass. Mopping and wringing, I continued the operation while fearing that someone going through the courtyard might spot me. My hands were dirty. I didn't have any water. I thought that this was the height of loathsomeness. But it was only my own urine. Later, I had to dip my hands into the urine of others. But the height of the horrible will probably never be attained. Human beings are intelligent. They are inventive. They will always be able to do better at extending the frontiers of evil.

Before leaving this prison, I must talk again of hunger. In my three previous palaces I had eaten very little. But this little had been nourishing. Milk, butter, meat, vegetables, fruit. Now what they gave contained nothing, for nothing changed from the content of the first mess tin. The change took place in me. The lack of appetite was followed by hunger. It got so that I waited impatiently for the soup that I had found inedible the first day and now found delicious. I counted the dried peas before eating them. Sometimes there were fifteen of them, sometimes more. What a wealth! All the moral fables for children are true. And all the proverbs. I was really very hungry.

A maze of corridors. All along the low ceilings, pipes of all sizes. A horde of rats scurrying in these pipes. A few dim light bulbs. Their dying light lapping at the cracked walls. The dark hole of the cell. The glimmer of light filtering through the square opening above the door. The hazy atmosphere. The crunching of the cement as it crumbled under foot. The iron cot. The more than doubtful sheet. The coarse blanket, heavy with grime. It was a very old prison.

I arrived there in the dead of night. At four o'clock in the morning, a guard rapped his stick along the walls, making the bars on the doors reverberate. The wake-up call. Signal for the "program." Before my turn came, I had long heard the prisoners' unsteady footsteps shuffling along the corridor, going past my cell. Sometimes a bump. A man, fallen. A wreck, unable even to crawl. It is a very old prison of torture and death.

A surprise, however. The soup here was nourishing. Hot, thick, full of cabbage, carrots, potatoes, tomatoes—a very good soup, really. Sometimes it even had a bit of tendon in it. Since my teeth couldn't bite through it, I could suck at it for a long time.

The toilet was dirty. By way of toilet paper, a pile of old out-of-date administrative papers. A directory of the former names of the country's towns and villages. Now scrap because of the dozens of localities bearing the names of members of the royal family or aristocrats who owned lands and villages. But the great majority of the municipalities, small towns, and hamlets had beautiful archaic names. With their various regional sonorities, these names could be recited like poems. I filched pages from it and stashed them under the mattress.

For me these books were treasures. With their pliable cardboard covers, I constructed a deck of cards. The size of stamps, fifty-two drawn with the burnt end of matches moistened with saliva. Lying on the bed, sometimes propped up on one elbow, sometimes on the other, I had to lean low over the game to make out the faint gray lines in the darkness of the cell. I don't remember the cigarettes, but I must have received some since I had the matches. On bits of paper, I even drew an old fellow in several comical poses. He and his rooster were the heroes of a children's story I gradually made up. Telling the droll situations of an old peasant going to market with his rooster friend.

The guards' surveillance was sketchy. I don't think they were unaware of my drawings or my deck of cards. But that didn't interest them. I probably was of no account to them. No investigation. No requests. I lay low in my kennel. Never giving anyone any trouble. Never knocking on the door. For the greatest service that these books did for me was, among other things, prosaic, mundane, and essential.

With a flexible cardboard cover, I made a funnel. A simple cornet held together by a match. To do what? To solve the onerous problem of evacuating liquids. I had found a simple solution for it. On the floor, between the bedstead and the rear wall, there was a main pipe outlet. One of those thick cast-iron disks which usually had a ring fixed to the center. By coincidence, my disk had a hole in place of the ring. About an inch across. This aperture gave me the idea of a toilet at home. But did this pipeline still exist? Wasn't it completely plugged? I didn't want to risk a new flood. I needed to put out feelers. I needed a probe. I had decided that six feet of emptiness would do. The edge of a frayed sheet supplied the thread. A tiny hunk of cement, the weight. I had only to let my six feet of probe slowly slip through the hole. No obstacle and the thread came out dry. It was perfect. Instead of knocking on the door, calling the guard, and waiting until he deigned to open up, I went behind the bed. I fit the cardboard funnel into the aperture and squatted a little, with only one concern, to get a proper aim. In the darkness at the rear of the cell, no risk of surprise. I hid the funnel under the bed, hooked to one of the iron bars of the bedsprings.

I was very dirty. During the two or three minutes of the Saturday shower, I only had time to get wet and dry myself as best I could. The soap was too hard to be useful. It wouldn't soften. Fortunately, I could not see my dirtiness. To see my black fingernails I had to raise my hand high enough to reach the faint beam of light coming at a slant into the cell and losing itself at the tops of the walls. My elbows gradually became covered with a hard crust. It didn't hurt when I made a vain effort to scratch it. Once back home, the first hot bath melted it away. It was merely grime.

I cannot bring back other details. I know that I lived for

more than a month in that ash heap. I look at the pack of cards. The drawings. I close my eyes. I see the rats. I hear the sound of the stick glancing off the bars. I do not see myself. I cannot re- trieve my thoughts, my fears. As if all this hadn't really happened to me. As if someone had once told it to me. As though I had read it in a book. As though, in this prison, they had locked up only a body. With no memory. With no past. With no soul.

One evening, rather late, they had me leave the cell. Go up some stairs. Go along corridors. Suddenly, breathable air. Lights. An office. A man. I recognize the interrogator from the previous prison. He receives me politely. Asks me some questions. Then he utters a few words and, from there, I remember. I come alive again. I feel my blood streaming toward my heart again. A searing flash. A start of all being. I hurry over to thank him. Yes. To thank him for saying: "You are free."

This man was no longer the interrogator. The jailer. He was force. Power. The master of destiny. And my heart overflowed with gratitude for this master of evil giving me the "gift" of freedom. So true is it that for those six months, before those six months, during the war, after the war, the ideas of law, justice, good and evil had degenerated in me, in us all. Satan had taken possession of the earth. Evil was the recognized master of the world, and Satan was man.

A guard led me to the clerk's office. Someone had me sign something. I asked to return to my cell for a moment to get my things. I took my cards and drawings from their hiding place un- der the mattress. The guard let me be.

I find myself outdoors. In the night. But why am I not alone? Why is this man walking so close to me? Next to the sidewalk, a large black car. Why is he urging me to get in? Behind me, how- ever, the prison door has closed. I will not get in this car. The in- terrogator said it. I am free. Where does this man want to take me? It takes him some time to persuade me. It seems that I am not al- together presentable. That it would be better to avoid the risk of unsuitable encounters. Besides, he had been ordered to drive me home by car and we must both follow the order.

My house? What house? It had been April when I was ar- rested. Now it was October. Did I still have a house? I give my parents' address.

Peering through the blackness with my face glued to the

window, I agitatedly follow the car's path. The direction taken is reassuring. But it is only at the third turn that certainty comes over me. I know that at the end of these childhood streets I am returning home.

That was in October 1948. I was arrested again on January 17, 1950. My freedom had lasted fifteen months.

PART THREE

The Penitentiary

6 Dumbraveni

Day 1 of penitentiary—April 15, 1954

We've been driving a long time. For hours. In a confined space, made for a single person, pressed up against each other, I listen to her speak. She speaks nervously. Hurriedly. For years, like me, she has not spoken to another human being. At the trial, I had merely noticed her. Heard the prosecutor's allegations. She had been sentenced to only eight years. Hence, innocence itself. The equivalent of a prize for virtue.

I had lived the final three days in a state of utter despondency, for on April 12, around six in the evening, they had dragged me to an office. One of the three officers present notified me of my sentence.

Twelve years of hard labor for the crime of high treason, ten years for counterrevolutionary activity. Twenty-two years? The shock was lethal. I have never fainted and I am still sorry for that. I would have gained a few minutes of amnesia. But I felt my knees trembling. The prosecutor hastened to explain the law. He was benevolence itself. The law, with the same benevolence, exempted me from the minor punishment and wished very much to take the years of investigative detention into account. Thus, he concluded, you face only about seven more years of imprisonment. A mere bagatelle! He also told me that at the penitentiary I would have companions and work "in your specialty."

In the morning, at dawn, they had me get into a police van. A narrow central corridor lined with tiny cells. Our whole trial must have been there. Headed for the penitentiary. I felt Harry's presence close by. I had learned only about my own sentence and that of the woman. Not those of the others. How would I have known, alas, that not all of us were present? One of us was no longer of this world. They had liberated him (Pătrăşcanu) . . . definitively.

For lack of space they had me squeezed in with this woman. In the darkness, terror-stricken by the sudden intrusion of this alien body on her body, she had let out a heartrending cry. Now she was happy to not be alone. She too had made up poetry. She told me about her childhood, the family home, her parents, her brother. She talked about the trial. "All of it was untrue," she said calmly. "But the Party is never wrong. It must have had some reason we can't understand." Furthermore, she didn't feel she was really innocent. She had dared to doubt the Party. So she was guilty in thought. Because of her husband's disappearance. She knew nothing about his fate. She believed he was in Siberia. But they had given her time to reflect. To understand. And she had understood. It was the Party who had been right and her husband wrong. She had been influenced by him. She deserved her eight years of prison. Finally, she told me that her own suffering, the separation from her little girl, the loss of her husband carried little weight compared to the supreme disaster, the irremediable calamity, the unspeakable anguish of the passing of Comrade Stalin.

I can't get over it. Stalin died? Yes. In 1953, and she was still just as disconsolate. With horror, I recognized her mystical adoration. It was the hysteria of the German women raising altars to Hitler.

I lose all pity for this woman. My proximity to her makes me feel vaguely nauseated, but I have no room to back away. And I continue to feel this body quivering with a demented amorousness against my body. This woman is insane. Truly insane. She herself says so, moreover. She claims to have been unable to bear the sexual loneliness. Tells me about her nervous breakdowns. Her suicide attempt. Through suffocation. She stuffed her throat with all the padding from the shoulders of her coat. A guard intervened just in time. She had been saved, then insulted, and finally punished.

Around noon, the van halts. One after another, at short intervals, the doors open and close. Our turn comes. They tell us to get out. A vast, barren plain. For some time I had been feeling the vehicle going uphill. The sullen sky of a chilly April. Piles of stones. An occasional bush. Not a single leaf yet. But some ten militiamen, weapons in hand. Guns aimed at two women with blinking eyes and quaking knees. In front of and behind the police van, two jeeps. Are they really afraid of us?

I can finally see the woman. Her scrawniness. Her pathetic little black coat. Her emaciated hand clasped over her flat chest to hide the tatters of her blouse. Her pasty face. Her brown hair streaked with gray and, on her face, the reflection of my fear. Has this place been chosen for a discreet execution?

We look at these men. These men look at us. Finally one of them breaks the silence:

"Relieve yourselves."

"Of what?"

He puts it crudely. All right. But . . . where? Here. I ask them to turn around. No. When all is said and done, it's all the same to me. As discreetly as I can, I lower my panties while squatting. A liquid stream splashes on the pebbles and trickles through the meager grass. I get back up. She is still motionless. Her eyes frenzied. Her face overtaken by her crazy eyes.

"Don't you need to?"

"Yes, I do. But I can't. I can't do it in front of them."

"Yes, you can. You must. Later on it will be too late."

I get in front of her. Very close to her. I block them from her sight. But I can't bear her face. I turn my head away. One of these human apparitions put a half-loaf of white bread and a hunk of cheese on the fender of the van. He chews with a look of bliss on his face. At my feet, a gurgling. A second stream slowly advances toward his boots.

We start up again. In the compartment, total darkness. There is indeed an opening, but it is obstructed by superimposed strips of sheet metal. Only the cold gets through. She goes on talking. Feverishly. The noises outside suggest that we are going through villages. A city. A second halt. All the doors open but ours. They have all the men get out. The woman says that, judging from the time elapsed, we must be at the Aiud Penitentiary. She is very disappointed. She had supposed that we would all be together. Men and women. As in the USSR, she had told me nostalgically. Earlier she had given me a detailed account of the charms of our new life. We were finally going to be able to take care of "our men." Wash their linen. Darn their socks. Have a cultural life. Hold lectures. Even put on shows. Every one of us, in turn, teacher and pupil. She had imagined a number of things. She had been slightly mistaken. Nothing surprising. She was a militant communist. A Stalinist. But she had never been to the USSR. Her only experience, a few months in one of the country's prisons under the old regime. She still had a lot to learn.

They now open our cell. Have us get out. A square courtyard. Tall buildings. Barred windows. We get into one of the jeeps. Next to the driver. They blindfold us. I am seated next to the door. The woman between the driver and me. An armed militiaman in the back. We drive off again. Making grimaces and knitting my brows, I manage to raise up the blindfold a little. Out of the corner of my eye I see waterlogged fields go by. Village houses. It is raining. This doesn't tell me where we are going, but I have the satisfaction of foiling the surveillance. Cold comfort, but seeing these woebegone villages drowned in the watery vapors merely increases my own misery.

A third halt. A gate creaks, however, and while the wheels clatter over a threshold, a bell breaks the silence, resounding discordantly. A huge courtyard. On the left, low buildings, most likely annexes, stand nestled under the tiled roofs. The jeep stops in front of the large building on the right. With some difficulty we go up the few stone steps. We are in one of the numerous prisons built by the empress Maria-Theresa of Austria in this province of Romania that struggled mightily to regain its freedom. A very old prison. How many rebels must have trampled over these stones, for having worn them down to this point? Made them so smooth, so sloping, and slippery under our feet. Feet stumbling from fatigue. From cold. From hunger, perhaps. We hadn't had anything to eat or drink all day. We are spent beyond measure. This prison fills us with fear. Fear of the life awaiting us. We are only two useless burdens, and how contemptible.

Beyond the steps, a vast enclosed space. The central hall of the penitentiary. Very high above our heads, the ceiling. All around, here below and on the upper two floors, the cells. A low grillwork lines the access corridors. And from the two upper floors, hung on this grillwork, dangle the shrouds and all the ghosts of the world. The sheets had been hung there to dry because of the rain.

The floor of the hall is gray. Cement. All around it, along the cells, a line, about three feet wide, painted black. Between the black and the vast gray, a thin line of white chalk. We go up to the second floor. The same worn steps. They have us go into a large room. Freezing. Empty, save for a long table and several dozen mattresses heaped up in a corner. The militiawoman leading us is young, almost pretty. Without saying a word she positions us there and turns the key. It is cold. Dark. The woman rejoices at not being alone. She feels much calmer with two of us being there. Her nervous breakdowns were due to solitude. She is glad to be with me. She tells me so. She should not have said so aloud. One must never tempt the devil. The door once again opens. They take her away. I will never again see her, but I know she is alive. During my year there, I would often hear her shouting and furiously stamping the floor. Both of us have been sentenced to hard labor. In real terms, this means, for me, merely total solitude, for her, a sentence of madness.

I didn't yet know that the prosecutor had lied. For the time being, I knew that I was in a penitentiary. You don't remain alone in a penitentiary. There are a lot of women here. All those sheets, all those shirts hung out on the upper floors were proof of it. I have just arrived. Tomorrow everything will be better.

A racket in the corridor. I hear the footsteps of the women leaving the cells. The babel of their voices. Tomorrow I shall be part of them. The prospect causes more than a little anxiety. I have remained too long alone. I feel I have become uncivilized. To make out what they are saying, I press myself to the door. Three quick taps make me jump. A quiet voice questions: "Who are you?"

I murmur my name. The woman who spoke goes off running. A few minutes later she returns:

"Several women here know you. Micaela Catargi sends you a kiss. Dorina P. had just gotten out. Also Mariuca V. You'll be with us tomorrow. You'll see. Most of the women are nice. And the system isn't too harsh."

"Who are you?"

"Me? Adrienne R. Do you want to have a look at me? I'll open the peephole."

I glue an eye to the round hole. She stands back a little. I see a lovely oval face. Splendid green eyes. She smiles at me. She is charming.

"Do you smoke? Yes? Wait!"

She goes off. Returns. Slips two cigarettes under the door. A voice growls: "What are you doing there?"

"Nothing, ma'am. I'm just coming back from the toilet."

The militiawoman opens my door. I have already hidden the cigarettes in my coat pocket and am some distance from the door. She has brought me a mess tin of barley porridge and a spoon. She tells me to take a mattress and go to bed. I cannot swallow the undercooked grains. I prefer to go to bed. I pick up a mattress. Put it on the floor in the middle of the room. The door opens again. What do they want from me? This time a whole outfit of militiamen and women overrun the room. One of them, wearing an officer's uniform, says something to me. I don't understand what he said. Then they all turn around, and the door closes. I hear lots of doors opening, closing, boots clattering down the stairs. It's over. My first night in the penitentiary has begun.

I lie down on the dirty, nearly empty straw mattress. I cover myself with my golden sheepcoat. The fur side toward me. This holds the heat in better. Once I had parents. I had sisters. Friends. A house. A bed. I had the sky, the sun, water, bread. The whole earth. Now I have nothing. Nothing but a coat. I love you, coat. You keep me warm. You caress me. Your wool retains the heat of the herd. The fragrance of meadows. You are my sole possession. My only friend.

I should now think only of those who lack even a coat to keep their hearts and bodies warm.

Day 2 of penitentiary—April 16, 1954

The next morning another militiawoman led me to a wing of the prison. To get there we went through the courtyard. There was an infirmary on the ground floor, but these two upper floors were absolutely empty. On the second story, she had me go into a large room whose walls had been recently whitewashed. The smell of the paint was still strong. The wooden floor had not yet been cleaned. Covered with white paint and trash. A mattress placed on the floor in the center of the room. A chamber pot. A cast-iron stove, cold. A water pitcher. A window, and the militiawoman's footsteps fading away down the corridor.

Once again I was alone. Alone in the penitentiary. Alone and

my hands still empty. Now, no more hope. Seven years. Exactly
seven years. Inexorable. Before me, no questions, no answers. Everything had been said. Standing before the window, I slowly re-
flected. With difficulty. The shock of the sentence had been too
unexpected. It had been scarcely five days ago. I was still incapable
of reacting.

Nevertheless, my eyes gradually were beginning mechanically
to perceive the space spread out before me. The window, a normal
window, came down to my waist. Beyond, a second courtyard as
large as the first. In the middle stood a beautiful old fountain with
a waterwheel. Near the fountain, four long wooden tubs, similar
to watering troughs. On my left, the large prison. In front of me,
at the rear of the courtyard, over the top of a high wall, the roofs
of the town. On top of the wall, the guards' watchtower. I could
see the whole wall of the large prison, the corner of the building
and a small part of the wall on the second side. At every floor, only
two small square dormer windows were visible from mine, most
likely the toilets. All these details were important for me during the
two weeks I spent in that cell. All my interest, all my attention was
concentrated on that prison courtyard.

I remembered the cigarettes. I had hidden them in a corner
of the room, simply putting them down on the floor. Along a wall.
I had gone away from the window for only a few minutes; where
had all these beggar women in rags come from? These gypsy women
in full flowered skirts? Some twenty women were there. Some were
filling the tubs with water, others bringing baskets full of dirty
linen. And the sound of their raucous voices rose up to me. Unfortunately I couldn't get a good look at them. Without glasses my
vision was blurry. I couldn't make out their faces. Vainly, I squinted
my eyes, until they hurt. Stretching them with my two index fingers as much as possible, I could see more clearly. But this eventually proved painful. But I still wanted to get a better view of them.
Who were they, these pitiful women? Political prisoners in rags or
human trash? Thieves? Prostitutes?

And suddenly I heard my name. In a sort of whispered shout.
The call repeated, I realized that it came from one of the dormer
windows on the second story of the women's prison. Since the
window was in the shade, I guessed more than saw the pale spot of
a face.

"Can you hear me? Yes? Hi! It's me, Adrienne."

"I'm still alone."

"Be patient. That's the way it is sometimes. A few days of quarantine."

I asked her if the women washing the linen were political prisoners. She burst out laughing. They were the common-law prisoners. Since the political types were not allowed to work, the common-law criminals did the cooking and laundry.

"Uh-oh! She's coming! We all send you a kiss. See you tomorrow!"

This was our second encounter. The third took place eight years later. After I was released. She had learned that I had come home and she came to see me. Some months later she was leaving the country for good.

A blessing on you, Adrienne. I would love to know that she is happy. Many years have gone by since our meeting. She is certainly no longer young. But behind my closed lids, her face will forever keep the beauty of her radiant smile.

This brief talk had given me a bit of hope. Of peace. A friendly contact had already been initiated. A bit of patience.

Around noon, a militiaman brought me a mess tin with a little cornmeal porridge. Very little. He showed me the place in the corridor to empty out the chamber pot. I had cursorily washed up with the water from the pitcher above the chamber pot. So the pot was rather heavy. I still managed to carry it and empty it. A short time later, I was visited by a young officer accompanied by two militiamen. The penitentiary's political officer. I later learned that the women had given him the nickname *Il Duce*. He was—tall, handsome, and authoritarian but fair-minded.

It took me several days to learn the customs of the place. Every morning and evening, the commandant or his aide, followed by the whole troop of militiamen from the day and night, did the official rounds of the cells. They called them "opening time" and "closing time." After the evening visit, no militiaman was allowed to enter the cells. It took me several days to realize that the bell that had rung at the time of our arrival did not signify the entry of a new prisoner into the penitentiary, but merely the mealtimes.

The Duce had advised me to respect the regulations if I wanted to stay out of trouble. How much longer was I going to remain alone? No reply.

Around ten in the morning, the criminals left the courtyard. Naturally, with no watch, I could determine the time only approximately. According to the light, the shadows, the bell and the various sounds. Gradually, with the help of habit, I managed to "feel" the right time, give or take a few minutes. After the common-law criminals left, turning the corner of the prison was a long line of women. They came slowly, one behind the other, and no murmur of voices came with them. I heard only the crunching of sand and pebbles, and sometimes some woman's dry cough. Only the hearse was missing from this lugubrious procession winding around the courtyard, filling out the corners of the space. They were not wearing prison uniforms. Their clothes were generally dark, for it was cold, and their coats were black, gray, or brown. Here and there, a little green or red. According to their gait I could make a rough guess as to their ages. The young ones had a springy step, the more mature women with heavy gait and bulky figures, the few elderly women walking in tiny, hesitant steps.

The column turned several times around the courtyard, then the militiawoman clapped her hands and gave the signal to depart. The woman at the head of the line entered the passageway, and I lost sight of them, one after another. Soon, a new procession came on the scene and this repeated itself several times until the bell for mealtime. I waited a long time for my turn to go walking. In vain.

The afternoon was harder to bear. The courtyard remained empty and silent. I had a physical sense of the great void around me. Not a sound broke the weight of this silence. After the evening meal, the militiaman coming by to fetch the empty mess tin ordered me to go to bed. Still no sheet, no blanket, no pillow. Still in the cold. Even worse. No light.

Day 3 of penitentiary—April 17, 1954

Adrienne did not call out to me today. At noon, they forgot to bring me anything to eat. I waited for a very long time. At the end of my patience, I went to the window and called to the guard in the watchtower. He was fairly far away. At last he heard me. I received my rations. The weather is cold.

Day 4 of penitentiary—April 18, 1954

Perhaps Adrienne has left. It seems to me that many fewer women were in the courtyard today. I have the impression that sometimes one of these women is looking up at me. Perhaps one of them made a little sign of greeting. Or was she merely readjusting her kerchief? It is still very cold. At night, the wind blows in under the door.

Days 5, 6, 7, 8 of penitentiary—April 22, 1954

It is raining. No walk. The courtyard is deserted. Puddles of water everywhere. I am cold. Perhaps they have all left. In the evening, after the closing, a militiaman comes in. In principle, this is forbidden. But no doubt he has been ordered to by the commandant. He tells me to come out in the corridor to help haul in a bed from the cell next to mine. A bed for me. Also near the stove in there is an armful of wood and corn cobs. He tells me I can use these to make a fire in my cell. A good fire. He goes to bring me some kindling. He really said "a good fire." I am touched.

The militiaman returns with a small shovelful of burning coals. He puts them in the stove and bids me good night. The door closes behind him. I am alone. The kindling becomes redder and redder. The stove draws well. The corn cobs still contain a few overlooked kernels. I carefully pick them off before putting the cobs on the burning coal. On top of them, the wood. The cobs flame up. The firewood crackles. The fire purrs. On my knees near the fire, I place the kernels of corn in the hot ashes. Very soon they noisily explode into large white flowers. I push the bed next to the stove. Put the mattress on the bed. I pick up one of the two cigarettes. I light it with the kindling. I lie on the bed. Cover myself with my coat. I eat the popcorn. The cell is warm. The fragrance of wood smoke, corn, and tobacco. I am warm. I am smoking. The coals cast red light on the walls. I can finally weep.

Days 9, 10 of penitentiary—April 24, 1954

The Duce has seen me at the window. I had opened it because of the sun, which had at last come out. He rushes in with all his band. Harshly, as though I were a child who has misbehaved, he asks me what the hell I was doing at the window. I feel that a line has been overstepped. The line of my patience. Yet I manage to say calmly: "Do the regulations of this penitentiary, which incidentally I do not know, allow you to address the political prisoners with such disrespect? And if the rules do so permit, must I address you in the same manner?"

For an instant he is taken aback. Behind him, the militiamen hold their breath.

"No, I do not have the right. But you do not have the right to go to the window."

"So why don't you brick it up?"

Day 11 of penitentiary—April 25, 1954

Despite the sunny weather, the women do not show up in the courtyard.

Day 12 of penitentiary—April 26, 1954

Once again I had to call the guard in the watchtower to get something to eat. The days are never-ending. I try to think of a subject for a play. What do I do? What do I think about? How do I live?

In the afternoon a militiawoman comes to fetch me. We go down into the courtyard. I am filled with emotion. I won't be alone anymore, for we are headed for the large building. We go inside. She has me walk across the vast hall and open a door. The room is quite a bit larger than all my other cells. Alas, however, only a single bed, mine.

The large slanting rectangular window is set very high up. To look through it I would have to hoist myself up on the water tub and the militiawoman warns me that this is forbidden. For here, in addition to the chamber pot, I have a large wooden tub for drinking water. With a wooden cover. I have a little tub as well, also wooden, to wash myself and to do my laundry in. The laundry that I don't have. The militiawoman informs me of the twice-daily "program." I must take out the chamber pot to empty it and the tub to fill it. Both seem very heavy. I don't have a great deal of strength.

On the bed, a clean sheet and a horsehair blanket. A pillow stuffed with straw like the mattress. I also have a bench, a coatrack, and a cast-iron stove.

Constantly on the lookout, alert to all the prison noises, time passed less slowly. I tried to "see" all the sounds. To see life in the prison. The noon meal surprised me. The rooms on the ground floor were served first. The mess tin the militiawoman handed me was fairly well filled. Since my arrival, the first dish had not had time to grow cold. I was moved by the pleasant heat of the food. I had become unhealthily sensitive. Because I'd been hit all over, everything in me hurt. I felt like a whipped animal. One that crawls off to hide. That wants to make itself invisible. But is only waiting to quiver anxiously with hope at the sound of a friendly voice. The least gesture, the vaguest shadow of a smile moved me. Arid land. Cracked. Lifeless land, sucking up the unconscious drop of rain.

I looked at the bed. The sheet. I waited impatiently for the signal to go to bed. To stretch out full length.

At last! I quickly took off my skirt. For the first time since I had been here. The stockings as well. But the blanket was rough, shaggy. I had to put my coat under it. Unfortunately, because the coat didn't completely cover me, my legs felt the unpleasant contact of the blanket.

So, once again I had to roll up into a ball. Turning over on my side, I saw something small and black running along the wall. Only a little mouse. Nothing serious, not a rat. I was nearly asleep, however, when the harmless mouse climbed onto my bed. This changed everything. Made it serious. Even very serious when a second mouse showed up. How could I go to sleep knowing that two mice were crawling over my blanket? And what if they slipped under it? And what if they took it in their heads to crawl over my face? I shook out the blanket. They disappeared in a wink. Five minutes later they were back again. I was sleepy. I was very tired. These mice were all I needed.

I knotted together the two strings I used as shoelaces. For my old shoes. Before I left the prison, they had taken back the new shoes from the trial. Attaching the string to one of the shoes, I could raise it up now and then and let it fall noisily back on the floor. But I still wanted to sleep. I had to catch the mice. But how? With what?

My eyes scoured the room. With what? I got up and lifted the wooden tub. Yes, the bottom of the tub was secured an inch or two above the base of the sides. Trying to make as little noise as possible, I slowly pushed the tub up against the wall and set a point of the tub's perimeter on the strip of wood surrounding the floor. Because the strip of wood was about an inch high, the mice would have enough room to wriggle under it. Unfortunately I didn't have even a crumb of bread to serve as bait, but I remained there, motionless, near the barrel, waiting for the mice to return. Indeed, in a few minutes one of the mice appeared and, its trust won over by my immobility, the poor thing calmly made a tour of the room, hugging the walls. On reaching the tub, it hesitated for a second and, instead of making its way back, it slipped into the trap. I had only to give the tub a sudden push to make it fall flat on the floor and the poor little thing was stuck inside.

For a short time I heard gnawing at the wood, and seeing that the other mouse did not return, I could finally go to sleep. The next morning, it was with a heavy heart that I watched the militia-woman carry off the lifeless little ball of fur on a shovel. But, when evening came I reset the trap. This time I even offered my victim a few crumbs. I have two more crimes on my conscience but no more mice in my bed.

One militiawoman told me that the woman with whom I had arrived fed a whole little family, nested in her stove. Doubtless, her interrogator never threatened her with the rat pit.

Days 13, 14, 15, 16, 17, 18, 19, 20, 21, 22, 23, 24, 25, 26, 27, 28, 29, 30 of penitentiary—May 14, 1954

The militiawomen are not bad sorts. They sometimes exchange a few words with me. Early in the day they even say "good morning." For the first time, I am allowed to walk outside. A militiaman fetches me. I am still required to cover my head and face completely with a hand towel. I pass beneath some women's window and they must not know that I am there. My jailers do not suspect that from the first day the exemplary grapevine had already been at work. But, neither did I know that the women who now filled the penitentiary were not the ones who had been there when I arrived.

I am allowed to walk only in the passageway between the two courtyards. No indiscreet window there. The passage is lined with a strip of grass next to the outer wall and an asphalt sidewalk along the building. I walk some thirty feet and then retrace my steps. Sticking to the wall. Crossing the courtyard, still masked, I was led to the laundry. There were several showers and long wooden tubs there. They gave me a sliver of black soap. It had to last a week. They also gave me a hand towel, a military shirt, and a pair of men's boxer shorts.

From the first day on, I have watched the judas. It opens only rarely. All I have to do is keep quiet and I am left in peace. I would like to be able to work. The only possible pastime is to make up verses. I think about the subject for a play for marionettes. I walk around the room thinking. I have already found the subject. I just have to carve it up into acts and scenes.

I walk almost constantly because of the bed. It is quite a problem. On my first day the militiawoman showed me the sophisticated way of making the bed. I am allowed to lie down on it only at ten o'clock at night. To wait for the knock on the door and the voice saying: "Go to bed." After this charming utterance, it is mandatory to be in bed instantly. It is forbidden to walk in the cell at night. Wake-up call at five in the morning. It is forbidden to remain in bed a minute longer. Meals at seven, noon, and six in the evening. The food is inadequate but acceptable. I start to feel hungry again. But this hunger still keeps a certain decorous quality.

I avoid the bench because of the bedsores. But so much walking wears me out and in the evening I am exhausted. I dream a lot. Very beautiful dreams, for the most part. I often awake during the night and am pleased. I try to impress scraps of my dreams deeply on my memory in order to keep them all alive the next day. I dream of my parents, their home—now, I often succeed in reaching it—and also landscapes, imaginary but always fantastical buildings, unfamiliar cities. But the dream that returns nearly every night in many variations is prompted by hunger. Mainly by the need for sugar of which my body has too long been deprived. Despite the pleasure had in dreams from eating a cake, these dreams depress me.

In general I treated myself with patience and caution. The first day I had given in to despair. This was fully justified. But I had to react. From time to time I carefully examined myself. I observed my morale. The despair was still there. The anxiety about my family. Rebelliousness. Sensitive spots. No need to insist. But there has been some improvement in one respect. Day by day, I feel the fear fading away. I am really no longer afraid. What would I still have to fear here below? I had been afraid of the trial, and rightly so. That critical point was gotten past. Be afraid of hunger? It is there. Of solitude? I am alone. What other hell to fear? The center of my fear was the waiting. Now I have nothing to wait for. Now I have nothing to be afraid of.

Nevertheless, I still had one secret fear to overcome. The fear of life. I was somewhat conscious that I had yet to overcome this fear. The fear of so many years to be lived out in prison. But I felt that to be able to live them, I had to want to live them.

I would have preferred to die. For the moment, however, I was living. As badly as could be? No. The bare essentials were not lacking. But I had to want to live better. The physical part did not depend on me. The mental part did. What solution could I find? I finally seemed to have the answer: the meticulous planning of my use of time. I had to form habits. The desire to stick to them rigorously. Become fanatical. I felt the need to be able to measure the time by actions.

All this didn't happen in a day. I summarized the effort made during my initial weeks at the penitentiary. As much as I can recall of it. Only a year later, however, did I achieve a genuine inner equilibrium, on May 18, 1955. That day was the most notable of the some 2,550 days spent in the penitentiary. Setbacks were certainly not lacking. But I knew that in the future they would be transient. Some surface ripples. As the basis of my existence I had taken pride in the mind and had contempt for the body. I concentrated all my will on this lone goal. Respect for, in a person of flesh, what is least fleshly. Respect for humankind in its uniqueness.

I spent only some twenty days in that room on the ground floor. During this period I realized that only the first and second floors were occupied. The third floor was vacant. Most of the inmates had to be young. Bursts of youthful laughter sometimes reached me. I was a bit surprised by this laughter. On the first evening, at the moment of the "program," all the doors opened at once. Now it seemed to me that the occupants went out in turns so as not to meet up. The change surprised me. Even worried me. Had they been punished?

Much later, when I finally started communicating with my neighbors, I heard the explanation for this mystery.

The country's largest penitentiary for women was the one in Mislea. Also the best, for there the inmates had the right to work.

Women generally keep busy with their hands. At dusk, when their day's labor is supposedly over, peasant women come to relax and chat on the porch, and always have their distaff or knitting needles in hand. One didn't have to dig deep to find this peasant stock in most of the women in the penitentiary. Books? Papers? Pen? Few of these women suffered from the absence of these things. Only manual labor had filled their lives. In our penitentiary, no work. The time dragged by heavily. In Mislea, the woes, the affective, sexual, or other deprivations were easier to bear because their hands toiled. Even the most mechanical work occasionally requires sustained attention. The train of thought is interrupted, for a few moments distress is forgotten and, from forgetfulness to forgetfulness, is eased. The work kept the prisoners from wasting away from boredom and heartache. Work, however, was a blessing most often denied us by our jailers.

Mislea was the country's only factory prison. There, the women wove flowered rugs in the folk tradition. They were also taught to make the knots of Persian carpets. The toughest work was the fabrication of fishing nets. Often drops of blood spattered the nets with brown stains. Most of the women, however, worked in the shops for making men's underwear. They cut and sewed the thousands of shirts sold in the department stores of Bucharest. With no label of origin. So as not to lower the number sold.

Mislea's second advantage was the remuneration for the work. They received far less than the union rates and almost nothing remained for the workers themselves, for they were forced to pay for their own upkeep. But with the trifling sums received, they had the choice of saving it through the penitentiary's savings account or being reimbursed in the form of purchases of basic articles at the penitentiary cooperative. The food, even though paid for by their work, was often inadequate to make up for the fatigue of eight hours of labor under strict surveillance. The "lucky ones" at Mislea thus had a cooperative at their disposal. There they could buy bread, sugar, marmalade, and cheese, as well as handsoap, toothpaste, absorbent cotton, and—the most important items for some of them—cigarettes and matches. The women in all the other penitentiaries had to do without any of these things. The cigarettes were a truly precious commodity. Because the heavy smokers didn't have enough money to afford all the cigarettes they wanted, they had to get them by swapping. Bit by bit superfluous items of clothing and sometimes even food changed hands.

Finally, the inmates enjoyed a semblance of freedom there, within the walls of the vast prison, in the central courtyard, in the orchard. Their nerves did not have to suffer the constraints of life strictly confined to a cell nor forced coexistence night and day in an enclosed and most often restricted space with a small number of women assigned by the head staff. Later, when I at last joined them in another penitentiary, one of the harshest, they spoke nostalgically of a storehouse for equipment—an old church, in fact—the chestnut trees surrounding it, the flowers and fruits of the apple trees in the orchard, this whole miserable paradise, but one in which they were free to choose their friendships and their loves from among these hundreds of women.

There, only inmates who refused all work were kept in solitary confinement. Some refused out of express opposition to the country's political regime. Others refused with their last strength to comply with the "capitalistic"—pardon, socialistic—exploitation. Joining this tiny minority were those women who were too old or ill to meet the mandatory work quotas. For, wages were received only by those who met or exceeded these quotas. Unfortunately, a quota, once exceeded, became the law. It was Stakhanovism run amuck. Hence the silent and dangerous war conducted by the near-totality of the women against those who attempted to top the established quotas and whom the staff sustained by illusory promises of every kind of advantage and even a speedy release. I later learned many details about the abusive methods used by the women supervisors to jack up the established quotas. Quotas that were moreover sufficiently hard and demanded great effort from the majority of these women.

According to what I later learned, some international commission, it seems, had done an inspection at Mislea and had forbidden that political prisoners be required to work. A great stir then took place in the country's penitentiaries. Mislea had been filled up with common-law prisoners and the political ones were evacuated to our penitentiary. This had occurred during my stay in the closed-up wing. The women I had found on my arrival were not truly tried-and-convicted political prisoners. They were what was called "administratives." Kept apart for a time from the political life as a punishment for having been wives, daughters, or close relatives of important members of the historical parties or of high officials from the time of the monarchy. Three or four days after my arrival, they had been released and returned home.

Going by my cell to go walking, voices pleasantly murmured "hello" and sometimes an index finger tapped lightly on the door. I would love to have recognized Adrienne's voice. How could I have guessed that Adrienne and her companions had been set free? They had been "held" for two years. Two years, for nothing. One of them had been only sixteen at the time of her arrest. Thus, she got out at eighteen, scarred for life.

In fact, entering our penitentiary were only political prisoners convicted for belonging to the fascist Legionnaire's party. Mostly young or even very young, they had formed the only organized nucleus of the Mislea penitentiary. Combative, intelligent, disciplined, led with a firm hand by their elders, high cadres of the Legion, they had infiltrated the offices, the staff, the accounting office, but mainly the good graces of the staff and, rather, its female director. It seems they had abused these positions. After their abortive attempt to strike, the director was accused of having shown favoritism toward them, because a number of them accepted to submit to her approaches.

For them, the penitentiary routine was a hard punishment. Closed rooms. No contact between the different cells. Separation from friends. A ten-minute daily walk. Underfeeding. Prohibition from any work. Only once a week, a needle and a bit of thread for the necessary mending of clothes. Strict surveillance. Even the two pieces of broken needle had to be handed back to the militia-women. Once a week a pair of old and rusty scissors to hack away at, not clip, nails and hair. The women who had the money, however, could buy soap and cigarettes through the mediation of the prison administration.

Day 31 of penitentiary—May 15, 1954

A move to the second floor. A room exactly like the old one. One improvement, a window. I will be able to see the comings and goings in the courtyard in greater security.

Days 32, 33, 34, 35, 36 of penitentiary—May 20, 1954

The next day, getting up on the tub, I had before me the whole main courtyard. The low buildings I'd noticed on my arrival were the kitchens, the wash house, the outbuildings. Only the common-law prisoners were allowed, or rather compelled, to work. They did the cooking. In twos they lugged the heavy tubs of food from door to door. But they were not allowed to see us. The militiawoman on duty personally handed the inmates the mess tins through the partially opened door. The militiawomen were also responsible for washing the sheets. The inmates did only their personal effects in the wash house. I was the only one to wash them in my room. One of the women on duty left a pail of hot water in front of my door. The militiawoman waited for her to leave before handing me the pail.

Thus, I had no direct contact with the common-law prisoners. Nevertheless, in an instant stolen behind the militiawoman's back, a face smiled at me. A friendly hand waved me a quick greeting.

All cagelings have a pressing need for hope. A vital need to hope for freedom. They feed this absurd, insane, and utterly groundless hope with hunches, premonitions, signs. And here I am back to signs. . . . For the prisoners, the slightest improvement in the food, a guard's smile, an officer's sudden politeness, everything is a sign.

From mouth to mouth, from wall to wall, this breath of hope would soon intoxicate the whole prison. The experience of many disappointed day-afters changed nothing. For the most frivolous and vain reason, a wave of madness would once again carry off the dark slave ship.

That day, set off by I don't know what, a new hope engrossed the whole prison. A powerful hope since it even came banging on my door. Around noon, while I heard the common-law prisoners toting the heavy tubs of food, several light taps sounded at my door. I responded by coughing. Then someone softly muttered: "In two or three days you will all be getting out of prison. It's absolutely certain. Good luck!"

Two days, three days, four days. No. The good common-law woman was mistaken. But she had given me the gift of a few hours' hope.

The common-law prisoners. Thieves, criminals, prostitutes, embezzlers of public funds, speculators, wandering Gypsies and pilferers, their routine was much better than ours. They had the right to the visiting room, to receive letters and packages. We political prisoners were denied these things. An injustice that not only shocked the common-law inmates, but in some way humiliated them. Born for the most part of the peasant class, they had been reared in the tradition of kissing the hand of lords, masters, gentlemen. This respectfulness, their innate goodness, and dedicated hatred of their jailers impelled them to help the political prisoners, who, of necessity, belonged to the category of "gentlefolk." In the second and final penitentiary, where I spent more than six years, the male common-law prisoners were very often devoted companions in adversity. For us they displayed great respect, great pity, and often faced the danger of punishments to come to our aid.

Days 37, 38, 39, 40, 41, 42, 43, 44, 45, 46 of penitentiary—May 30, 1954

Early one morning, about two weeks later, I had just gotten up on the tub to gaze out on the courtyard when I saw a militiawoman nudging toward the infirmary, or perhaps the office, a woman whose head and face were covered by a dark kerchief. The figure . . . the gait . . . I held the image in my head a long time. I knew that woman too well to be mistaken. It was Pătrășcanu's wife.

Thus she in turn had been judged. Convicted, since she was here. I watched for their return. I saw them go through the courtyard and into the penitentiary. I heard them coming up the stairs. Go along the corridor. Very close to me I heard the jangling of the militiawoman's set of keys. A key inserted in the lock. A door opening. Closing. I didn't dare breathe. It was the door of the cell adjacent to mine.

How could I not let her know that I was there? I tapped three times with the knuckle of my index finger on the wall between us. Like an echo, three taps were struck just as softly on the other side of the wall. Using the only language possible, I tapped twenty-three times for the letter *w*, eight times for *h*, and so forth: "Who are you?" It was indeed she.

For three days on end, cautiously and with infinite patience, we managed to talk at length. She had been convicted two weeks after us in a group of thirty to forty persons more or less associated with our trial. She had been sentenced to fourteen years. She began violently accusing Herbert Zilber. Betrayal and lies. What did she know of the huge sum of money that I had supposedly hidden at her husband's request? Nothing, but under pressure, she had ended up declaring that she had brought it to me herself, not even knowing anymore whether all this was true or false. She also told me she had been gravely ill several times.

On the third day, a militiawoman caught her at the wall. In punishment, her mattress was taken away and she had to sleep three nights on the iron lattice that served as the bedsprings for her cot. They punished me in quite a different way. I was placed on the floor above. I had a cell just like the other, but as the black sheep, I had no next-door neighbors. All the other cells on this third floor were empty.

Days 47, 48, 49, 50, 51, 52, 53, 54 ,55, 56, 57, 58, 59, 60, 61, 62, 63, 64, 65, 66, 67, 68, 69, 70, 71, 72, 73, 74, 75, 76, 77, 78, 79, 80, 81, 82, 83, 84, 85, 86, 87, 88, 89, 90, 91, 92, 93, 94, 95, 96, 97, 98, 99, 100 of penitentiary—July 23, 1954—1,834 days of detention

One hundred days of penitentiary already! Adding to that the 1,550 days during the investigation and the first six months of detention in 1948, I had already spent 1,834 days in solitary confinement. Alone for 1,834 days.

Every morning, going out to empty the chamber pot, I could see, as though down a well, the whole interior of the penitentiary. The ground floor, the two upper floors, the iron railings alongside the narrow corridors on which all the cell doors opened, the funereal gray cement of the floor. I was thus over twenty-five feet from the bottom of this pit. The railings were low, easy to step over. Step over, let myself fall . . . I had a last resort.

That pleased me. Gave me a comforting sense of security. The militiawomen had me under very light surveillance. I was alone. The walls would remain mute. Of what use was the fatigue of so many steps up and down? They were, however, obliged to do this more than ten times a day. "The opening," the three meals, the walk, "the program," and "closing time." Once again, I was the last one served. Almost every day I heard the cook scraping the bottom of the tub for me. When the mess tin arrived half full, I too was almost full. But because most often the mess tin was not even half full, I was hungry. Hungry all day long. And at night, I again dreamed of eating. To tell the truth, hunger in this penitentiary never approached real suffering. I had grown used to the pearl-barley, the basis of our food. Sometimes it contained shreds of meat. I never figured out what this odd meat was. From what part of what strange animal did it come? One morning I finally had the key to the mystery.

I had climbed up on the tub and was looking out at the courtyard. The large covered entranceway had just opened and a heavy cart, drawn by two strong horses, noisily clattered into the courtyard. On the cart, a massive crate, painted green. The cooking staff spilled out of the kitchen. Two of the women got up on the cart. They opened the cover of the crate. Inside, a mass of red meat. Leaning over the tub, the two women filled their arms with quarters of blood-dripping meat. It must have been extremely heavy, for I saw their bodies brace themselves under the effort. Below, around the cart, the other women raised their arms to receive these enormous skinned heads of cattle. One of the women displayed childish delight. She burst out laughing, taking in her arms the heads with blood still fresh and dripping. One morning during the walking period, an old guard in a chatty mood had told me that one of the kitchen women was a vampire. The woman who laughed. As soon as the poor soul found a nail, she hastened to drive it into her body, for the pleasure of seeing the blood spurt forth.

I often saw the cart and the crate arriving. Sometimes the crate contained only large, rubbery pieces, thin and pliant. They were wet and dirty beige. The women rinsed them over and over in the fountain. The next day, in the barley porridge, were little squares of something gelatinous, fairly resilient, and of a rather pinkish white. It was the tripe from cattle, bleached from cooking.

The food was generally unspoiled and acceptable. It was often inadequate, however, for I was always the last to be served. In the morning I received a little cornmeal porridge. At midday, a hunk of bread and a dish of noodles or a soup of dried beans, cabbage, potatoes, or pearl-barley. The thick soup of dried peas they sometimes gave us seemed a treat. But I was never given fresh vegetables, no lettuce, no fruit. Just as no milk, cream, cheese, eggs, or sugar. Once a week, on Saturday, the pearl-barley was lightly, very lightly, sugared. They had added a little marmalade to it. I always kept a bit of it for Sunday morning. Cold, the pinkish mush seemed a little sweeter. I kept it in a little enamel pot I was allowed to have in the cell. I had to hide it under the bed, sometimes under the mattress, for it was forbidden to keep food in the cell overnight. This prohibition had a valid rationale. Some foodstuffs turned sour and hence could cause diarrhea.

Gradually, I managed to allocate my seventeen hours of the day. Mandatory wake-up at five o'clock. Make the bed. Wash. Calisthenics. Sweep up. Keep an ear out for the approach of the militiawoman. Hear her coming up, trailed by the whole gang. Look at all of them through the open door. Wait for the corn porridge. Eat it as slowly as I can. Or rather suck on it to make it last and savor the peaceful feeling of a mouth full of food. The militiawoman, "Miss," for that is what I had to call her, returned to fetch the empty mess tin. (Not knowing the ranks, I said "Commandant, Sir" to all the male members of the penitentiary staff.)

Until lunchtime, I slowly walked the room. From the door to the window. I had before me a large rectangle of sky. Often a cloudless blue. Sometimes filled with strange animals, castles, mountains, blue lakes, and all those images passing by in slow motion subtly metamorphosed into other mirages. I came back toward the door. Solid. With iron bars. Deeply set into the heavy wooden frame. Covering the door, the frame, painstakingly carved names, initials, dates. Bit by bit, however, the sky, the window, the door, the whole cell disappeared. I didn't see them anymore. I didn't see anything anymore. Nothing but a little boy talking to his dog. Surrounded with grass, flowers, a white apple tree, the light of a sunny sky. Here and there, several sheep. Lambs. The dog answered the child by barking and the child understood its language. The child also had a magic flute. Yet he had one more desire. The child wanted all of mankind to be good. For everyone to be happy.

Finding a subject had reconciled me with myself. I did not yet know how the action would take on scale. But I was now sure I would be able slowly to make progress on this unknown path, which brought me a new view at every turn. Every day, deaf and blind, distant and unfeeling, I would have the certitude, along the winding, upward path, not of walking on the road with my bruised feet, but of spreading my wings of escape to reach the culminating peak. I was in no hurry. No one came with me. No one would be waiting for me at the summit. It was, as I knew all too well, only an uncertain life buoy. When the play ended, I would plummet back to earth. Would I find new strength, new courage to start over again?

The afternoons were harder to bear. My health left something to be desired. I felt weary. No pain in particular, but a great general fatigue. Together with a faint, constant hunger. Which was an advantage, all things considered. For to appease this hunger somewhat, just eating the penitentiary's tasteless pap gave me a faint pleasure.

Once a week I washed the floor. In the cell I had a broom and a cleaning rag. But only one wooden tub in which I washed myself and which I didn't want to get dirty. To clean the floor, I thus did not soak the rag in the tub. I scrubbed small areas of the wooden planking by pouring a little water directly onto it. I wrung the rag out over the chamber pot and tried to rinse it there as well. Trodden upon by so many feet since the empress Maria-Theresa, the floor was knotty and worn down. Long and wide, seven planks took up the whole cell's floor area. And each one now was no more than a long gutter in which water accumulated. I wasted a lot of time and energy, hunched over for so long, trying to dry them. With great difficulty, I managed to wash the floor all at once. How to do it? Kneeling? Squatting? Leaning over? My knees, my back, each in turn, ached. A whole morning spent this way.

In the first weeks, I was taken to the laundry every Saturday. For a quick shower. Soon, however, the militiawomen found it unnecessary to go to this bother just for my sake. They got into the habit of bringing me a bucket of hot water and emptying it into my tub. I washed up in bits and pieces. From my head to my waist, from my waist to my knees, from my knees to my feet. In the same water. Next, my linen. The solitude of the "great secret," the strictness of my regime, made them behave more offhandedly with me, more cavalierly than with the other women in the penitentiary. I was alone. I had no way to defend myself. No witness to substantiate my words in the event of some injustice. So I was completely at their mercy. Whether under interrogation or at the penitentiary, my situation was the same. Hence my wise decision never to contradict them. To behave so that they would be convinced that vigilance over me was pointless.

One day, a militiawoman brought me a needle and some thread. A few yards of white thread. She told me that the regulations allowed me two hours of sewing a week. After sketchily darning the worn elbows of my wool jacket, I had a bit of time and some thread left. Since it was white, this thread gave me the idea of sewing the triangles of a backgammon board on my green kerchief. With some bread and moistened soap, I formed fifteen little disks. Fifteen others by darkening the paste with some soot taken from inside the stove. Finally, two tiny dice. As a child I had often played the game with my father. So I chose him as my first opponent. I threw the dice first for him, then for me. I also played with my sisters and with Harry. The match was always accompanied by lively chatter. Some afternoons thus went by more quickly.

One night at "closing time," however, the duty officer asked me how I'd spent the day. I was naive enough to tell him that I had been playing backgammon.

"What? You've been playing backgammon? With whom?"

"Just myself."

"And where's the board?"

I showed him the scarf.

"But . . . don't you know that games of chance are forbidden in the penitentiary?"

He couldn't see that this rule was valid only when the winner could strip the loser of the bare essentials. In my case, no chance. Wasn't I both the winner and the loser every time? Nothing to be done about it. Alone or not alone, games of chance were prohibited. An order to undo the backgammon.

It was replaced by the window. Perched up on the tub, I

gazed at the comings and goings in the courtyard, which I already knew. From the third floor, however, the world became much larger. Much richer. Behind the kitchen buildings, there had to be a street. I could see neither the pavement nor the sidewalks. Nothing but the top of a wall and the back walls of two houses on the other side of the street. Beyond the wall, jammed in between the two houses, a garden. Or rather a green tangle. Some trees engulfed in a mass of greenery. Behind that, a second wall, broken by a door. When it opened, on the other side, it was still green, but a green raked and combed. Circular plantings of flowers, a lawn. One of the two walls of the houses, the one on the left, had three dormer windows, like three sightless eyes, boarded up I think, for they were always hermetically sealed, and, beneath the three black holes, a door at the top of four steps. Was this house a hospital, a hotel, or merely a restaurant? Nearly every day, sometimes even several times a day, three women loaded with large round baskets would come into the garden. In turn, the three women took out twisted masses from the large wicker baskets filled with white linen, shook them, held out their arms, and the shaken linen became large white squares or rectangles. They made them snap in the air, drops sparkling in the sunlight. They stretched these splashes of white row by row on clotheslines, but the clotheslines were too short for them, so the women spread them out on the bushes, covered all the bushes with them, and the garden turned all white. They put clothespins everywhere to keep them from flying away, but when the wind filled them, they were no longer sheets or perhaps tablecloths, but huge flags, and in the evening, when all three women or only two returned, they gathered up the now-dry linen and folded it up once, twice, three times, and when the filled baskets had been toted off, the garden turned green again, but a darker green, already invaded by the darkness of the night, advancing, devious.

Two of the women were young. I could see clearly only the dark hair of the one, the red curls of the other, framing their oval faces. Slender, well-dressed, and—so I had decided—very pretty. The third was an old woman with a white chignon, in a long gray dress. But perhaps it was only a large apron with sleeves, over which she wore another old-fashioned, blue bib apron. The old lady—plump, clean, charming—gave me great pleasure. Sometimes she would enter the enclosure all alone and discreetly, daintily lift up the hem of her dress, bend her knees a bit, and pee on the grass. How could she know that on this normally vacant third floor of the penitentiary an unknown woman was tenderly gazing down on her?

Sometimes the door beneath the windows slowly opened and, against the dark background of a hallway, no doubt, stood out only the pale spot of a face. Then a tall, vaguely feminine form came slowly forward in my direction. Finally, she was there, on the doorstep, quite striking, quite dark, all alone, even more so than I. As though regretfully, she decided to descend the few steps. The black lengths of her dress flattening the wild grasses, she went between the rows of linen, lost and found again in the soft flapping of the great white pieces of cloth. The stump of a tree trunk received the heavy mass of this lifeless body. In the quivering of the grass, leaves, wind, and clouds, she remained there, indifferent to everything. Was this strange woman mortally ill? Was she insane? I felt she was stricken with a hopeless melancholy, obsessed by the death of a child or the loss of a lover who had died. She remained there for hours, transfixed. At dusk, the old woman entered by the rear door. She stayed for a moment on the threshold, looking at her. Slowly approached, as though not to scare off the dream, then, taking her by the arm, she led her back up the few stone steps, and the black door silently closed behind them. Perhaps the old lady was the ghost's mother and I was sad for her.

One morning the three women entered with their arms full of copper basins and pails. There were two men as well. In shirt-sleeves. Comings and goings. A flash of silver gleamed in the hands of one of the two men. The other nudged an animal into the courtyard. High-pitched squeals rose up to my window. A pig? Yes, they were slaughtering a pig. There was also a fire. Did I really detect the smell of singed fur? Or perhaps it was only the memory of that odor, of the same scene, as it had happened in this village in a distant time beyond the grave?

Out of caution, out of fatigue, I couldn't remain constantly perched at the window. I went back to a slow walk, repeating from one end to the other all the poetry I'd already completed. I had learned to measure time by the poems' different lengths. One tale lasted about fifteen minutes. Another about an hour.

I had used my heartbeat as a measure of time, sixty-five beats to the minute. That made four to-and-fros a minute. With a thread of wool taken from my skirt, I had made a kind of rosary with fifty knots. At each to-and-fro, I slipped a knot between my fingers. Mechanically. At the end of fifty knots, I knew that twelve minutes had gone by.

The older my verses were, the better they were imprinted on my memory. By dint of repetition. Upon my departure from prison, I managed to make a word-for-word transcription of all the poetry from my first years in prison. Because this took up a good deal of time, a life of freedom almost completely eradicated the rest from memory.

At six in the evening, the militiawoman opened the door. Handed me the mess tin. A little later she came back to fetch it. Around seven, the duty officer, followed by the whole troop of daily and nightly guards, did the evening inspection. They called it "closing time." The morning inspection, "opening time." Each time, I was supposed to say a formula. In the morning: "Room number nine is opening with an inmate." In the evening: "Room number nine is closing with an inmate." Inadvertently, I happened to mix up the two phrases, saying "closing" in the morning and "opening" in the evening. Then I had to repeat the silly words.

I still had three hours to fill. Or, rather, kill, until bedtime. A void of 180 minutes. I had found a mind-numbing solution to fill up this oppressive void. A childhood game of geography. Finding as many names as possible of countries, cities, rivers, mountains, and so on, beginning with the letter *a*. The letters *b* and *c* followed, and so on. After ransacking my memory, redrawing all the maps from school, and noting that the largest number of these names began with an *a* or an *m*, I had to go on to another series. Still in alphabetical order. I counted the writers I knew of or had read. The poets, the musicians. I counted the plays I'd seen, the films, the concerts I'd heard. I counted the names of artists.

I counted the names of fruits and vegetables. Flowers. Trees. Animals. Birds. Fish. The names of fabrics. The whole inventory of a bookshop. The notions in a fabric store. The foodstuffs in a grocery.

I counted my friends. My acquaintances. I counted my days of happiness and days of woe. And when all this was counted, squeezed, and dried up, I just started over again.

With the help of my memory, the first sixty minutes went by reasonably well. It was much harder to fill up the second hour. My steps grew slower and slower, my body heavier and heavier. My mind grew dim. My memory gave out. I had to give up ransacking. I was at the end of my fatigue. Aching all over. My back hurt. My legs hurt. My shoulders hurt. My feet hurt. I hurt all over.

When the second hour subsided, drunk with sleep, numb, stupefied, I dragged the final minutes behind me, stumbling, bracing myself to pull them out of the ruts. And I went on moving my legs, asleep and awake, conscious and unconscious, dead and alive. Dying, in fact.

Finally, I heard the militiawomen down below going from door to door, commanding the inmates to go to bed. I still had to wait for the end of the bedtime ritual on the floor beneath me. Their steps came heavily up the staircase. I had to wait for the judas to open. I had to wait for the saving words "Go to bed" to be uttered. Finally I was allowed to unmake the bed. To arrange the sheets so that it covered me. To stretch out this exhausted, worn-out, tortured body, my anvil body, my doormat body, my scrawny and mangy dog of a body.

Every evening I had to repeat all the stages of this ordeal, without shouts that would whip my pride, without tears of pity that would lend me courage. I was alone.

For these three hours, the hardest ones, the bed was there, within reach. From time to time all day long, I stretched out on it. Just for a few seconds, to ease the pressure on my painful spine. After "closing time," however, the lax surveillance of the day turned vigilant. The militiawomen arrived fresh and well rested. They had no doors to open, no "programs," nor walks to supervise. Just one assignment. To patrol us. To keep us from lying down on our beds. To keep us from resting. From sleeping. From forgetting.

They had been instilled with a few preconceptions. Every inmate was by definition an enemy of the regime. A priori dangerous. Inclined to do evil. We had all exploited the proletariat. Some of the more simpleminded militiawomen sincerely believed this. One day, one of them asked me if it was true that I used to bathe in champagne. Because they were all happy to earn, with no effort, much higher wages than factory workers, they took pains to satisfy their employers. Who, moreover, offered them the benefit of free uniforms and underwear. Also the benefit of inspiring a cringing fear both in and out of prison. Of seeing people efface themselves in front of them in the street and in stores, where they were the first ones served. They were very proud to see themselves lifted up on a pedestal of fear, and took this as their due. But the less small-minded ones felt the contempt and hatred rise up under their steps and slink in their wake. They took out their revenge on us, on me.

It is some excuse for them that they themselves were under permanent surveillance. In constant danger. Not knowing whom to suspect, of whom to beware, they suspected everyone. Officers, colleagues, and inmates. For at that time, innocence was an unknown commodity. A useless one. To be innocent did not give you the right to a peaceful sleep. Any accusation whatever, any slander, got a hearing. Every denunciation, even the most outlandish, was considered. Out of caution, out of fear, out of cowardice. Not to give free rein to a denunciation was equivalent to an act of complicity. Even a lousy inmate was taken seriously when he accused a guard of conniving with another inmate. The militia were thus obliged to apply the regulations with the utmost severity.

No doubt some of these women were merely unfortunate types with no profession. Only too happy to have been solicited by the militia. Very few of them were genuinely malevolent. Except two or three who really took pleasure in torturing us. The others, when they were absolutely sure of the honesty and solidarity of a cell's occupants, dared to risk a human gesture. Over time I had several demonstrations of this. I was alone. Unwitnessed. With no potential informer. I had gradually learned who they were. Knowing that I could stretch out on the bed when a certain militia-woman was on duty. That day I might even be lucky enough to receive a little more food. Even a surplus, the remainder of a medical diet. Semolina, noodles, rice. On some days, the aroma of cheese, toasted cheese, mixed with noodles from the medical diet, entered my cell, making me salivate unpleasantly. Sometimes the door opened and the rest of the dish was mine.

One of the militiawomen even sparked a certain affection in me. A comforting feeling for someone in solitary confinement, just as starved for friendship as for bread. For the moment, however, during those first days in the penitentiary, I was the prison's number-one danger for them all. They eyed me very warily. Past history, education, profession, trial, conviction, solitary confinement—everything pointed to me as the focus of their vigilance. Of their class hatred. They felt their inferiority complex more acutely with me.

It was during the first days spent in this room that I heard Pătrăşcanu's wife coughing. Just beneath my cell. If the sounds came up to me distinctly, through the floor, perhaps she could hear me as well. I tried changing my walk into language. Each of my steps struck the floor a little harder. Each becoming a letter of the alphabet. I began with the three words of every beginning. "Who are you?" (Only two words in Romanian.) I still had to make sure it was indeed she. So twenty-three steps for *w*, pause; eight for *h*, pause; fifteen for *o*. Three quick taps of the heel to mark the end of the word, and so on. The attempt seemed absurd. Nevertheless, I repeated it several times. Contrary to all credibility, the answer came through clear and distinct. Why did she think she was speaking to a stranger? Why didn't I tell her? We exchanged only brief messages, mainly good morning and good night.

Until the day when, around ten in the morning, a siren began blasting away. It terrified me. An air raid? War? How? Against whom? That seemed crazy. Still the siren sounded, constantly going up and down, screaming on and on to death. No. Death itself danced about, bellowing with joy. War? All my loved ones were far away. Here with no news, no communication, how could I bear the anguish of a war? The horror of a war? But hope? Freedom at this price, for nothing in the world. I would rather spend my whole life in prison.

When the siren died down to a final groan, however, when there was absolute silence, a message came up to me, an obscure message. Yet I had paid close attention. Counted each letter of the four words that I couldn't catch. Abruptly, from repeating them several times, I seemed to see them, and then the words took on a precise meaning. Pătrăşcanu's wife had spoken in French. She thought she had sent a message of encouragement: "Things are picking up." Oh no! Above all, don't let things pick up that way.

The solitude weighed on me more and more. Here, at the penitentiary, it seemed harder to bear. The prosecutor had assured me of a normal prison life. I had had my fill of existing only within myself. Of being the center of the world. I wanted to finally get rid of myself. Share the life of the others. To experience solidarity. Several times I had asked the commandant (the title of the chief officer of the penitentiary but which could be used for all the personnel) how long my special situation was to last. He answered with the ritual "Wait!" So I decided to act. To force them to respect the "law" of the penitentiary. The law. What a ludicrous expression.

The only weapon within my reach? A hunger strike. I thought about this for several days. It wasn't easy for me to accept the idea of an absolute and voluntary starvation when the slight but constant hunger I was experiencing was already hard to bear. Finally, assuming that my strike would not last long and that after three or four days my solitude would be ended, I made my decision and one morning refused the corn porridge. Let the militiawoman make her report. I declare a hunger strike to protest my solitary confinement. She made no comment, but a half-hour later she returned. A sheet of paper. A pen. Declare the hunger strike in writing. My reasons. Sign it. This surprised me. I was expecting something else. An officer. A discussion.

I communicate my decision to Pătrăşcanu's wife. This takes a long time. When she finally understands, she tells me, "It's the wrong thing to do. They'll let you die of hunger." Perhaps she is right. I am worried by the statement they so promptly asked of me. But the morning goes by uneventfully. Disregarding the "lower instincts" brings me real satisfaction. I am not the least bit hungry.

At noon the militiawoman obliges me to take the mess tin. The rules are definite. I am allowed a ration; the penitentiary must give it to me. "You can just not eat it." I put the mess tin on the stove. Despite myself, I occasionally go over to it. Look at it. I feel my mouth salivating. I turn my back. I drink a little water. It isn't hunger yet, but this mess tin bothers me.

It isn't sensible to walk all the time. Too tiring. But the bench is hard. It hurts. The bed? No. I must pay attention to the militiawomen. And suddenly I'm hungry. Really hungry. The mess tin is getting on my nerves. This mess tin is a temptation. Why did they give it to me? Perhaps because they don't want me to die. Think of something else. Shake off the nightmare. Convince myself that all this is mere appearance. It is impossible for this cell to be real. It is impossible for my presence to be real in this unreal cell. Impossible that in this unreal cell, my unreal presence is tormented by a pitiful mess tin half full of some pitiful porridge.

. . . Blue sky . . . sun . . . grass . . . flowers . . . forest . . . brook . . . waves on the sand . . . wet sand . . . the coolness of the wet sand beneath bare feet . . .

No. A woman locked up in a cell. Miserable. Contemptible.

Humiliated. A woman who is hungry. Who is ashamed of being hungry.

That evening, the militiawoman takes away the mess tin. Leaves another one. The evening rations. Without a word. The same silence at "closing time." The officer on duty asks me no questions. Perhaps my neighbor hadn't been wrong. She knew them better than I did. The evening goes by with difficulty. Not because of the hunger. It had been only thirty hours since I had eaten. The discomfort was not yet suffering. But I was afraid. Of the next day. Of the days to come. Of this death drawn out too long. Of this passing away in snatches. This loss of blood drop by drop. Fear mainly of suffering in vain. Of a death I had not wished. Solitary. I had wanted only to escape my solitude. I wanted "others."

I again clearly see the pitying face of the militiawoman the next morning. She speaks to me in a kindly way. Explains, murmuring, so as not to be overheard, how futile this strike was. My life in the cell did not depend on the penitentiary's authorities. The report to be sent, the answer to wait for, all that could take a lot of time. Why ruin completely your already fragile health? What if they got orders to force-feed me? With a tube?

My hunger strike ended. Only much later did I understand how right that woman was. My sentence called for total seclusion.

Days 1835, 1836, 1837, 1838, 1839, 1840, 1841, 1842 of detention—July 31, 1954

A week later, no doubt because of my abortive hunger strike, the commandant gave me permission to make some drawings with soap on the windowpanes, by getting up on the tub. He set one condition, however. That he have a look at the drawings.

A problem. What to draw? What subject might please him? In any event, something anecdotal. Within his grasp. Hence something related to prison life.

One night I had been awakened by a commotion. Boots hammered on the cement. Doors opened. Orders were barked out but I didn't hear them well enough to understand. From my bed, my heart pounding, I listened for the alarming noises. No light at the window. So it must be the middle of the night. The noises rose to the upper level. I finally heard a few words clearly: "Take out your baggage!" Were we leaving this penitentiary? Fear returned with a premonition of disaster.

The boots come up once again. The key turns. Quick! Get up. Get dressed. When I am ready, the militiawoman opens the door for three men. Three militiamen. "She doesn't have any baggage," she tells them. Then they lift up the mattress, bend over to look under the bed. One of them even opens the grate of the stove. Just a search. A first for me, here. Later, there were countless others. These three men and this woman were searching an empty room. The pointless absurdity of it, that would be the subject of my drawing.

Because the soap left rather thick marks, I had to sketch only a few lines, the two militiamen coming up the stairs, the third ending up under the bed, the fourth, half swallowed-up in the stove. The better to impress the commandant, the drawing was accompanied by an epigram. I remember it, more or less: Why all this fuss? What are all these crazed militiamen looking for in the women's prison? To see if the women haven't somewhere hidden away . . . a man.

The noon guard saw the drawing. Listened to the poetry. She sent the others to admire my drawing. The commandant was away. For the two days he was absent the whole prison staff marched into my cell. Finally, on the third day, at "opening time," the commandant, followed by his whole staff—who were almost as excited as I—made his appearance. He crossed the cell. Looked up. The whitish lines of the drawing stood out clearly against the blue sky. He gazes. Smiles. Turns toward me. Listens to the epigram. "This deserves a reward," he finally says. A shiver went through the crowd. A spectacular pause.

I couldn't believe my ears. A reward? Behind me I had already felt the guards' sudden chill. They had entered all smiles. Crestfallen, they followed their boss out, their heads bent. A half hour later, the officer on duty came to fetch me. He appeared embarrassed. He had me go down to the ground floor. Right under the staircase, he opened a small hidden door. In front of me, a black hole. He pushed me inside and shut the door behind me. The key turned. Instinctively I had turned around. Between the boards shone chinks of light. Sudden, total darkness. The sound of a hammer. They were nailing a cover over the door. The commandant had punished me. "Two days in the hole." I had blundered.

Forgotten that humor is a weapon. The subtlest one. So in prison, there is only one place for humor: the hole.

I had to spend two days in this blackness. I needed to study the space. I held out my arms. No obstacles in front of me. The void. But to the right and left, my hand felt rough brick walls. This cubbyhole was barely three feet across. I felt the floor. Stone. I took a short step. Cautiously, fortunately, for my foot found nothing to stand on. Is it a well? No. Stairs. Slowly I went down five steps. Below, a floor of hard-packed earth. Two steps more and my outstretched hands bumped into a second door. I grope for the doorknob. I give it a very slow twist. It gives. The door is unlocked. What's on the other side? I am scared to find out. All kinds of lurid stories read or heard a long time ago suddenly pop into my mind. Burst into my mind, freezing me with fear. Tortures of the Iron Guard, sadistic instruments, irons reddening in the fire. It is a very old prison.

Spend two days in this hole? How? It was cold in there. The floor, the walls were damp. Where to sit down? How to remain standing? Lean up against the walls? I was much too frightened even to touch them with my fingertips. I was soon tired. Forced to sit on the first step. But the cold of the stone goes right through me. I go back down the steps. I feel the floor with my foot. Carefully. Something rolls under my foot. I get down. I touch the thing. It's wood. A piece of wood. I feel the convex part of a log. The bark. Two flat surfaces. Firewood, no doubt. I set the wood down on the step. It keeps me from making direct contact with the stone.

Why has no sound reached me? This silence is frightening. The darkness, frightening. I must stop hearing the silence. I must stop seeing the darkness. Close my eyes. Concentrate. Hypnotize myself. Not be there. Work. Repeat the last lines of my play. Once, twice. Take flight. Tie up the thread. Make the words come. New words . . . and the words slide slowly toward me. Melodious words. Luminous, living words. That fly. That arrange themselves into measures. Strong syllables. Weak syllables. A dancing rhythm. A falling rhyme. I search. Change. Repeat. A minute? An hour? A lifetime? I've made up two lines. But again I am cold. Aching. In my kidneys. In my back. I must get up. Move. Warm up. And I need to pee. This is all I needed.

I knock on the door. Nothing. Knock again. Nothing. I

knock louder. Could it be that no one can hear me? That no one will respond? I experience an instant of desperation. What to do? It is because of this damned cold that the need is so urgent. On the floor? And then? Step in a puddle? I must open the second door. What is there to be afraid of? There can't be any danger behind this door. Too bad if there is. I go down the stairs. I take two steps. I hold out my arms, find the doorknob. Very slowly I open the door. I see nothing. Everything is black. My outstretched arms find no obstacle. A single step through the doorway. That's that. It's done. I feel better. I close the door again. Get back on the piece of wood. I cross my arms. I lean over. My arms resting on my knees. My head in the crook of my arms. How difficult it is to live and how difficult to die.

Die? I am going to die. Everything here is so black. Could a grave be any blacker? Has time stopped? I am suspended in time. Interred. It's the end. The end of everything. Nothing more desired. Nothing more felt. Infinite peace. The void. Nothingness. I am dead.

They let me out around six in the evening. For close to ten hours, no one had come to see if I was dead or alive. No one had brought me a crust of bread. A cup of water. Besides, I had stopped knocking on the door. I had gone twice more through the second door. Not been brave enough to go farther. The militiaman who brought me out of there said that the commandant had spared me the rest of the punishment.

Days 1843, 1844, 1845, 1846, 1847, 1848, 1849, 1850, 1851, 1852, 1853, 1854, 1855, 1856 of detention— August 14, 1954

If this third cell wasn't hell, it was certainly the next thing to it. To tell the truth, on objective examination, the precise replica of the two others. Same length. Same width. Same flooring. Window set at the same height. One floor below. But I did the objective examination only much, much later. At the time, immobile, my breath taken away, leaning on the door long since locked by the militiawoman, I looked at the cell. I was alone and yet assailed from all sides. Vertical, horizontal, slanting, superimposed, in a jumble, metal teeth, racks, lances—an incomprehensible and malignant metallic armor mercilessly assaulted me.

Iron cots. The cell was jam-packed with iron cots. Full to bursting. Full to suffocating. Four beds to the left lining the wall. Four beds to the right lining the other wall. Four more beds on the left, set on top of the four on the left. Four more beds on the right, set on top of the four beds on the right. Sixteen black iron cots. Sixteen thin folded mattresses, in canvas, black with grime. Barely filled with straw, ground into dust by the bodies and nightmares of so many men and women. Stopping the light. Transforming each bed into a mortuary niche. Catacombs devoid of everything, even their dead ones.

A passageway between the two rows of beds. So narrow that, only with difficulty, could I thread my way through or turn around between the beds. Sixteen women? This cell, inhabited by sixteen women, must have been unbearable. Piled up on one another, clearing a way with difficulty in the narrow corridor, climbing on the bars, clinging to the metal legs, hoisting themselves up on the beds to sit, dangling legs brushing against the heads of the women sitting on the lower beds. Even so, this monkey zoo would be lit by the white of sixteen sheets producing a chiaroscuro in the blackness of the niches. Human faces would drive away the ghosts. Human voices, sometimes even a burst of muffled laughter would drive out the evil spells. I, however, was alone.

To escape the fear of the gloom, I wanted to fluff up the mattresses a little. I had to give it up. Through the filters of the worn canvas, a dense suffocating dust filled the cell. I was coated with it.

The militiawoman brought me a sheet and blanket. Because of the lack of space for a bench, I was allowed to sit on the bed. I chose one of the upper bunks, up against the window. But getting up and down was strenuous work. My dangling legs became heavy, red, and swollen. The next day I regretfully had to change levels. I had acquired the habit of walking for hours on end. Until I was extremely tired. In the long run, the forced immobility was just as fatiguing. I had pins and needles in my legs.

The first evening, I had asked the officer on duty to have the beds removed or change my cell. He promised to do so. Day after day, to each militiawoman, to each officer, I repeated, mortally afraid, the same request. Finally, to the commandant himself.

During those two weeks in that cell, I at least had the joy of getting word about my family. One morning, taps on the wall. Seated in the shadow on one of the beds, I could answer without fear of surprise. Of course it began with "Who are you?" My name was familiar to her. She had also known one of my sisters. She knew that the whole family was in good health. My brother-in-law, the professor, took part in congresses abroad. Each time, my sister accompanied him. The fact that this news dated from the previous year was of no importance. Now I finally knew that, despite my conviction, their life was normal. I was happy to know that I had not brought them misfortune.

Only two days later, a change of cell. On the same floor and with only one bed.

Days 1857, 1858, 1859, 1860, 1861, 1862, 1863, 1864, 1865, 1866, 1867, 1868, 1869, 1870, 1871, 1872, 1873, 1874, 1875, 1876, 1877, 1878, 1879, 1880, 1881, 1882, 1883, 1884, 1885, 1886, 1887, 1888, 1889, 1890, 1891, 1892, 1893 of detention— September 20, 1954

Long, interminable, always alike, the days went by even so. The nights turned cool. I developed a cough. Felt washed-out. And my teeth began aching again. I had, for a long time, but in vain, been asking for some medical treatment. Finally, through my insistence, I was taken to the infirmary. The doctor said he didn't have the resources to treat me. He wasn't a dentist. The best he could do was to pull the tooth. But the tooth was broken. His several attempts to get a grip on it with pliers broke the rest of the walls of the tooth completely. He had to intervene with a lancet. Without an injection, without even a pretense of anesthesia, he dug into the quick. Then, making a circular movement, he began hacking at the gum around the root, to take it out. Blood spurted forth. Filled my mouth. Ran down my chin. He took up the pliers again. Groping, searching, he finally got a grip. He squeezed the pliers, pulled, and I heard the root break in my brain. Looking for bits, taking them out one by one, was a real feat of butchery.

Each morning I went out to empty the chamber pot. Though not very large, it was made of cast iron and too heavy for me.

There were some latrines at the end of the corridor but I was forbidden to use them. Only to go there to empty the chamber pot and give it a quick rinse. There were also the trash bins. The contents never ceased to amaze me. Not only leftover food, particularly the barley porridge, but also cigarette butts, many butts and burnt matches. Where could all these butts have come from? I later happened to learn. One morning the officer on duty entered, notebook in hand. He asked me how much money I had deposited at the penitentiary and what purchases I wished to have made. Money? I didn't have a penny. The devaluation that occurred shortly after my arrest had evaporated what I had in my purse that day. That was at least what I had been told on my departure after the trial. But had the purse itself and its contents, gold watch, glasses, and so forth, been gobbled up by this providential devaluation? They were never returned to me.

When I had entered the cell, the first thing I noticed was a sheet of paper stuck to the wall. The yellowish, fly-specked sheet was titled, "inventory":

1 bed
1 bench
1 coatrack
1 tub for water
1 chamber pot
1 barrel
1 light bulb
1 stove

I was rich! I immediately took down the paper and, folding it eight times, hid it under the board of the bench, fitting it into a groove. Why? For no particular reason. A prisoner's reflex. But this paper gave the idea of making off with some butts. Of hiding them at the back of the stove. It was unthinkable to ask the militiawomen for a match. But I granted myself the pleasure of anticipation. The prospect of winter changed its complexion. Winter . . . cold . . . fire! Fire in my stove. Hot embers. From then on I would wait for the embers that would lend their flame to my first hand-rolled cigarette.

A pilfered little square of pink cloth from a trash can was invaluable. For a long time it was my only handkerchief. But I couldn't understand why the prisoners threw so much porridge in the trash. In the earliest days I too had had trouble swallowing it. But by now I had reached the point of looking with envy at the gray and gluey stuff. Looking at the trash with envy. I didn't know that the regulations granted each inmate a full dipper of food. Because the dipper was large enough, the other inmates did not suffer from hunger. At least, in this penitentiary. I, however, was given very little. Always the last to be served, moreover, the dipper was not used. The tub was already empty or nearly so. Setting the dipper aside, the cook scraped the bottom with a wooden spoon to collect my ration, and the resulting noise each time saddened me. I so wished, I too, at least once, to have the luxury of throwing some porridge in the trash. But was this a special order? A starvation diet? Chance? I never received a full dipper.

Gradually, monitoring the sounds from the corridor, I learned the penitentiary's customs. I thus realized that my neighbors on the left enjoyed certain privileges. In the morning I heard the militiawoman ask them if they wanted milk or café au lait. Several times, too, around noon, the doctor's voice. With modulations that were human. Even friendly. Asking them if they were satisfied with their diet. There were three, perhaps four of them. Very young, their voices suggested. A militiawoman told me that they were ill. Consumptive. So this doctor was a monster only on orders.

Owing to the lack of a table, I always ate while seated on the bench, bent over the mess tin on my knees. Now, because this position made my back ache, I was forced to eat standing up. I walked around the cell, the dish in one hand, the spoon in the other. The coatrack was made of two long, vertical boards, connected by two other horizontal boards a bit more than three feet long. The first at mid-height, the second, at the top, fitted with wooden pegs. At a right angle to this second board, a fifth board, about a foot wide, formed a shelf. One day it occurred to me to push the coatrack under the window. Standing on the barrel, the mess tin set on the shelf, converted into a table, my eyes just reached the bottom of the window. It was pleasant to forget the taste of the food while looking at the sky. The Duce, making an unannounced inspection at mealtime, saw me by the judas and entered, asking what I was doing up there. He found my explanation unlikely and ordered me to move the coatrack away and "eat like everyone else." "Like everyone else?" I couldn't, really. So I resumed walking and, while walking, several times heard the suspect noise of the judas. Finally the Duce came in again. He gave me permission to use the coatrack, but not to put it back under the window. Thus I had only the wall in front of me, but it was enough for me to turn my head a little and once again the sky was there. The Duce was not as nasty as the others, but one had to stand up to him. Being unafraid of him disarmed him.

Days 1894, 1895, 1896, 1897, 1898, 1899, 1900, 1901, 1902, 1903, 1904, 1905, 1906, 1907, 1908, 1909, 1910, 1911, 1912, 1913, 1914, 1915, 1916, 1917, 1918, 1919, 1920, 1921, 1922, 1923 of detention—October 20, 1954

Days? Weeks? Months? From scene to scene my play was taking a definite shape. The main characters—my one little girl and six little boys—asserted their distinctive personalities. Really lived their lives, each in his or her own way. The action was off to a good start. The crisis was already becoming clear and drove me toward the final episode. Each evening I recited the whole thing, trying to hear it with an objective ear. My greatest pleasure was to add further difficulties in order to challenge myself to the utmost. By combining dialogues, for example. The end of one character's line of dialogue occupying only part of the line of verse, the other part being completed by another character's short answer or the start of an answer.

Because it was a children's play, it had to be funny. How could I accomplish this? By interspersing a comical situation or response, a witty remark, within the serious or lyrical passages. Another comical effect was repetition. I wanted to be moving, and then to provoke laughter. It was truly difficult work. Taking up all my attention. Alone within four walls, I had good days and bad days. The long-sought success of a verse, a scene, created a hope for better days. I don't think a pencil and paper would have made my life any easier. Only this purely mental labor could completely absorb my memory, my attention, my will.

I was in my fifth year of complete isolation. Without this work, how could I have escaped the despair, the sense of helplessness, the horror of the next seven? Without those long hours of perfect escape? Wasn't there madness there? Waiting to pounce? I was content to be able, from time to time, to thumb my nose at it. Despite the hunger, the solitude, despite my weakness and their strength, to thumb my nose at all of them.

Wake-up call in the middle of the night. The noise of doors being opened, closed, slammed. The voices of the militiawomen. "Get dressed! Bring out your belongings! Quickly! Quickly! Faster! Baggage on the floor. Show your things!" Another search. The militiawomen rifled through the baggage. The militiamen, the cells. When my turn came, this time I trembled for my hidden property. The luxury of a new emotion. A certain category of inmates savored this sensation of fear mixed with pleasurable triumph when the militiamen left empty-handed. Playing with fire and not getting burned. Losing out sometimes is the rule of the game. I believe that what makes the game sexy is not the idea of gain but that of the possible loss. I too let myself get caught and later played the game to the hilt.

Over the days I found two more subjects for drawings and epigrams that pleased me but I refrained from expending humor on the commandant.

First subject: Hearing sharp whistle blows early one morning, I had gotten up on my tub (I was still on the second floor). Down below, close to the fountain, an ancient hand-operated pump. Connected to the pump, a long garden hose spread its flat coils all over the courtyard. An officer and several militiamen were eyeing the nozzle. Two by two, four red-faced and sweaty militiamen were applying themselves to the pump handle. With ferociously energetic and rapid up-and-down movements. Finally, the hose appeared to spring to life. A shiver went through it. It rounded out a little, and in a first and very last convulsion, it must have spit out a driblet of water, for I saw a little dark stain spread out on the ground. A new whistle. Exercise over. Proof established. If a match thrown by one of the regime's enemies caused a fire in the penitentiary, the energetic and courageous personnel would, by a superhuman effort, succeed in extinguishing . . . the match.

Second subject: The fact is real. The verses easy. But the hunger that day was genuine.

In a mess tin
A clear soup.
    In the clear soup
    Some large green peas

In each green pea
A fat little worm.*
  The little white worms/verses
  Are children worms
But on the surface
Those that lounge around
  Large, fat and white
  Are the parent worms.

Seeking to recover my past life, I realize that with all my might I avoided thinking. Thinking about myself. About the human condition. About causes and purposes. About God or the devil. All this was taboo. "Danger." I preferred to talk twaddle. I was unhappy enough already. Let the philosophers—clothed, sated, warmed—scribble their bitter phrases on the pointlessness of it all, that is their right. Let them publish them if they find a publisher, and let them sell them if they find readers. All the better for them. If one of their readers kills himself, too bad for him, after all. Within me as well, there was the latent thought of suicide, but at the same time this thought gave me the strength to live. If one day this thought became an act, I would be driven to it not by metaphysical theories, but by the suffering felt in my unconscious and vulnerable flesh. When this suffering transgressed the limits of my will, of my desire to live. When the body became stronger than the mind.

Alas! My certitude of being able to get it over with at the moment desired and determined by me was illusory. Perhaps the sun shone more brightly that morning. Perhaps I went out to empty the chamber pot earlier than usual. Or later. Why until that morning had I never noticed the iron netting shining between the three floors? I had thought I could, by stepping over the low railing, plummet down to the cement, in the abyss of the stairwell. But they had thought of everything. We had to live out our suffering to the end.

Days 1924, 1925, 1926, 1927, 1928, 1929, 1930, 1931, 1932, 1933, 1934, 1935, 1936, 1937, 1938,

* In French, the language in which the poem was composed, the word *vers* creates a double entendre, meaning not only "worms" but "verses."

1939, 1940, 1941, 1942, 1943, 1944, 1945, 1946,
1947, 1948, 1949, 1950, 1951, 1952, 1953, 1954
of detention—November 20, 1954

For several days it did not stop raining. I was cold. An unfamiliar cold. Odd. Impossible to describe. Concentrated in a single part of my body, my thighs. A deep, painful cold. In the muscles surrounding the bone. When I complained to the doctor on one of his rare visits, he made a quick diagnosis and that's as far as he got. The knowledge that I was suffering from "rheumatic cold" did not warm me up.

On one of these nights of monotonous rain, I was awakened by a gnawing anxiety. I thought I had just had a nightmare. But the anxiety persisted. In the penitentiary, the usual nocturnal silence. Nevertheless, a muted clamor filtered into the cell. Stealthy footsteps. Muffled whispering. In the distance, the sound of doors. The momentary gleam of a flashlight swept over the rectangle of the window. Something secret and ominous was going on in the courtyard below.

Take a look? How? The tub? Too low. From this second floor my eyes could no longer pierce the depths of the courtyard. The bed? Yes. Close enough to the window. The iron bar of the armrest, just the right height. The corridor, silent. The militiawomen? Probably in the courtyard.

Quickly I got up on the bed and stood barefoot on the armrest. In the middle of the courtyard, some women, many women, huddled together. The feeble light of the penitentiary window barely lit up the streaks of rain, and puddles of water weakly glistened. Shrouded in darkness, the image of the women was murky. My head, silhouetted against the background of the cell, could easily be seen. I became frightened and, seeing little, went back to bed.

Down below, the noise grew louder. A piercing whistle blast made me jump and distinct words, loud and clear, rose up to me:

"You are leaving this penitentiary. Attention! Line up by fours. Close ranks. Faster! Faster! Now, no one makes a move, and listen to the orders. When the signal for departure is given, you will all leave in complete and total silence. I order you to maintain your starting alignment during the trek. Keep your eyes fixed on the back of the woman in front of you and follow in her steps exactly. You are expressly forbidden to talk or cough. You are forbidden to stop or get out of line. You are forbidden to slip or fall. The order is strict. No reason will be accepted for excusing a stop or a departure from what is prescribed. It is raining. The road is wet. The road is muddy. You will walk in the water and you will walk in the mud. Any action hindering the order to march will be considered sabotage and punished as such. Any misstep will be considered an escape attempt and punished on the spot. The militiamen around you are armed. They have orders to shoot. No pity for the enemies of the people! Anyone who tries to escape will be shot down like a dog! A mad dog! And now . . . attention! Prepare for departure. Guards! Open the doors! Attention! I will count to three. Attention. One . . . two . . . three! Forward, march!"

This is more or less the speech I heard as I lay trembling in my bed. But I cannot reproduce the voice's brutality. I hardly heard the sounds of their departure. I heard only a muffled noise as a background to the heavy hammering of boots.

I knew nothing about these departing women. I knew nothing of those who came to take their place. Where had they gone? Where did they come from? No rumors reached me. My days were still the same. It sometimes seemed that I endlessly started the same day over and over again with no perceptible change.

Days 1955, 1956, 1957, 1958, 1959, 1960, 1961, 1962, 1963, 1964, 1965, 1966, 1967, 1968, 1969, 1970, 1971, 1972, 1973, 1974, 1975, 1976, 1977, 1978, 1979, 1980, 1981, 1982, 1983, 1984, 1985, 1986, 1987, 1988, 1989, 1990, 1991, 1992, 1993, 1994, 1995, 1996, 1997, 1998, 1999, 2000 of detention—January 6, 1955

Yet, I had reached my two thousandth day of prison . . . and it, too, was just like all the others.

With a few pieces of wood and some ten lumps of coal in a little box, winter had officially entered the penitentiary. A little later the militiawoman brought in a small heap of burning embers on a shovel. I had had time to take out the cigarette butts I had hidden there.

The stove drew well. I had put only two pieces of wood on the lighted kindling. The wood crackled and took flame. The fire

was a problem. Maintain a good fire and burn up all my com-
bustible material in two or three hours or, rather, keep a very small
fire going all day in order to have some remaining embers for the
evening? To be able to sit on the floor in front of the stove. To put
some wood on the burning kindling. To listen to the purring of
the fire. Finally, to open the little door of the stove. And during
these hours, the hardest to bear of the whole day, to remain there,
a good heat penetrating me, gazing at the flames.

It is not easy to keep a fire from burning without altogether
extinguishing it. This took up a good part of my time all winter
long. From morning to night, I managed to maintain a fire that
barely glowed. I burned up all the coal but I kept half the wood.
Impatiently I waited for "closing time." Finally, doors opened, then
closed. It was my turn. Yes. My turn to take my leftover wood out
into the corridor. It was forbidden to have a fire in the stove or any
wood in the cell at night. But the wood was given back the next
morning.

For the whole winter, I conducted a quiet struggle for this
fire, and always victoriously. They never managed to find my hiding place. Never guessed that I simply hid my wood in the stove.
Behind the fire. A low parallelepiped on legs fitting into a large
cylinder about three feet high, the whole surmounted by a long
pipe driven by an elbow joint into the wall and the chimney, this
stove was very peculiar. The first part was occupied by the grill pan
and thus the fire. The cylinder was merely for giving off more heat.
When I received my wood in the morning, I put a few pieces of it
at the back of the cylinder. With the anemic fire I sparingly kept
going all day, no danger threatened my stockpile. The wood became drier and that was all. Even at "closing time," they would occasionally inspect the stoves, but only to put out the still-burning
fires. So before the "closing," I carefully hid my last embers under
the ashes. Later, I merely had to pile them up against the left side
and put my arm all the way into the rear to get back "my wood."
To blow to reignite the kindling. Artistically arrange the three or
four bits of wood. Sit on the floor in front of the stove. Listen to
the voice of the fire. Open the little gate. Gaze at the flames. Let
the heat from them warm my face. How painful it all was.

And then there were the cigarette butts. But I prolonged the
pleasure of anticipation. The tobacco, the paper, the fire, everything was finally within reach. I treated myself to the luxury of

postponing my pleasure. Moreover, how could I be lavish? Four cigarettes, with a chance of five—I had to choose my moments. I took a certain amount of care rolling my first cigarette. The tobacco, dry and skimpy. The paper, too thick. The taste, acrid. But the smoke curled up in a spiral. The gestures were the same. I was smoking not a cigarette, but the idea of a cigarette.

Days 2001, 2002, 2003, 2004, 2005, 2006, 2007, 2008, 2009, 2010, 2011, 2012, 2013, 2014, 2015, 2016, 2017, 2018, 2019, 2020, 2021, 2022, 2023, 2024, 2025 of detention—January 30, 1955

The end of 1954 and the beginning of 1955 have left no memory, but the story of my fire is still long and filled with adventures. After "closing time," I still had to outwit the guards' surveillance. Fortunately, they were not allowed to enter the cells and could not see the stove from the judas. Even less, the little gate. On some days, too involved in my work, I forgot to stoke the wretched little fire in time. Nothing glowing on the grill pan. I rooted around among the embers and if I found at least two red bits, with infinite patience and three or four splinters of wood torn off with my fingernails, I managed, by blowing for a long time, to reignite my fire. But when the ash no longer hid anything, if the militiawoman on duty was not one of the ones who let herself be moved to pity, my stove remained cold until the next day. I consoled myself by thinking of the wood I'd saved and of the somewhat more luxuriant fire the next evening. Moreover, all day long, the cell was nearly as cold with or without the fire, but the walking made the cold more tolerable. My coat of golden sheep as well. I wore it with the fur turned toward the inside. The fur was still long enough and it kept my chest and back warm. Its satin lining was increasingly dirty and threadbare, but this was an unimportant detail, as I was not altogether clean myself. Particularly my hands—I could no longer keep them at all clean. I was given only a small piece of black laundry soap. Very hard, hardly making any suds, I had to make it last a whole week. I had asked in vain for some additional soap in view of my special situation. In a cell with several inmates, they could take turns tending the fire, while I, being alone, was the one who could do this. Nor did I have much water. So I couldn't wash my hands very often. My fingers were calloused. My fingernails black. Because of the cold water, deep cracks cut into the corners of my nails. They were very painful. I had to find a cure for them. Once again, the trash cans came to my aid.

Some rags, filched over several days from under the militia-woman's nose, were transformed, in a day's sewing, into fingers for gloves. I slipped them on before handling the wood or coal. But there were also the ashes to take out. I always rolled up the sleeve of my jacket before putting my arm, up to the elbow, into the cylinder to get out the hidden wood. Despite all my precautions, however, the right sleeve became much dirtier than the left, but I was lucky never to get it, or myself, burned.

Only twice did my stockpile catch fire. A cup of water thrown in the back of the stove calmed its ardor. This gave me the idea of putting out the embers to make them into charcoal. I picked up an ember between two twigs and dropped it into the cupful of water. The ember went out with a hiss and all I had to do was let it dry out in the hiding place. From then on, when I found only bits of embers in the ashes, I could use my charcoal. Carefully collecting the fragments into a pile so that they didn't fall from the grill pan into the ash pan, I set two or three small pieces of charcoal on top of them; all I had to do then was blow forcefully several times to reignite—much more quickly than with the splinters of wood—a flickering little flame of which I was extremely proud.

Handling wood, fire, and flame had always given me pleasure. Wood is noble. Fire has forever been connected with mysteries, with sacrifices, with all religions. I received rather slender cut logs. Their bark was pleasant to look at. But how beautiful was the smooth and shining bark of that unknown essence. It was probably very green wood, no thicker than my wrist, round, and when I reheated it on the stovetop, it gave off the bittersweet aromas of violets, wildflowers, and sun.

At night it was always very cold. In the earlier prisons, I had always had a semblance of heat, even at night. Here, nothing. The iron—or maybe cast iron—of the stove, I don't know, the iron—the white metal of the cylinder retained no heat. As soon as the fire was out, the stove acted more like an air cooler. It brought me the cold wind swallowed up by the chimney. The blanket was thin. Woven of waste cotton and wool, it could not hold warmth. In the evening when I undressed, I arranged my skirt, the jacket, the hand towel, my whole outfit, even my stockings, on the sheet. I wore only the white canvas military shirt. Over all this I laid the blanket. I then rolled up these layers to make a long tube. A shroud, even furnished with a mummy's wrappings. A cord made of knotted rags. Used during the day to tuck my coat around my waist, it served to bind up my shroud at night where my ankles came together. I put the coat over it, but unfortunately, it didn't completely cover me. For the truly glacial nights, I stuffed myself under the blanket wearing the coat over my shirt.

Day 2026 of detention—January 31, 1955

A few moments before, I was still walking peacefully in the cell. Working, as usual. Trying to merge two verses into one. To make them more forceful. Concentrating too hard to pay attention to a slight warmth in my left lung. Unconsciously my right hand came to rest on my chest. Over my heart. And mechanically my feet went on moving.

Blood. It was blood I was looking at now, stunned. Dark red. With clots. Blood spattered on the floor in front of me. My blood.

A slight warmth in my chest, my hand placed over my heart, and suddenly I had felt my mouth full of something. So full that, on its own, despite myself, my mouth had opened, for I would have liked to go spit in the chamber pot but I didn't have time to and it spattered on the floor, with spots all around, and I saw that it was blood, a rather large spot of blood but not so large that I couldn't have covered it with one of my outspread hands, then it began again and the spot grew larger and it would have taken both hands to cover it, and then there was a third spurt and this was the last one but I had to spit several more times to clean out my mouth and get rid of the flat taste, and the spot had become a pool and I now would have needed four hands for it was slowly spreading, encompassing the spatters, and the blood wasn't completely liquid but viscous and its color was darkening, becoming brown and I stood there, bewildered, looking at it and thinking that it was blood and that blood is hard to wash away and that I had to ask the militiawoman for a rag to wash it, provided that she brought me one quickly, before it dried completely, and then I was a little sad because I had a hemoptysis and was ill and was in prison and at the same time I thought of my neighbors, the ones who were tubercular, and that they were well cared for and could not be hungry, and after I knocked on the door several times, I heard the steps of the militiawoman, and she opened the judas and I told her that I had spit blood on the floor and needed a towel to clean it up before it dried completely, and she saw the blood through the judas and I think she became a bit frightened for she left in a hurry and soon came back and opened the door and threw me a piece of canvas but said nothing, and I had to remain bent over for a long time to remove the blood but not completely and the floor was still a bit stained and one could very well see how much blood had flowed to leave such a large spot and I begged the militiawoman to call the nurse and she said "yes," but he didn't come, and I lay down on the bed without asking permission and the militiawoman opened the judas several times and each time she saw me on the bed and each time she said nothing.

Two days later, after taking the chamber pot to the latrines, I had a second hemorrhage. Right away, the militiawoman on duty that day immediately had the nurse come. The nurse told me that he was going to call for the doctor. The doctor told me nothing at all because, quite simply, he didn't come. I waited for him the next day as well. In vain. I waited for him every day for ten days. On the eleventh day, he had me come to the infirmary. He examined me very cursorily and sent me back without even taking my temperature. A little later a militiawoman came in to tell me that the doctor had given his permission for me to sit on the bed during the day and to go to bed by "closing time." Starting the next day, I began receiving, every morning, five pieces of sugar, about three ounces of solid marmalade, and a tablespoon of oil. The hunk of bread was doubled and, five times a week, I received a little cup of milk. A quart a week. But at noon and in the evening, no change of diet.

The nurse gave me ten injections of I don't know what. Only ten. No other medication. I realized that my diet was totally different from that of my neighbors. The regulation TBC (tuberculosis) diet. For me, a simulation. I understood that it was not really the doctor's ill will. I also explained to myself the ten days' wait.

The commandant had no doubt sent a report to his superiors. Had waited for the answer. Special instructions for a special case.

The sugar and marmalade gave me pleasure, but it was hard to get the oil down quickly. The guard opened the door, handed me the spoon of oil and was always in a hurry to get it back empty. I asked for a little bottle in which to keep the oil, to wait and mix it in with the noon rations and, to my great surprise, I got the bottle.

After some careful consideration, I decided to make some cakes. I had all the necessary ingredients, most importantly the fire. After making a thorough study of my wood, I managed to remove from it a strip already started by an axe. Some three inches wide, about six inches long, it was just the dish I needed to bake my cakes on. I had long hidden away a sort of wooden knife that I had managed to make almost sharp. With care, I cut two thin slices of bread I had dried out on the stove. In the evening I coated them with oil and moistened sugar, crushed with my knife. A little marmalade spread over it. Pushing the embers aside, I made a place on the grill pan for my tart dish. Five minutes later, the sugar caramelized, the marmalade crackled, and my oven emitted a delightful aroma. It seemed to me I had never eaten such a delectable cake.

It was just the right time to roll a cigarette. The next to last.

Well-being? Yes. Ridiculous? Perhaps. A little bread with the aroma of a fancy cake. A cigarette containing just a few shreds of tobacco in the thin tube of paper that saliva didn't succeed in glueing—how to admit that these two nothings can suffuse you with such keen pleasure? Even the most destitute of derelicts would have vomited it up. But for what free man would these vulgar nothings have evoked such memories, dreams, so much pity for himself and others?

At the same time, I was also a little afraid. Afraid that these odors, creeping through the chinks in the door, would tickle the nose of some alert militiawoman and that she would confiscate my goods. Several times my tarts were slightly burned, but they were no less delicious. The milk gave me less pleasure, but I was delighted, thanks to the additional bread, to have my hunger appeased.

The solitude from which I suffered so was now salutary. My cell was not polluted by the breathing of others. Moreover, I kept the window open despite the cold. Not having anyone to talk to was also good for my lungs. The new diet, as meager as it was, provided the minimum of calories, of which I had so long been deprived.

Unfortunately, exactly a month later I waited all morning for my diet, in vain. When the guard handed me the noon mess tin, I shyly recalled her forgetfulness. Her answer was short: "Ended!" Several days in a row I asked to see the doctor. After a week he came to see me and declared, with an air of irritation, that I was cured.

"But you haven't even examined me."

"What's the use? The infirmary isn't heated and you could catch cold."

I had to be content with this answer. He surely did not have permission to do more. In any case, those thirty days of rest had been a help. The illness progressed no further. I had no more hemorrhaging. I knew the disease was there and that I had to defeat it myself. I gave up the excessive fatigue of my continual walking. Particularly in the evening. Obviously, I was once again prohibited from sitting on the bed and could now retire only at ten at night. From time to time, I sat down on the bench and, if all was quiet in the corridor, I lay on the bed for a few minutes.

I'll say it again. Not all the female guards were truly malevolent. When they could do so safely, they closed their eyes to this behavior of mine. I was alone. Always quiet. Never giving them any trouble. I had accepted my fate. They were not responsible for it. What right had I to ask them to take the slightest risk on my behalf? I was grateful for even a hint of a smile. For the "good morning" sometimes whispered in the morning. For a mess tin a little fuller than usual. The one who helped carry my chamber pot one day had made a serious, and for her dangerous, gesture.

I now knew their names and personalities. I would never have begged them, even the best of them, for something against the rules. I didn't even claim to ask them for absolute respect for these rules. They didn't always have the time or desire to waste ten minutes just so a single inmate could go for a walk. Sometimes, on Saturdays, instead of taking me to the showers, they brought a pail of hot water into the cell. My rations never strictly conformed to the rules. I never complained. I particularly avoided, in tone or in words, anything that these simple and limited creatures might have interpreted as a sign of humility or lack of dignity. My attitude eventually imposed on them a similar attitude or nearly so toward me.

One of them, a Hungarian called Erji, was truly nice to me. A charming face, always clean and well groomed, she shared a friendly dialogue with me just in our exchange of glances.

Days 2027, 2028, 2029, 2030, 2031, 2032, 2033, 2034, 2035, 2036, 2037, 2038, 2039, 2040, 2041, 2042, 2043, 2044, 2045, 2046, 2047, 2048, 2049, 2050, 2051, 2052, 2053, 2054, 2055 of detention—March 2, 1955

End of special diet.

Days 2056, 2057, 2058, 2059, 2060, 2061, 2062, 2063, 2064, 2065, 2066 of detention—March 13, 1955

One day, despite the demands of my work, the meticulous analysis not just of each line, but also of each word and syllable, the search for alliterations, onomatopoeias, for rhythm and uncommon rhymes, a final line of verse brought my play to a close. It was called *Limpid Days*. I was both pleased to have brought it to a good end and worried, distressed. Would I be able to hit upon a new subject? This was the fourth play that I had finished. Like the others, it was made up of about two thousand lines of verse.

All together I composed eight plays. After my release from prison, I managed to write down only three of them. The time it took to write them down, normal life—unsettling for me—erased the other five from memory. I did not go to the trouble of retrieving them. A more objective assessment of my literary abilities led me to judge the effort useless. My three plays are lying at the bottom of a drawer. No one has read them. What's the use?

In pursuit of a new theme, waiting for inspiration, I went back to poetry. But it was short-lived work. I needed difficult, methodical work. Only one of the poems from that time has remained in my memory and it gives me pleasure.

It is intimately connected with that chilly day in the month of March. With a gray sky. With rain, with sparrows shivering and wet on the windowsill. It had a complicated rhythm. One line very long and one line very short. Like the uneven gait of a lame person.

Days 2067, 2068, 2069, 2070, 2071, 2072, 2073, 2074, 2075, 2076, 2077, 2078, 2079, 2080, 2081, 2082, 2083, 2084, 2085, 2086, 2087, 2088, 2089, 2090, 2091, 2092, 2093, 2094, 2095, 2096, 2097, 2098, 2099, 2100, 2101, 2102, 2103, 2104, 2105, 2106, 2107, 2108, 2109, 2110, 2111, 2112, 2113, 2114, 2115, 2116, 2117, 2118, 2119, 2120, 2121, 2122, 2123, 2124, 2125, 2126, 2127, 2128, 2129, 2130, 2131, 2132, 2133, 2134, 2135, 2136 of detention—May 20, 1955

March, April, May . . . and still the sparrows. In my prison life, as in the one with my husband Harry, the sparrows sometimes were important and helpful characters. His stories of sparrows are so beautiful that they tug at your heart, and no one can hear them with a dry eye. My story about sparrows is violent.

In the very thick wall of this very old prison, in an upper corner of the window, on the outside, of course, a couple of sparrows had come to make their home. Finding a chink in the masonry, they had warmly lined it with down, dry grass, bits of wool, and they had made it their nest. With silky rustlings, they soared out and returned. Each day, I sacrificed a few crumbs of bread or polenta on the windowsill for them. The sparrows pecked away, hopping and peeping. I was sometimes tempted to deny them this beakful of my bread. But each time, I was moved by their tiny birds' bellies. I very much wanted to touch them. Caress their plumage with my fingertips. I never managed this, but it was a joy and a consolation to feel them close by and to be able—I the destitute one—to provide for them and, in my ugliness, to admire their beauty. They gave me the blessing of my tenderness for them.

So many days and nothing else to say about them. I must have lived these days in some way or other since I reached this day, May 18, 1955, a crucial day of all my days of prison, past and future.

. . . and the story of the sparrows continues . . .

On May 17, a new political officer rushed into my cell. The Duce had gone elsewhere. The officer entered with a wild look. He made a few steps, paused, and began looking around. He appeared so totally absorbed in eyeing the bed, the bench, and the coatrack that I couldn't keep from asking if he was looking for anything in particular and I even offered to help him with his search. He turned his back on me and went up to the window. It was a luminous spring day. On the windowsill, the striking yellow of the sunlit polenta stood out sharply against the blue of the sky. Finally unglueing his thin lips, he asked if my ration of food was excessive. On the contrary. Quite insufficient. Then how was it that I threw some of it out? I don't throw any of it away. I do without these crumbs for the sake of the two sparrows. Since I am forced to be alone, they are my only companions.

Should I have answered otherwise?

An hour later, a militiaman escorted me to the walk. It lasted longer than usual. Upon my return to the cell, the sparrows appeared panic-stricken. They went round and round, hurried to the nest, banged up against the wall, left again, came back, began again, and I couldn't understand the cause of their confusion. I saw some sticks coming from the nest, but it seemed impossible that they had put them there to destroy the nest. How could I believe that a political officer had gone to the trouble of ordering that a ladder be brought up, that someone climb up it and destroy a nest of sparrows by plugging it up with twigs only for the sake of depriving a woman in solitary confinement the company of two tiny little birds?

With tears in my eyes, unable to come to their aid, for the nest was beyond my reach, I watched the two birds struggle, their beaks and talons clutching the twigs, beating their wings feverishly to keep themselves at nest level. After an hour, however, I was delighted to see them settle in anew. Piece by piece, they had succeeded in taking everything away.

Day 2137 of detention—May 21, 1955

The next day, a new outing, a new devastation. But this time the sparrows had to give up. The hole with the nest had been filled with cement. The two birds flew away forever.

For years I felt myself sinking. Going down ever deeper into the black water, day after day. Suddenly, however, on that May 18, 1955, my feet painfully hit the bottom of the abyss. My fall was so hard that its impact propelled me to the surface in a single bound and I felt that my trouble had been broken, that its fragments were carried off by the agony, and with them any resignation, any despair, and any idea of death. No more room for all that. In neither my head nor my heart. Anger had cleaned the slate.

Sadness makes you weak. Anger, powerful. I chose resistance. Made the decision never to weep again and since then I have never wept. To be receptive to hope, and I moved beyond hope. Certitude took root in me. The certitude of regaining freedom, joy, my loved ones. I will conquer the illness. Finally, justice will be done. I was not deluded.

In 1968, we were granted a new trial. By the decision of the new Party secretary. The country's Supreme Court recognized our complete innocence. But the Supreme Court couldn't raise the dead. At the investigation occasioned by the new trial, I told, among other things, of the murder of the nest. It seems that at all the Party meetings at which the acquittal of Pătrăşcanu and the other defendants was announced, the political officer's behavior was cited as an example of how badly we had been treated, and it provoked the audience's outrage! The wind and the years gone by since those days of outrage have erased all trace of them, and oblivion has fallen heavily on the graves of the dead and of our murdered youth.

Thus ends my story of the sparrows.

Days 2138, 2139, 2140, 2141, 2142, 2143, 2144, 2145, 2146, 2147, 2148, 2149, 2150, 2151, 2152, 2153, 2154, 2155, 2156 of detention—
June 10, 1955

Around noon a few days earlier, they had me leave the cell and escorted me to an office. I was given a paper to sign and a package of food. Without any explanation, a militiaman drove me through some side streets to the train station. There, in front of me, on an empty siding, a single railroad car with tiny boarded-up windows. In the distance, on my left, the station building. Green trees. A little grass on the embankments and militiamen everywhere. They had me get into the railroad car. A corridor, two doors to the left, a door at the end. A militiawoman was there. She opened one of the two doors and had me enter a tiny compartment almost filled by a wooden seat. The window was not plugged up as I had thought. It was simply covered by narrow overlapping metal slats and let through very little light. And even less air. It was terribly hot in there. The seat could be raised up to uncover a toilet. Every amenity. My cynical assessments weren't quite right—this comfort was real. The whole rest of the penitentiary, who had arrived after me in trucks, was crowded together in the common compartment—the third door—a real can of sardines for so many women. The sun beating down hard on the sheet metal made the heat suffocating, and after an hour I had to take off my thick military shirt and remain in my tattered petticoat. But the line for the toilet? I was truly privileged.

I opened my package. A quarter loaf of black bread. A hunk of cheese. A square of marmalade, perhaps three to four ounces. A slice of bacon. I had forgotten the existence of bacon and cheese. The trip promised to be a pleasant one.

The wait was a long one. The sun went down, the cell became darker, when a lurch and a creaking signaled that our car had been coupled to a train. After several maneuvers, yet more waiting, and finally the train came definitively to life, began slowly moving, and took on speed. A dim light bulb went on in the ceiling. Finally, a militiawoman opened the door and handed me a cup of water. She told me to knock on the door when I wanted some more. Putting my mouth to the opening in the window, I could also drink in my fill of fresh air, which smelled of wood and hay. I was really the passenger in a first-class sleeping car.

From time to time, the train stopped at a station. I listened to the human voices. Judging from the accent, I knew that we were still in Transylvania, and often Hungarian could be heard. With pleasure, I started in on my package. I was seated with my legs almost extended along the seat, my back against the side wall. But I couldn't sleep. The wheezing of the railway engine. The pleasant rocking. The hammer banging the wheels in certain stations. The strong taste of the cheese. The whistle blasts. The calls of a woman's voice. The perfume of fresh grass. The sweetness of the bacon melted by the heat, just right with the crust of black bread. The light of dawn laying pale gray rays across the window. I had to intoxicate myself with noises and odors. Take them in with every pore. Be attentive with all my memory and all my body to this nocturnal euphoria. When the daylight burst forth, on my knees against the window, I even saw green trees, grass, a little patch of sunny sky. I had finally become drowsy when the train came to a final stop.

The coach was uncoupled. I heard the train start up again without us. It had to be about eight in the morning. We had arrived. But where had we arrived?

7 | The Walls Speak

Miercurea-Ciuc Penitentiary

Day 2157 of detention—June 11, 1955

Low houses. Red tiles. Flower gardens. The canvas-topped truck pitches and bumps on the dirt road. Sitting next to the driver, I glance at the passersby. I would like to attract someone's gaze.

An old woman on a doorstep looks at the truck coming, looks at it going by, but the old woman doesn't look at me.

Pink houses. Blue walls. Small windowpanes and white muslin curtains. I would like to encounter a smile. But the young woman in the flowered dress goes by, indifferent, and does not look at my smile.

I would like to meet someone's gaze. A single gaze. But the two children playing in the street do not turn their gaze to me. The old man passing by does not look at me. The young man coming up does not look at me.

No one pays attention to this truck, to this canvas-topped truck going by, bumping over the ruts. They do not know. They cannot know. No one knows. Alone, a dog, sprawled out in the shade of a wall, raises its head, sniffs and, detecting the unquestionable smell of some penitentiary livestock huddled under the canvas cover, alone, the dog looks at me, and I hear it, for a long time, barking in our wake.

An archway. A large courtyard surrounded by buildings. They have me get out first and cross through the courtyard. Through a little door in a wall more than six feet high, I enter a second square courtyard. Three-sided, a U-shaped prison. On the ground floor, as on the only floor above, wide, completely glassed-in corridors onto which the cells open.

The ground of the courtyard is studded with round stones of different sizes. Nearly every day for seven years, I will circle round and round it. Ten minutes a day. Limping more and more, I will learn to steer clear of the bumps and slow down my pace where the stones have disappeared and the bare earth seems soft to my feet. Sometimes, when my legs hurt too much, the militiawoman will allow me to use a long-handled rush broom as a crutch. Other times, she will let me simply sit on the ground, with my back to the wall, and I will be happy to do so.

That first morning, however, four stone steps. An entrance hall. On the left, a corridor going off at an angle. Five doors. In front of the third one, the elderly militiaman halts, selects a key from his ring, inserts it into the lock. Apprehensively, I follow him with my eyes, but when the door finally opens, a miracle. Dazzled, through the window I see only a great deal of green against a huge expanse of blue.

The window is fairly low. My head just reaches the bottom of it. My cell looks out on the courtyard behind the penitentiary, some fifty feet wide. A high brick wall separates it from a garden that surrounds a very large building, only a part of whose sloping roof I can see. On the left, in a corner of the courtyard, a watch-tower, set high up. Along the wall, a wide strip of lawn protected by a network of barbed wire. On the wall is a notice-board. Despite the distance, I manage to make out the wording because it is written in large capital letters: "It is forbidden to approach the wall or stand on the grass on penalty of death." Up above, the guard, gun in hand. On the other side of the wall, just in front of my window, the supple branches, the graceful and tender green of twin acacia trees.

I cannot take my eyes off all this. I look at the trees with love. With passion. And while I breathe them in with all the intensity that I concentrate in my nearsighted eyes, a small elf makes a sign of friendship with his arm, all laced with green. I have a perfect view of his head with a pointed cap and his other arm hooked to a branch and his feet in a skirt of ornamented foliage. A light gust of wind made my little man dance and he never stopped wishing me a good day.

He was a merry little lad, and from time to time all day we exchanged greetings and words of tenderness.

The cell was clean and just as large as the others. In fact, I had a space designed for at least four persons. Actually, it was the same bed, the same bench, coatrack, tub, chamber pot, and stove. But the chamber pot was much heavier, and the stove was unfortunately situated differently. The low part with the grill pan, the ash pan, and the little door were fitted flush with the wall. In the cell, only the large cylinder and the pipe going into the chimney by a bend. The fire was thus maintained from the outside, in the corridor, and no longer depended on me. In a corner, a rush broom and a rag.

After taking possession of my cell, I had to get to know the rest of the prison. For the moment, only silence. Not a sound. Not a murmur. The judas remained closed for hours on end. According to the sun, noon was long past. My package had been a long time ago. I was hungry. Finally hearing the sound of footsteps in the corridor, I began knocking loudly on the door. The same elderly military man opened the judas. You've forgotten to give me something to eat. But no, he hadn't forgotten anything. Hadn't I received a package of cold food when I left the penitentiary? That, it appeared, was my ration for the next day. But they had forgotten to tell me so. All I could do was be patient for twenty-four hours. Late in the afternoon, the two cells next to mine were in turn occupied. With my ear up against the wall, an indistinct medley of voices came through. Later I heard the voice of Pătrăşcanu's wife speaking with the militiawoman. She occupied the last cell. Between the two of us, a buffer cell, empty.

Starting the next day, my next-door neighbors on the right tapped gently on the wall. Despite a certain uneasiness, I had decided to give up any communication and left the call unanswered. What was the use? Besides my family, nothing interested me. There was little likelihood that these neighbors knew of my loved ones. Luck doesn't repeat itself every day. Why risk losing my tree and my elf?

The head of the penitentiary was an elderly Hungarian, plump and a good fellow, but obsessed with military discipline. Respect for rules. Absolute prohibition against sitting on the bed. Out of cunning, he instigated a very special way to make the bed. Impossible to lie down on it without messing it up completely. I had to rest on the wooden bench. A position that my lack of flesh made increasingly painful. However, the food, without being more abundant, was better and more nourishing. Potatoes, cabbage, green beans, noodles, pearl-barley, and Saturday the porridge slightly sweetened with marmalade. A dirty pink color, it turned a bit gelatinous as it cooled, and I got into the habit of eating only half of it in the evening and hiding the rest in the little water pot kept under the mattress. To treat myself to a Sunday breakfast. Giving up eating anything in the evening was to remain hungry but I always managed to do it. I made it a matter of dignity! The relation between porridge and dignity may seem ludicrous, but a rule that one lays down for oneself always has a moral value if one manages to observe it.

Days 2158, 2159, 2160, 2161, 2162, 2163, 2164, 2165, 2166, 2167, 2168, 2169, 2170, 2171 of detention—June 25, 1955

Two weeks went by, bearable. Once again I had found a subject for a play. I had gone back to working. My time was planned meticulously. But every day my neighbors insisted on disturbing me. My silence did not deter them and I felt my resistance crumbling. In any case, I was almost peaceful when, one bad morning, the political officer entered the cell. It was, alas, the political officer of the sparrows! As soon as the door opened, he shrugged, then planted himself like a post in the middle of the cell. He gazed for a long time at the window, and without saying a word he left the place as angrily as he had come in.

Around five in the afternoon, an unfamiliar noise caught my attention. I could not look out at the courtyard without risk. I was on a slightly elevated ground floor, and the orderly was right nearby at his surveillance post. I soon realized that it was only the sound of a saw, on the other side of the wall. I froze in my tracks with a premonition. Not even daring to breathe, I looked at the lacy foliage that had begun to tremble. The imp jumped and made great signals of friendship. But the saw continued to rasp, and suddenly, beating the air with its tousled branches, the first acacia came down behind the wall in a heartrending crash. My sprite, shaken by the shock, feverishly waved to me and perhaps said farewell or perhaps he called to me for help, and I could do nothing to save him, and the saw went back and forth in my flesh and sawed my heart and took away my breath and I stood there sobbing my eyes out and unable to take my eyes off the little fellow to whom I had murmured words of love and I begged him not to abandon me, the way everyone had abandoned me, not leave me once again all alone and I told him good-bye, my tiny green imp, good-bye, a few minutes more and I shall lose you forever, you, my final illusion, and how can I leave you without tears and I promised never to forget him and to keep him in my heart and he has remained there, more real, more present than those whom I had loved and for whom I had suffered and whose memory now makes me neither hot nor cold, as if I had never known them, but he, the nonexistent, still lives, and I want to forget only the noise of the saw and his last dance and that not having the strength to see him vanish I closed my eyes and also forgot the groan of the tree trunk and the sound of the twisted branches and only recall that I kept my eyes closed for a long time without having a premonition that the miracle, once again, was there.

Nothing but sky. Three clouds crimped with gold. On the horizon, a hill, all green with trees, and now I saw the whole beautiful roof of pink tiles, and on one of its tall chimneys, previously occluded by the two acacias, a white and black stork in all its majesty.

I had not wept from grief. I did not weep from joy. But it was much more beautiful than before. There is a regulation in our country's prisons. I don't know whether it exists in other countries as well. This ruling is flexible. But the political officer had hatefully applied it. No grass, plant, stalk, leaf, bud, flower, bush, or tree is allowed to come up, grow, flower, or bear fruit within the sight of a political prisoner. If—despite the ruling—this happens, he is punished with death.

The grass growing between the stones of the courtyard was burned alive under pounds and pounds of salt. The officer murdered each blade of grass, each tiny flower, as he had murdered my two acacias and my winsome green elf. What law in the world punishes these crimes? I hated him. In all my impotence. But this hatred was of no concern to him, while I was suffocated by it.

Days 2172, 2173, 2174, 2175, 2176, 2177, 2178, 2179, 2180, 2181, 2182, 2183, 2184, 2185, 2186, 2187 of detention—July 12, 1955

That morning I was going round and round the courtyard when I saw him. Behind the windows on the second floor, he stood motionless, spying on me. In the right-hand corner of the courtyard, where the right-hand wing of the building ended, the latrines were located in a recess. Two cubicles closed by slatted wooden doors and a long gutter that served as a urinal. Next to some trash cans. While walking slowly around the courtyard, I had noticed in one of the trash cans, on top of the other trash, a long leaf of green onion, thrown away by one of the militiamen, for the prisoners did not get any raw vegetables. I glanced at the militiawoman and, taking advantage of a moment's inattention, furtively leaned over, grabbed it, and hid it in my closed fist. A few minutes later, the officer came down the steps, hurried over to me and, to the militiawoman's dismay, asked me, shouting, what had I put in or taken out of the trash. I at first pretended not to understand, then to be afraid, and after letting him rant and rave threateningly, I held out my arm and slowly opened my fist, revealing the crumpled blade of onion. "Take it if you need it." Fuming, he turned his back, and the militiawoman's barely contained smile evaporated my hatred. I had made him look ridiculous. How could one hate an idiot, even a sadistic one? I had other problems to solve.

My clothes were falling to bits. No way to repair them. I asked the commandant for permission to write my family for the bare necessities. He sent the warehouseman to my cell. It was the first time I saw him, but the nice impression he made on me never faded. Behind his surly looks, he always took the trouble to help us as much as he could. So I received two yellowish and grimy pairs of boxer shorts and an old pair of pants no doubt left by one of the thieves that had preceded us in the prison. I showed him my shoes. The soles still held but the upper parts were in shreds. He fetched a pair of dreadful, very worn-down laced boots with malodorous linings. Despite all his eloquence, he couldn't persuade me to take them. I would have preferred to walk barefoot. I begged him to give me a length of thick material to make some slippers. He provided me with a scrap of woolen military cloth, scissors, a needle, and thread. The militiawomen were directed to bring me some hot water and an additional piece of soap. It took me two days of continuous washing to get the stuff clean. I reinforced the knees of the pants, took in the waist, shortened the legs, and the result was better than my translucent skirt. I made myself a pair of slippers that I wore with the soles strapped over the instep by a leather strip.

But I still had no stockings, skirt, blouse, or warm jacket. I continued to insist at each of the commandant's visits. I needed underwear and warm clothes for the winter. To ask my family for clothes was the only way possible to show them that I still existed. He finally capitulated or perhaps he received instructions in this regard, for one day a militiawoman brought me a postcard, a pen, and a bottle of ink. With permission to write out a list of things I wanted, the words: "I am in good health and I kiss you," and my signature. All I had to do was wait.

The subject for my new play was rather complicated. The action took place during the revolution of 1848. The main character, a boy of fourteen. Not wishing to use any neologisms from modern speech, I ransacked my memory for authentic Romanian words. My next-door neighbors still insisted. The idea that they might be of help to me put an end to my obstinate silence. One morning, using the alphabetic language, they again asked me: "Who are you?" I finally answered by giving my name and the trial I had been involved in. I, in turn, learned that there were five of them in the cell, all convicted of belonging to the Iron Guard, the pro-Nazi movement. The idea of having this party, which was also called the Legion, and its members, "legionnaires," as neighbors sent a chill up my spine. But I overcame my repulsion. They were in prison like me, and I didn't want to judge anyone. My own judges had left me forever disgusted with judging. I merely told them I hadn't enough patience for long conversations. So many taps for each letter was tiring and I had my work to do. They proved very tactful. Three of them were students and much too young to have taken part in the Legion's crimes. We talked only a few minutes a day. Each morning, we wished each other a good day and in the evening, good night. A week went by in this way, then the one who was their spokeswoman offered to teach me Morse code.

Without paper, without pencil, pen, or ink, I had to go back through the centuries and use a wax tablet and a stylus. The tablet? One of the faces of a bar of soap. The stylus? A broom straw. I began by carving all the letters of the alphabet on my tablet. She then dictated the various corresponding combinations of dots and dashes. The dots were light taps on the wall with the fingernail or the knuckle of the index or middle finger, or with some object. For example, the handle of a toothbrush, if one had one—as was not true in my case. The dashes, a scratch of about three inches on the wall, lightly so as not to leave a mark on the lime.

After rehearsing my lesson well, I rather quickly learned to talk, that is, rapidly strike the letters of each word of my text. But it took me much longer to learn to receive messages. To instantly decode the sounds I heard. To be able to make of them not isolated letters but words and sentences.

With infinite patience, G., my interlocutor, tapped a letter, and if I didn't recognize it from memory, she gave me time to consult my tablet. The letter finally picked up, I gave a short tap on the wall, the signal that it had been received. Only then did she dictate the second letter, and so forth until the end of the word. Once the reflex for Morse is acquired, when the sounds unconsciously become words, the language is really very rapid. Because of the dryness of the wall, the sounds came through clearly. In order for the militiawomen not to catch us, one also had to be attentive to the noises in the corridor. Also to take care to hide or erase the tablet. It was absolutely forbidden to communicate with one's neighbors. The militiawomen took a malicious pleasure in surprising and slapping us with the "seven days," that is, seven days in the hole with only bread and water.

Soon I was able to have extended conversations with my neighbors, or rather with G., for she was the only one who tapped on the wall. She was always extremely discreet. Respecting my hours of work. Only something unexpected drove her to the wall to inform me or warn me of some danger.

G. gradually let me enter the secret life of the penitentiary world. For more than a year, I had lived on the fringes of it. She began by teaching me the telegraphic code of alarm. I now knew that a forceful fist blow on the wall meant *danger*. Two blows meant *search*. My job was then to hurry over to the other wall. To relay the alarm. She told me of the feverish agitation triggered in the cells after the two fist blows. The iron wires for knitting, the needles, the works in hand quickly vanished. The filched spoons, whose handles had been sharpened, the pieces of glass for cutting fabric, all the thousand little things prohibited by stupidity or spite were hidden in the straw of the mattress, under the slats around the floor, in who knows what other hiding place determined by ingenious necessity.

In Morse code, the letter *L* had become my signal: dot-dash-dot-dash. It was my initial. I could respond to it in complete confidence. They had the corridor under surveillance. No danger. But one of my other neighbors took the precaution of remaining on watch near the door, listening for any suspicious noise. Later, when this language became familiar, I could easily listen to the wall with one ear and to the corridor with the other. I finally understood my neighbors' insistence. It was neither curiosity nor lack of discretion. A mute cell broke the chain. They had had to overcome my resistance. To knit up the link of solidarity.

And there's the word I've been waiting for. Solidarity. The Larousse dictionary gives a first official definition. I cite only the beginning. "A state of two or more persons each of whom is committed to each other and to the whole."

Yes. Each of us was committed to each other and to the whole.

The great mass of the women in our penitentiary was amorphous. A political prison? Political prisoners? What an irony. Except for the group of legionnaires—if that!—among the hundreds of women whom I knew "through the wall," personally or by hearsay, how many would that term cover? About ten. The rest? Illiterate peasants arrested for the mercenary or sentimental harboring of partisans, escapees, or parachutists. For resistance to land collectivization. Women convicted of an "omission of denunciation." They had omitted to denounce a father, son, or husband. Women in love. Women who had wanted to flee the country, and so on. Nearly all these women observed the penitentiary's regulations. The fear of the terrible "seven days" was certainly in force. But also their simplemindedness. Their basic lack of initiative, culture, or interest in anything outside their everyday plebeian frame of mind. The condition of women who had always been subject to some sort of authority. That of a father, husband, priest, public opinion.

Fearful? Not really. On the contrary. But their courage became manifest only on rare occasions. When they were pushed, almost despite themselves, by the strong, affective, and completely feminine sentiment of solidarity.

The women, all those admirable, miserable women of the penitentiary, demonstrated solidarity. For seven years I had time to come to know them. To study them. Young and old, peasant women, workers, and members of the petite-bourgeoisie, ill and well, they all stood up for those who maintained the ties. For, in each cell, there were always one or two women who scorned danger, loved risk. Most of them young. As I think about it now, it seems to me that nearly all of them belonged to the category of genuine political prisoners. Guilty or innocent, they had been, like me, implicated in a real trial. In addition, they had a certain amount of education. To learn to speak in Morse code, to use tablets, one had to know how to spell and have fairly quick comprehension and synthesis. They wove together the postal network linking all the cells. The passive ones were grateful to them for keeping them in the know about the closed life of the penitentiary. For transmitting messages among friends who had been separated by a change of cells. Sometimes, even a message from the outside brought by a recent arrival. For helping them to live by doing something solely for the benefit of others. For all. For the whole. For, the threat of the "seven days" was no mere scarecrow in a wheat field.

G. had explained to me what the "seven days" entailed. The cunning, circumspection, auditory acuity, and a spirit of observation that were needed to avoid them. The punishment of an inmate was generally requested by one of the militia, a witness to some infraction of the rules. At the close of his report, he had the right to determine the punishment himself. In fact, one and only one punishment, the "isolation room." But he also had the right to set its duration. Three, five, or seven days. Unfortunately, it was always seven days. The commandant and the penitentiary doctor had to approve the request for punishment. But no one had ever heard of a single doctor ever daring to interdict the punishment for even the most mortally ill of the inmates. It goes without saying that very often a mere suspicion was enough for a militiaman to make a report of culpability.

The "isolation room" was a small cell that was completely bare except for a chamber pot. From five in the morning until ten at night, one had to remain standing or walk around hugging the wall. For seven days. It was forbidden to sit on the floor. At ten o'clock, they threw in a straw mattress. With no sheet, no pillow, no blanket. In winter the cell was unheated. At five in the morning, the mattress was removed. No way to wash. For seven days. All this was very hard but seemed to them insufficient. The punishment was stepped up through a substandard diet. They starved us. For seven days. . . . The first two days, nothing but a cube of polenta. Length, width, height less than four inches. The regulations also allowed for three mess tins of lightly salted hot water. But the water was most often either cold or too salty. The third day, a normal diet. The fourth and fifth day, a new cube of polenta and hot water. The sixth day, normal. The seventh day, polenta. So one was starved five days out of seven. If, by some misfortune, you received two punishments in a row of seven days each, you were allowed, between the two "isolations," three days of normal diet with a return to your usual cell. But it could happen that those three days were denied you. You then did fourteen days of isolation with ten days of starvation. G. tells me that the only consolation for the woman punished was the certitude of the warm welcome of her comrades on her return. On the bed would be piled hunks of bread, polenta, or any other food received that day in the cell and which the women did without to help her get her strength back.

This solidarity of our penitentiary was the staff's nightmare. It was primarily against the solidarity that the commandant and all the militia had to struggle. Using ever more barbaric means. "Seven days" after "seven days," handcuffs, and even gas masks. But even when the individual punishments were angrily replaced by collective ones, the bulk of these women did not lose heart. They submitted to all the punishments without flinching, without denouncing us, without criticizing us. They did not even ask us to halt the postal network, that major delinquency. Eventually, however, being unable to stand to see them suffer, we stopped nearly all our secret activity. Nearly all, for it was impossible for us to remain completely inactive.

As I have said, my next-door neighbors were legionnaires. At the head of the movement, a mixture of pro-Nazi intellectuals, discontented and ambitious pseudointellectuals, and high bourgeoisie fighting against "Jewish financiers," decadent aristocrats, and a few visionaries. The proselytes, wooed from among the exploited and limited peasantry, priests, schoolteachers, high school and university students, and the dregs of the poorer outlying areas, eager for plunder and pogroms. What held them together were basic Eastern Orthodoxy, some imported Nazism, chauvinistic patriotism, obscurantism, the morbid cult of death, and above all, anti-Semitism—that is to say, hatred. These young women, at the instigation of their families or boyfriends, had wanted to establish a fascist dictatorship. Exterminate the Jews.

I asked them questions. Theoretical ones. They answered *The Protocols of the Elders of Zion*. Nevertheless, they got lost in the legionary adventure impelled by certain real, positive characteristics. Constant thrills. A need for action. A taste for risk. A true desire for "better," fundamentally miserably distorted, going as far as the acceptance of the supreme sacrifice. But also driven by a character defect. By fear, the inability to assume responsibility for oneself. A docile and disciplined herd. Absolutely needing a leader. A wolf in sheep's clothing.

Now my neighbors were confused. They were asking themselves certain questions. Suffering in the face of the clarity of the answers that they still refused to accept. It is easy to intoxicate oneself with the idea of sacrifice in full carnivalesque parades, sheltered by banners and icons. With the idea of the triumph of death in howling patriotic songs in marches led by the banners of priests promising them an apotheosis for their crimes. Besides, isn't the idea of death ridiculously abstract? But prolonged confinement—five to six years already—had taught them suffering. Sinking their teeth into their own flesh. Bloodying their own heart. I had come to wonder by what right they had wanted to impose this on others. Above all, while brandishing the cross of Christ and in the name of the archangels Michael and Gabriel. Three of my neighbors were very young and, despite the fascist indoctrination, deeply innocent and decent. I never dared ask them if they would have carried out the order to kill a Jewish newborn. But I was sure that my two other, older neighbors would have done so. Their role in the movement had been too active for them to admit the bankruptcy of their goal and the criminality of the means employed. They made an effort to keep up their influence over the young women and managed only by rousing the mystical and obscurantist side of the

Legion. A poison that no former legionnaire would ever manage to vomit up entirely. For them, their leader, a raving mad apparition on his white horse, still cut a heroic figure. The bloodthirsty nonsense of the former royal dictatorship had catapulted him into "martyrdom." My background did not predispose them in my favor. A communist trial? And yet, hadn't I been convicted? Finally my long solitude dictated a certain respect from them. They in turn asked me questions about communism. I replied as best I could. It is true that I understood the subject only through Pătrăşcanu's opinions, which were not very orthodox since they had landed him in prison. It was only much later, through a militia-woman's indiscretion, that I learned that he had been executed the day after the trial. So they could not doubt my sincerity. Didn't they claim to have tried to establish a new social justice? Perhaps they were beginning to discover that hatred, whether fascist or communist, could never open the way to a better humanity.

Two of them had attended the famous meeting in Cluj between Pătrăşcanu and some students at the time of the chauvinistic clashes between Romanians and Hungarians, in 1945. Learning that I had been present as well brought us together. We had a memory in common. They also knew that Pătrăşcanu's conciliatory attitude, making the greatest possible effort to calm the students and open the prisons, had weighed heavily on his fate. And rebounded on my own fate. Out of necessity we had mutually accepted our proximity. Apprehensively. But the same bars, the same padlocks, did violence to us in the same way. Gradually our relations were transformed by a genuine friendship. I approached the wall with pleasure. I was no longer alone.

A few months later we were separated. Then neighbors again. And again separated. The clandestine postal system made up for the distances. It went through the walls, as numerous and thick as they were. The letters began circulating among us. But that is another story, of which I shall speak later.

Our friendship grew stronger all during my years in prison.

Days 2188, 2189, 2190, 2191, 2192, 2193, 2194, 2195, 2196, 2197, 2198, 2199, 2200, 2201, 2202, 2203, 2204, 2205, 2206, 2207, 2208, 2209, 2210, 2211, 2212, 2213, 2214, 2215, 2216, 2217, 2218,

2219, 2220, 2221, 2222, 2223, 2224, 2225, 2226,
2227, 2228, 2229, 2230, 2231, 2232, 2233, 2234,
2235, 2236, 2237, 2238, 2239, 2240, 2241, 2242,
2243, 2244, 2245, 2246, 2247, 2248, 2249, 2250,
2251, 2252 of detention—September 16, 1955

September 1980. It is nine o'clock in the morning. Sun. Warmth. Calm. I am in Ouchy for two weeks with my husband Harry. Since our exoneration, in 1968, it has been easy to get permission to travel. We go to France, where Harry has a brother, and to Switzerland to see his sister.

The weather is splendid. Both of us are still able-bodied and pleased to be here together. Why did I suddenly decide to get on with my story? When it was broken off two years before, I thought I was incapable of going on with it. It is hard to do a piece of work to no purpose. I know that these notebooks will remain hidden and that I will never be able to publish them. Nevertheless, I would very much have liked to know what people would think of them. After my death, it is all the same to me. In beginning to write them, I even dreamt of a rather odd glory. Was I not the only woman locked up, all along, for more than eight years?

The only woman trying to tell how she managed to fill those years, how she managed to live. Escaping in thought, by strength of will, through obstinacy even?

So I was still alone in my cell but contact had been made. I had friends now. I knew about life throughout the penitentiary. I took part in it. I heard the latest news. Letters were exchanged between cells. Written on cloth. With the methylene blue that we were given to disinfect the receptacles. With a black powder—for treating diarrhea, I think—mixed with water. Sometimes even in a stitched Morse code.

But I had trouble walking. Diffuse pains in my legs. The chamber pot was heavy. Full of water and filth. Liquid and solid. Walking along the corridor. Going down the stairs. Crossing the courtyard. Stumbling on the round stones. I could no longer make the trip in one go. This annoyed the female guards. To my great displeasure, my neighbors were assigned to take over for me. I only took the chamber pot with its wooden cover out into the corridor. Once my door was closed, theirs opened. I heard them scurrying about. I was always on the lookout by the door, and heard them murmuring: "Good morning, Lena!" Sometimes they even managed to open my judas to sneak a peek at me.

When the militiawoman had her back to us, one of them would open the judas and hold it open while standing back a bit so that I could get a look at her. After returning with the chamber pot emptied and cleaned, they would wait for the sound of my door closing, then for the militiawoman's steps fading away, and the "dot-dash-dot-dash" would call me from wall to wall. "Today you saw G." Or B., or somebody else.

One sewing day, I told them that I had just put a piece of cloth on the heel of my one pair of stockings. A few days later, G. summoned me to the wall after bringing back my chamber pot. She told me to look under the cover. I would find a present there. To be in prison. All alone. Then a wall speaks. Everything perks up. Friendly faces smile at me. I even receive a present. A touching pair of socks. They had knitted them for me in secret. With makeshift needles. With bits of rough wool in all colors. I put on the socks. They are soft. Warm. I have new socks. A present. Is this possible? I must not weep.

Smile instead. Relish the humor of this inconceivable present. After six years of solitude, three members of the Legion have offered me a pair of socks. A week later, a second, more elegant pair. They must have sacrificed a scarf. Its dark red wool was very fine. I never understood why the militiawomen pretended not to notice my new socks. They knew perfectly well that I had only a single pair of stockings darned from top to toe. They knew that these two pairs of socks hadn't fallen out of the blue.

Days 2253, 2254, 2255, 2256, 2257, 2258, 2259, 2260, 2261, 2262, 2263, 2264, 2265, 2266, 2267, 2268, 2269, 2270, 2271, 2272, 2273, 2274, 2275, 2276, 2277, 2278, 2279, 2280, 2281, 2282, 2283, 2284, 2285, 2286, 2287, 2288, 2289, 2290, 2291, 2292, 2293, 2294, 2295, 2296, 2297, 2298, 2299, 2300, 2301, 2302, 2303, 2304, 2305, 2306, 2307, 2308, 2309, 2310, 2311, 2312, 2313, 2314, 2315, 2316, 2317, 2318, 2319, 2320, 2321, 2322, 2323, 2324, 2325, 2326, 2327, 2328, 2329, 2330, 2331,

2332, 2333, 2334, 2335, 2336, 2337, 2338, 2339,
2340, 2341, 2342, 2343, 2344, 2345, 2346, 2347,
2348, 2349, 2350, 2351, 2352, 2353, 2354, 2355,
2356, 2357, 2358 of detention—December 31, 1955

It is not true that $0 + 0$ = zero. Arithmetic is wrong. One after another, I added up 120 zeros. Total: 120 days. Nothing + void + nil = four months.

Fall had come. Fall had passed. My cell had become cold. The food, still inadequate. My body, scrawny. My bones showing through the skin. My sleep, intermittent. My bed, a sack filled with broken straw. All had turned to dust.

Under the weight of my body, the dust of the mattress piled up. Releasing large stems. The stems dug into my flesh. Sawed at my bones. Lying on my back, I had pain in my spine. On my side, in my hips. The pain woke me up. Undo the bed. Turn the sack over. Put everything back in place. Go back to bed. Wait for the heat to build up again between the layers of rags. Repeat the operation two or three times every night. Life went on.

Wake-up call at five in the morning. Bully my body. Force it to leave the gradually accumulated heat behind. Take off the shirt. Splash my body with the icy water in the glacial cell. Rub myself with a bit of canvas. Get the blood back into circulation. Warm myself with fists and slaps. Despising the militiaman who often had an eye glued to the window. Get dressed. Raise my arms, hold them out, whirl them around, lift my legs, do deep knee bends. What a bore. Make the effort of these gestures day after day, each time wanting to give them up. Overcome my weakness. Get my body under control. This enemy on whom I nevertheless had pity. Force it to make the bed. Sweep the floor, and finally say good morning to my neighbors. Yes, things are okay. Yes, I slept well. Yes, I had sweet dreams and that finally was true. I really had sweet dreams.

The morning stretched out. Work went forward. Around eleven o'clock, I heard the door of the stove opening in the corridor. I counted the pieces of the single daily load of wood . . . four . . . five. The two scoops of charcoal lumps, thrown helter-skelter into the stove, hit the sides. The match, with an explosive pop, ignited the gasoline in which everything had been drenched. The purring of the fire. The cylinder gradually became warm. I pressed my palms, my arms, my chest to its heat. The noon mess tin arrived. Disappointing, as always. The surface of the cylinder was now burning hot. All around, warm air. Push the bench up next to the stove. Finally take off my coat. Lay it out on the bench. Stretch out on the fur. The water in the little pot sitting on the stove was hot. Drink it in little sips. Recollecting my dreams. Reliving them in detail. Fantastical landscapes. Unknown cities. Greenery and marble. Flowers and statues. And above all, going home. My mother's face. Her smile. The illusory joys of that empty day's zero.

The fire had gone out. The stove became tepid again. Then cold. The cell, glacial. It was about four in the afternoon. Only four o'clock. Wrapped up in my coat again, shivering just a little, go back to walking. Moaning my tirades. Waiting for the evening, the night, and the beginning over and over again.

One hundred twenty zeros = one hundred twenty days. And, even so, life went on. Soon, six years of detention. Half my sentence. Those first six years had lasted an infinity. How could I manage to bear six more? Better not to think about it. No longer think of anything. My neighbors had much more cause for complaint than I. All three were very young. So young. On their arrival in prison their lives had barely begun. I had lived half of mine. With highs and lows, like everyone. I had to go forward, by choice or by force. Besides, as one of my intelligent interrogators had told me one day, was I not housed and fed? So I had everything I needed to live.

Day 2359 of detention—January 1, 1956

December 1955? January 1956? Rather December . . . but what can I do to recall it more precisely?

The heat of the sun. The blue of the sky. The white foam and golden shimmer of the water. The lapping of waves on the sand. It is clear. It is blue. All along the beach, brown against a blue background, men, women, young people, elderly people play, dance, sing, bask, sleep, splash about, and swim. With no complexes. Next to me, even Harry is sleeping. His sleep is peaceful. He breathes in, breathes out, his chest gently rises, sinks, rises, his face is relaxed. Today, even he had slipped through the mesh of his usual nightmares.

It is good. It is warm. It is blue. It is June 14, 1981. It is ten in the morning. I feel good. I have no pain anywhere. Not in my feet. Not in my back. I have a book. Cigarettes. Even some chocolate. Swiss. Bordering the beach is the village street. Some shops. A bakery. There, every morning, we buy bread. Our bread. Dark or white, round or long, the one we want, as much as we want. A whole heavy golden loaf for today's hunger. But how can we appease the hungers of the past? And here the demon has returned. Again it pushes me, claws me, orders me:

"Close your eyes! Put out the sun! Concentrate! Remember! Go back to your hell! Take up your burden . . . your pains and your hungers . . ."

December 1955? January 1956?

Plunge into the fog. Find that day, the officer, the militiawoman. Leave your cell, your shell, your habits, the now-silent wall. Go with them, once again up the stairway of stone steps toward the unknown. Go up them slowly, carefully; they have become sloping and slippery through wear. This stairway that I will go down and go back up day after day, for months, for years, limping, hobbling more and more. That I will go down for the final time on June 14, 1961.

Once again the same anxiety, the same rebellion, seizes me. Why? What's the meaning of this cell? The darkness. The obstructed window. The shutters, overlapping wooden slats letting in only a vague half-light. Why, demon? Why?

Two or three days before, G. had summoned me to the wall. We were going to be leaving. Changing penitentiaries. Definitely returning to Mislea. Finally, I too was going to profit from the workshops, work, the orchard, in the semifreedom in the former monastery she had so often spoken of. Over with, my closed cell. My solitude. Together. We will soon be together. They had just been ordered to get their things together.

"They will come tell you, too. Wait a little while."

I waited. All morning. From time to time, G., very excited, called me.

"Did they come?"

"No."

"Wait, they must be coming."

I waited. I waited all afternoon. Toward evening they left. Without me. A final fist blow on the wall. The dragging of their footsteps at the corner of the corridor, gone. A shroud of silence stealing through the prison. Enveloping me. No noise. No echo. Empty. The penitentiary was empty. The world was empty.

Yet the next morning the cell door of Pătrăşcanu's wife opened as usual. I heard the plaintive murmur of her voice. So I was not utterly alone.

Several difficult days went by. I felt my neighbors' absence acutely. I felt unhappy, persecuted. Soon I would miss this respite. The hole of unhappiness has no bottom. Outside of death, I sank more deeply into its mire. The ominous cell on the second floor.

Days 2360, 2361, 2362, 2363, 2364, 2365, 2366, 2367, 2368, 2369, 2370, 2371, 2372, 2373, 2374, 2375, 2376, 2377, 2378, 2379, 2380, 2381, 2382, 2383, 2384, 2385, 2386, 2387, 2388, 2389, 2390, 2391, 2392, 2393, 2394, 2395, 2396, 2397, 2398, 2399, 2400, 2401, 2402, 2403, 2404, 2405, 2406, 2407, 2408, 2409, 2410, 2411, 2412, 2413, 2414, 2415, 2416, 2417, 2418, 2419 of detention—
March 2, 1956

It seems like I'm down there once more, still rooted to the spot. Not daring to move, I feel the officer and the militia-woman once again behind me. The silence of our total immobility is abruptly broken by an explosion of violent sobs. More like cries. Almost groans. The shock of this nearby despair wakes me up with a start. I turn toward the officer. I implore him. I beg him. That he take me back to my cell. Does he not know it? Perhaps he doesn't know that I have been all alone for five years. With diseased eyes. Rotten. Without glasses. I don't want to go blind.

I do not sob. I do not weep. My eyes are dry. My voice is dry. It burns my throat. My voice makes the officer uncomfortable. He makes vague promises. It is still winter. It is cold. The shutters are there to protect me. In the spring. Yes, in the spring. The door closed. Silence has returned. It is over.

Convinced I had heard Pătrăşcanu's wife crying, I go up to the wall and tap the four letters of her nickname. On the other side of the wall, someone asks me to repeat it. Surprised, I begin again.

The third letter of her name required a cedilla. But I had learned Morse code without a cedilla, apostrophe, hyphen, comma, or other diacritic. Without a cedilla, her name made no sense. But she should have understood it. She must have doubted that her new neighbor was I. Why did she ask me: "Who are you?"

I finally realized that there were three of us. An unknown woman had been placed as a buffer between us. Without answering her question, I ask her to go to the other wall to tell the woman there, the one she heard weeping, that Lena is here. That my window is boarded up. That I am just as desperate as she. This little drama went on for some time. A few days later, my neighbor confessed that she had felt bounced back and forth like a ball from one wall to the other by two madwomen. In fact, there were four inmates there. There were two in cell 10. Involved in the same religious trial. The one to whom I had spoken was an Englishwoman married to a Romanian man, sentenced to fifteen years, and a young Romanian woman, sentenced to eighteen years.

To escape the darkness of the cell for a bit, I pressed myself to the wall, under the window. Between the wooden slats, I could see long thin strips of sky. Deep blue, very bright, better than nothing.

And something else besides. Between the base of the shutters and the windowsill, some four inches of emptiness. I pushed the water tub over. I got up on its cover. Joy! I could see a part of the courtyard next door. The courtyard of the barracks with the acacias. Glimpse the snow. Several tree trunks. Two long, wooden watering troughs. I did not clearly grasp the layout of our floor until several days later.

The next day, our corridor was blocked off from the rest of the prison by a high wooden partition, pierced by a door that was always locked. The sound of the key turning reached us quite distinctly. No danger of being caught in the act of communicating between cells. So we could speak without fear. In the next few days we realized that the rest of the building had been filled with common-law prisoners. Well played. Who would have thought we were hidden there? They must have considered all four of us political prisoners more dangerous than the rest.

Our militiawomen had also left us. The first day, when the door opened in the morning, I fearfully searched their unfamiliar faces, and it seemed to me that they too, men and women alike, accustomed to common-law inmates, looked at us with the same rather nervous attentiveness. In this great den of thieves, criminals, and prostitutes, we were the "ladies." A hateful but also envied social class. Contemptible yet admired.

In the large section of common-law inmates, yelling, squabbling, filth. In the other, calm, politeness, cleanliness. We didn't want to give them any reason for ill treatment. To them we made no complaint. In spite of themselves, the militiawomen eventually showed us a certain respect. The important thing for us, however, was to get them to ease up on their surveillance.

My next-door neighbors eventually found protracted cohabitation unbearable. They were separated by everything—their social origins, circles of acquaintance, traditions, material means, age—all in the Englishwoman's favor. The only point of contact was the militant Catholicism that had brought them together and then sent them together to prison, but that did not succeed in filling the gap. The inactivity, the privation, the cramped cell, the impossibility of a single instant of solitude, and finally the Englishwoman's self-centeredness, her airs of superiority, had produced an animosity that the two women could no longer hold back. My arrival was a real boon for them both. The Englishwoman, leaving the other to the diversion of listening to us or of completely ignoring our conversation, took full possession of me and the wall. A jealous and passionate possession. Spoiled by life from childhood on, pretty, rich, admired, she had been stripped of everything overnight. Even of the secret of a clandestine love affair, revealed in the investigation. Hence the contempt of the untainted virgin. The Englishwoman thus transferred to me all her repressed enthusiasm, all her frustrations, and her affection for me took on a tinge of love. When the Romanian woman also wished to speak to me, she needed the pretext of some malaise and to give up the daily ten-minute walk.

The Englishwoman went to all kinds of trouble to find things in common between the two of us. Some of them were not fictions. We were the same age. We had both studied in Paris at the same time. No doubt we had often walked simultaneously along the Boulevard Saint-Michel, for both of us had lived there. I had known her first husband, a Romanian, moreover, like the second. Accompanying a cousin, a Scottish folklorist who had come to study in Romania, she had made a short trip with Harry.

Moreover, he had talked to me about it. Finally, we had read the same books, attended the same cultural events.

With G., conversations had rarely gone beyond five minutes. Now the wall took up most of my time. We talked. Of everything and anything. With humor, she told me of her family, her childhood, her studies in Spain, her love affairs, her marriages. Her typically English and charming tales of her childhood enchanted me. I never wearied of hearing her talk about her dogs, cats, pony, white mice, the rabbits, and even caterpillars. When my turn came to entertain, I set about making up, as I went along, comical adventures about an imaginary tour of Italy. Together, of course. A great many preposterous adventures that sometimes made us burst out laughing, and our cells were flooded with the Italian sunlight.

When, however, the charm of novelty wore off somewhat, I felt guilty for all the time taken from my work. To salve my guilty conscience while keeping me at the wall, she suggested giving me English lessons. Soon, with a minimum of vocabulary, I set about making up short poems in English. When I couldn't hit upon a rhyme, all I had to do was tell her the word I wanted to rhyme with, and every word she proposed was in some way integrated into the poem. The result was often bizarre, absurd. Really crazy.

February. March. We were waiting for spring. The verses. The English. Repeating my old poems. Cleaning the cell. Washing the linen. The wall primarily filled the daylight hours. Sometimes, in the evening, after "closing time," a young militiawoman, rather limited but harmless, sneaked in her husband's socks for me to darn. Huge holes that I darned with artistry. In return, she sometimes gave me a piece of candy. Never two.

But the major event of those days was my receiving a package. The commandant came in person to preside over the ceremony. This took place in room 8, which was large and empty apart from some iron cots, and on one of them, a big open suitcase. In the suitcase was everything I had requested from home. A sleeveless sheepskin vest with white fur. A blue wool jacket. My green overcoat with its matching skirt. A silk blouse. A woolen blouse. A pair of underpants and a downy cotton flannel undershirt. Three yards of lining for my coat. A pair of shoes. A scarf. Stockings. A small canvas bag containing thread in all colors. Needles. A comb. The commandant gave me permission to take everything except the overcoat which was kept in the suitcase at the depository. It remained there until the day I was released.

On returning to my cell, after I had reassured my neighbors, who had been alarmed by my abrupt departure, I carefully inspected all of the objects in the package. Convinced that I would find some "messages" where the prison officials had seen nothing. Four signs. I was looking for four signs. Letting me know that all four—my parents and my two sisters—were in good health, or at least alive. I could feel those signs. They were there. For me that was a certainty. I simply had to find them. There, on the clothing heaped up on my bed, I had to pick them out. To doubt this was to doubt my mother. Inconceivable.

Four signs? No. Six. All by my mother's hand. No doubt to bear the full responsibility for them. The bag full of thread was itself a sign. That of the house. My mother had cut it from an old worn tablecloth. For years on end, I had seen it covering the dinner table. On the cloth were squares of faded green, four large letters written in pencil in barely visible traces: *MAMA*.

On the wool blouse, a small multicolored, crocheted bouquet. Three little flowers, two little green leaves. How many of these bouquets had ornamented our dresses when we were children? Finally, the three handkerchiefs, bearing three monograms. A *C* for my father, a *Z* and a *V* for my sisters.

My mother had managed to slip between the bars. She had come into my cell to tell me the most important thing. Everything.

The head of the prison had given me permission to sew in the new lining of my coat. For several days, I had the pleasure of work. With the remaining fabric, I delighted in making a large bag full of pockets and compartments for each of my things. I later learned that bags with many pockets are one of the prisoner's characteristic obsessions. My bag, all decorated with white stitches, was a truly beautiful bag. Very well designed. Too well designed, even. Two weeks later, on returning to the cell after a search, I found all my things thrown in a heap on the bed. The bag had vanished into thin air. Vanished also was a pair of slippers whose thick soles I had made by layering cotton wool and cloth. No reason. No explanation. No way to protest. A tangle of vipers writhes in your belly and you are obliged to digest it. For a few days I had had warm feet. Now I was even colder.

My new comb, too brittle for the ill-washed matted thicket covering my scalp, quickly lost all its teeth, one after another. I had heedlessly thrown away my old one which still had five good teeth.

What could I do? Comb my hair with my fingers. That took time but the result was unhoped-for. My sick hair, dry and splitting, falling out in fistfuls, came back to life. The continual scalp massage was an ideal remedy. It is true that this result was achieved only after a few months. I had several times asked for a comb. One day a militiaman brought me a tiny little comb. A doll's comb. But so clogged with grime that I felt queasy just looking at it. Touching it, washing it would have been beyond me. I decided to make one myself.

For some weeks I was as sparing as I could be with the soap I received every seven days. Hiding the remaining slivers. Then, slowly moistening them, kneading them, molding them until I had achieved a malleable paste. Giving the paste the shape of a bar about two inches long and wide and a half inch thick. The straws in the broom were held together by a thick iron wire. At four inches from the joint, the branches had been cut together and bore a clean diagonal cut. I set eight four-inch lengths of cane very deeply and very close to each other into my bar of soap, leaving only half of each one showing, with the diagonal cuts facing the same direction. After a few days, the paste hardened and the comb was functional. I used it for a long time. It made the militiamen angry at every search. They confiscated it several times, but each time the militiawomen went to recuperate it. One prosecutor was also impressed by it. I would have thought that the use of such a comb by a political prisoner would cause him some annoyance. Absurd. All smiles, he congratulated me on my ingenuity.

Prosecutors? Some time earlier, following a bloody scandal in a penitentiary for political prisoners, some military prosecutors were assigned to make a check of the penitentiaries. In principle, as representatives of the prisoners, and with the duty of imposing respect for their rights. But after the horrible crimes perpetrated in this other penitentiary, what could they find to condemn in ours? In the other one, legionnaires, the dregs of the society, and trained in a spirit of stupid cruelty and obscurantism, had been assigned by prison staff to the job of educating their fellow prisoners by every means. This had been paid for in broken bones. Gangrene. The most degrading tortures. To the point of washing the floors by licking them, and even eating shit. The only way to get out of it was to go over to the side of the torturers. What could we have to complain about? The cold? Hadn't one of the prosecutors, with his leering eye, advised us to sleep two by two and to warm each other up? Hunger. Weren't we sufficiently well fed since we had the strength to remain standing at attention before him?

Then I was ill. Fever. Chills. The medical office. Some pills and permission to stay in bed for three days. The militiawoman helped me to push the bed next to the stove and make the most of the hours of warmth. I also was allowed a double ration of fuel. That must have happened in March, for one day shortly afterward the stove remained cold and I knew that spring had arrived.

My mother knew a great many proverbs. Their folk wisdom was a consolation to her in life's vicissitudes. One proverb had seemed utterly meaningless to me as a child. With age I adopted its optimism and I made it my motto. Translated literally, it is: "All the evil, toward the good." Certain misfortunes can set off a chain reaction, ending in prosperity, joy, success. Thus in spring and in its wake the icy stove that made us suffer from the cold—all it took was an idea of my neighbor's and we were enchanted by it.

Since two adjoining cells had a single chimney for drawing their two fires, why couldn't we communicate directly from one cell to another by taking the elbows of the pipes out of the chimney as though for cleaning out the winter's soot? Each of us pushed the bench next to the stove. Carefully pulled out the pipe, took out the elbow of the chimney. Looked through the round hole, and there we were, face to face, both faces framed in the hole, just a foot-and-a-half from each other. What really captivated us, however, was not seeing each other but the chance to talk without using code. Just to talk. To hear all the subtleties of intonation enriching the words. Also the chance for material exchanges. Thus, on May 21, for my birthday, I received a fine cotton handkerchief, a piece of perfumed soap, and a little medal of the Immaculate Conception, in a tiny canvas pouch. The Englishwoman had managed all this time to hide it under the guards' noses. I in turn could make it invisible to searches by several times resorting to a contemptible hiding place, for which the good Virgin would pardon me when the medal was taken out with me from the penitentiary, and I shall always keep it with me.

All during that spring and summer the hunk of bread—three ounces—received in the morning, went to the Englishwoman, who had little tolerance for the polenta and from whom I in turn received half her portion.

In the morning, after the "program," we would get up on our stoves and chat without fear until lunchtime. If by chance we heard the key at the end of the corridor, I had to put the pipe back in the chimney. Get down. Push the bench back in place. All this in a great hurry, and I was having more and more difficulty managing it. The pain in my legs was getting worse. Fortunately, in the afternoon, my neighbor changed walls. I took advantage of this respite to do some work.

Directly beneath my cell were some new common-law mothers with their babies. The law authorized them to keep their prison-born infants with them until the age of eighteen months. The penitentiary provided them with baby clothes and better food. In the afternoon, they went out in the rear courtyard, hence, underneath my window. Hearing their chatter, I would get up on my observation post for a look at them and their babies. They all appeared to me to be gypsies. Seen from above, with their many skirts of all colors and their children taking their first steps, they were really a delightful sight. When they opened the window of their cell, however, such a reek of turned milk and urine wafted up that I had to quickly shut my own window. Down below in a cell large enough for two, there were six or seven women and six or seven babies who had to be bathed and changed, and whose diapers had to be laundered and dried along with the women's own clothing. The anguish of the day when their little ones would be taken away from them, perhaps for years, to be sent to their families or a state nursery, the lack of space and the constant lack of privacy resulted in deafening squabbles, and a vivid stream of bad language and blasphemy reached my ears.

One morning, I again heard Pătrăşcanu's wife sobbing. I learned from the Englishwoman that one of the militiawomen had just told her that her husband had been executed immediately after the trial. Then her diet was upgraded. She was to work. She was given clay and spent her time modeling. It seems she made an ashtray. The ashtray was fired in the kitchen oven and ended up on the commandant's desk. For us, the permission to work was a sign, even a good sign, for some time later, a noisy to-do in the courtyard woke me up in the middle of the night. Her door was opened several times. I heard whispering, the footsteps of several people. The partition wall was once again locked, and finally the same heavy silence returned. I went back to sleep, worried. The next morning, however, the militiawomen told us in a veiled manner that she had been freed.

Unhappily, the good fortune of some means the misfortune of others. Her departure triggered the change of cells that we had always feared. They put me in her cell. Identical except that the stove was connected with another chimney. We were forced to resume Morse code. Our only consolation was the inevitable coming of winter and the fire that would have interrupted direct speech in any case.

But when winter came . . .

Days 2420, 2421, 2422, 2423, 2424, 2425, 2426, 2427, 2428, 2429, 2430, 2431, 2432, 2433, 2434, 2435, 2436, 2437, 2438, 2439, 2440, 2441, 2442, 2443, 2444, 2445, 2446, 2447, 2448, 2449, 2450, 2451, 2452, 2453, 2454, 2455, 2456, 2457, 2458, 2459, 2460, 2461, 2462, 2463, 2464, 2465, 2466, 2467, 2468, 2469, 2470, 2471, 2472, 2473, 2474, 2475, 2476, 2477, 2478, 2479, 2480, 2481, 2482, 2483, 2484, 2485, 2486, 2487, 2488, 2489, 2490, 2491, 2492, 2493, 2494, 2495, 2496, 2497, 2498, 2499, 2500, 2501, 2502, 2503, 2504, 2505, 2506, 2507, 2508, 2509, 2510, 2511, 2512, 2513, 2514, 2515, 2516, 2517, 2518, 2519, 2520, 2521, 2522, 2523, 2524, 2525, 2526, 2527, 2528, 2529, 2530, 2531, 2532, 2533, 2534, 2535, 2536, 2537, 2538, 2539, 2540, 2541, 2542, 2543, 2544, 2545, 2546, 2547, 2548, 2549, 2550, 2551, 2552, 2553, 2554, 2555, 2556, 2557, 2558, 2559, 2560, 2561, 2562, 2563, 2564, 2565, 2566, 2567, 2568, 2569, 2570, 2571, 2572, 2573, 2574, 2575, 2576, 2577, 2578, 2579, 2580, 2581, 2582, 2583, 2584, 2585, 2586, 2587, 2588, 2589, 2590, 2591, 2592, 2593, 2594, 2595, 2596, 2597, 2598, 2599, 2600, 2601, 2602, 2603, 2604, 2605, 2606, 2607, 2608, 2609, 2610, 2611, 2612, 2613, 2614, 2615, 2616, 2617, 2618, 2619, 2620, 2621, 2622, 2623, 2624, 2625, 2626,

*2627, 2628, 2629, 2630, 2631, 2632, 2633, 2634,
2635, 2636, 2637, 2638, 2639, 2640, 2641, 2642,
2643, 2644, 2645, 2646, 2647, 2648, 2649, 2650,
2651, 2652, 2653, 2654, 2655, 2656, 2657, 2658,
2659, 2660, 2661, 2662, 2663, 2664, 2665, 2666,
2667, 2668, 2669, 2670, 2671, 2672, 2673, 2674,
2675, 2676, 2677, 2678, 2679, 2680, 2681, 2682,
2683, 2684, 2685, 2686, 2687, 2688, 2689, 2690,
2691, 2692, 2693, 2694, 2695, 2696, 2697, 2698,
2699, 2700, 2701, 2702, 2703, 2704, 2705, 2706,
2707, 2708, 2709, 2710, 2711, 2712, 2713, 2714,
2715, 2716, 2717, 2718, 2719, 2720, 2721, 2722,
2723, 2724 of detention—December 31, 1956*

It happened well before the young Romanian woman gave up her walk so she could talk with me. To tell that she was sure of the pending release of her comrade. She knew (how?) that the British embassy had appointed a lawyer to take the necessary steps. Perhaps Pătrăşcanu's wife, already free for some time, had had something to do with this hope. In order to spare me distress, the Englishwoman had not wished to talk with me about this.

But when winter came . . . she was already in Bucharest, free, and it was with the young Romanian woman, S., that my life as a political prisoner went on at the penitentiary of Miercurea-Ciuc.

Once again it was winter. The weather was very cold. Nevertheless, how could I resist the call of that distant loudspeaker, placed no doubt in the small town's central square? At six in the morning, it broadcast the first news of the day. My next-door neighbor's hearing was much more acute than mine, but she had frankly confessed her fear to me. Of the cold. Of the punishments. So, standing precariously on the cot's narrow iron bar, my eyes closed in total concentration, with my hands cupping my ears, I made an effort each morning to catch the words fluttering in the frosty air. I often managed to reconstitute a coherent sentence, an exact meaning. Thus, we learned to our utter confusion that the Queen of England had been visited by the head of the USSR. That she had received and fed him very well. She had invited him to lunch! Learning that, with everything going so well in the world, we hadn't the slightest chance of finding anyone concerned about our hardships, that was really not worth the trouble of having one's nose, ears, and hands icy. And in addition, risking the "seven days." Nonetheless, I would never have found the strength to give it up of my own free will, so I was pleased when the broadcasts abruptly ended.

After the Englishwoman had gone, I went back to work. But, as to my total renunciation of English and English poetry—S. would have been able to keep up the lessons—I think that the Queen of England had something to do with it and hence should be truly remorseful.

Soon the partition was taken down. The common-law prisoners left. The political women all returned. And still others. A new phase of my life began. My old friends from the ground floor occupied the cell just beneath mine. Room 12, to my left, became the punishment or quarantine cell. So I was in room 11. Room 10 was S. Room 9, five women sentenced to life imprisonment. Room 8, some fifteen legionnaires. Then, where the corridor made a turn, the militia's little office. In the two other corridors continuing the prison's U layout, six more cells, large and small, with a whole hodgepodge of miscellaneous sentences, from two to twenty years. Which is to say from the innocence of a newborn to the venial sins deserving at the very most a few months of confinement. I never heard of more than five women who had really engaged in espionage.

All these newcomers had come from a work penitentiary. I heard that an international committee had intervened to "save" the political prisoners from mandatory labor. The men working in the mines no doubt welcomed this intervention, but the women were much displeased. The work in the shops at Mislea was, however, not easy. It was all but impossible to meet the quotas set (Stakhanovism was in full swing), and the women were often deprived of the tiny profits from their labor. Wages that enabled them to make some essential purchases at the penitentiary cooperative: soap, absorbent cotton, toothpaste, bread, marmalade, cheese, and above all cigarettes. The right to letters and packages. But mainly the privilege of being all together in the workshops and open cells. To be able to gather at will. To choose. Now placed in locked cells, groups, friends, and even sisters were separated overnight. This later produced a whole secret postal network and innovations of every kind to foil the inhuman regulations. In return, however, this loosed an avalanche of punishments, from handcuffs to the gas mask to the "seven days." Thus, the punishment cell, cell 12, was constantly occupied. Thanks to my neighbor's good qualities, I could be up to my neck in the underground activity without being caught. She had a sturdy, cautious character. Good sense. An excellent memory. In the first place, the keenness of her hearing helped her to "see" everything that went on in the prison and to warn me of any danger when I was conversing with one of the women being punished in cell 12. Which happened every day, for "they" always were finding new reasons for punishment.

Gradually I made the acquaintance of a large number of prisoners. They had all heard of the woman in solitary confinement, and my special situation inspired them with a certain respect, pity, and total trust. I even made friends. One woman who had done the "seven days" for some trifle returned for a new punishment. What mortal sin could she have committed? A needle. They had found it in her mouth. Hidden between the cheek and gum. A slender pointed needle concealed in her mouth so she could darn her tatters. Only once a week did the militiawomen bring some needles and a few yards of thread. One had to wait one's turn to do the mending in a hurry. Yet, these women had a good deal of time and a taste for well-done work. So they hid in the corners of their cells where they couldn't be seen from the judas. To mislead the surveillance, they piled up their clothes under the blanket, which then looked like a sleeping body. The regulations interdicted the militia from entering cells between "closing time" and "opening time." I don't know how they discovered that final buccal hiding place. Now, at each search, the nurse forced our mouths open with the handle of a spoon.

We were pleased to meet again. She said she was content with being punished, despite the regret about the needle. "Life together in a locked cell is hard. There are too many of us. All together in a heap . . . three beds, one on top of another . . . all classes . . . nerves on edge. . . . The chamber pot . . . the smells. . . . It's peaceful here . . . rest. . . . Hunger? Yes, but I know my companions are hiding provisions for me, everything they can . . . polenta . . . bread . . . marmalade . . . They are good comrades, but all those women, what with all the time we've spent together. I know them by heart. . . . But you are the unknown."

Some of these women did not know Morse code. Real penitentiary illiteracy. Then it became hard. I recall my neighbor, the nun. A peasant, almost illiterate, who came from a Moldavian convent with several other nuns and their mother superior. In principle, she knew the Morse alphabet. Making frequent errors, she managed to spell her name, but was unable to take in a single word. The sounds didn't change into letters and, even less, letters into syllables and words. At each letter, picked up with difficulty, she had already forgotten the preceding one. After two days of trying, I had to give up. I never learned what the gallant little nun might have done to deserve seven days of cold and hunger.

At certain times in the afternoon, the corridor was left without surveillance. Perhaps the militiawomen were writing their daily report. It was during one of these moments of safety that I tried communicating with a new woman being punished. Instead of her responding in Morse, I heard her say: "Talk with your mess tin!" That was too much. I went to tell S. that my new neighbor was crazy. With S., conversations were circular. Hardly had I tapped out the first two or three letters of a word than two short taps—"understood"—sent me on to the next word. When I mentioned the mess tin, I heard her burst out laughing. (Actually, I could hear only the little taps that in our personal code meant "I'm laughing.") She explained that one could put the opening of the mess tin on the wall and talk by touching one's lips to the bottom of the receptacle. On her side of the wall, my neighbor did the same thing, making an effort to find the exact corresponding place. Our voices were clearly transmitted by the two resonating containers.

In principle, the "seven days" punishment called for isolation. But the penitentiary was full to bursting. They managed to stuff twelve women in a cell the size of mine. In the larger cells, from fifty to sixty. The punishments multiplied at the same speed. They were forced to put several women in the punishment cell at the same time. Of course, only women from the same cell. Soon, one lone "isolation cell" became inadequate. Then there were two of them, then three, and, two years later, six. Some forty square feet of cement, a chamber pot, a window near the ceiling, open even in winter, and a straw mattress thrown into the cell at ten at night. Six cells, always full. I told myself that the saving of ten to twenty meals five times a week might explain the avalanche of punishments. Pocketed by the commandant? By the staff? A mystery.

So, every week I had new neighbors. At the same time I had a chance to get caught up with the old ones. I managed to make myself heard by tapping on the wall at the back, as far down as possible, next to the floor. They responded by tapping as high up as possible near the ceiling. Crouching down just opposite the judas, but too far from the door to hear the guard's footsteps in the corridor was neither convenient nor wise. But S. glued her ear to her door to warn me of possible dangers; and we limited ourselves to short and important communications: the transmission of a message, an event on the outside, filtered in in some furtive way, or an announcement of a search. To be warned in time made it possible to hide certain forbidden objects in the straw of the mattress.

Corresponding to the second-floor cells, numbers 8, 9, 10, 11 (mine), and 12 (the "isolation room"), were cells 1, 2, 3, 4, and 5 on the first floor. By tapping on the left wall I could call cell 1. Adjacent to the outside wall of that cell, in the courtyard, were the toilets. A little wooden construction. Two stalls with planks with holes cut in them and a long gutter running along the wall, a primitive outhouse. Because the two stalls were insufficient for the large rooms, the women were also obliged to use the inconvenient gutter. They seized the opportunity to block from view—with three or four women—one woman at the very back who communicated in Morse code with cell 1. A message telling where a particular cell up above would hide a message for some other cell. "X" in cell 8 for "Y" in cell 5, for example. The message received by 1 went through walls 2, 3, 4, and ended up in 5. Cell 1 housed a young woman of indomitable courage. And unfailing devotion. She stood up to the militia guards, adamantly denied her crime, proudly accepted every punishment. She had the painful honor of having the most days of isolation and famine.

My neighbor S. feared for me. After vainly attempting to dissuade me, arguing bad lungs, illness, anemia, and the like, she resolved to help me overcome the dangers. To thwart the guards' surveillance. She made me promise never to send or receive a call without giving her the agreed-upon signal. Then her blessed ears caught even the most surreptitious footsteps of spying militia-women. A light tap on the wall and I had already resumed my slow back and forth.

I also had my work. I had found a new subject for a play for marionettes: *Together*. A consequence of my experiences at the wall.

Of my relations with my neighbors. Of the reflections of a woman spending "seven days" in room 12 with her friend. I heard them laughing, whispering, and even groaning a little. "We're together," she told me, "the rest doesn't matter." The rest? Prison, hunger, the cold, almost nothing.

There would be a lot to say about friendship in women's penitentiaries. From the friendship of camaraderie to the friendship of self-interest, from the friendship of tenderness to the friendship of passion. At Mislea, this latter kind of friendship found freedom for a complete solution. Something impossible in our penitentiary, where each moment was lived within the sight and knowledge of all the other women. Whisperings, the language of the eyes, two hands entwined, furtive touches increased the ardor of love. Sometimes, by a subtle exchange of fluids, an otherworldly concentration transported them to the end of desire. But I learned of this only gradually, through the scandalized comments of prudish S., the Catholic puritan. Through certain questions, put to me by strangers from cell 12. And when my solitude came to an end, through the stories of the work penitentiary as told, in rustically crude language, by an intelligent and cunning peasant, but with a mind turned sour.

During my two final years in solitary confinement, the wall took up the most important part of my time. There I had a curious experience. I realized that one's manner of tapping is just as expressive as the timbre of one's voice. As one's handwriting. Sometimes even more so. For it is unaffected by the conscious censorship of the voice. Or the acquired control of gestures and facial expression. It was due to this gift that I could understand the inward trouble of the stranger who had become my neighbor for seven days. She asked me a question. It no doubt took courage to ask it. Her manner of tapping, both nervous and purposeful, was clear. It was not mere curiosity that had driven her to ask for my opinion of lesbianism. For her, this had to represent the major problem at this point in her life. She had a great need to quiet her pangs of conscience. She needed absolution.

According to S., among the hundreds of women at Mislea, only three were acknowledged lesbians. No longer in their first youth, they had a good deal of experience, self-assurance, and attracted a sufficient number of lovesick young women, some of them still virgins. Carrying out long sentences, knowing their youth would fade in this misery, loving—even a woman—was the most normal outlet for their frustrated instincts. It seemed to me unjust that my young neighbor should suffer for this. I felt her remorse, and it was painful for me. I responded to her soothingly, to set her mind free of pointless torment. Didn't the tortures of penitentiary life, beyond any measure, already go beyond the unbearable? Two years later, she left the penitentiary weeping. Some months later she was already married and pregnant.

I come back to my play, *Together*. If the sisterly friendship of my neighbors was then such a support, how could I not have understood the mysterious power of love? Of even an impure love. In my text, the magic embellishing the cloudiest sky with azure shimmers, I transferred everything that the walls had taught me.

Two children, a brother and sister, live happily in a village at the shore of the ocean. It is spring. Two little birds return to their nest. The children understand, in their way, the birds' language. It seems to the little boy that the male birdie longs for the warm countries from which it came and he is filled with a burning desire to go away. The little girl hears in the lady bird's song the joy of returning home. The little boy's desire swells the sails of his dinghy and he is carried far off. While strange adventures befall him in a medieval country—for I took pleasure in making his dinghy drift backward in time into a fairy-tale Middle Ages—he feels more and more unhappy, despite the love of a grateful daughter of a king. The sister does not understand why the spring and her country's beautiful blue spring sky appear more and more cloudy and sullen. Finally, reunited once again, they see the rainy sky of November adorned in all the colors of a sparkling rainbow. They are together.

My mornings were once again taken up with work. Assembling words. Choosing one from among all the others. Surrounding it with other words. Making the text flow. Squeezing out meaning. Pruning. Getting lost and finding my way back in the maze of words, suddenly inserted into the place finally found for them as the only, the inevitable one.

My neighbor was a Uniate. Or rather, she had been. Her militant faith and the interdiction of this religion after the communists came to power had led her to prison. Condemned of spying for the Vatican. Deeply feeling the blessings of prayer, she proposed to teach me the most salutary ones. One need not have faith in order to pray, she told me. Even mechanically reciting prayers brings relief and peace. I didn't want to refuse her this pleasure. Moreover, having spent three years as a child at a Catholic boarding school in Paris, on the rue de la Pompe, the rosary and litanies of the Virgin were an intimate part of my childhood.

This part of my account may have created the illusion of a life that had become pleasant. No. The prison was just as unbearable for me. It is impossible to get used to bars. To padlocks. To a life of vegetation. To mental and bodily pains. To hunger.

Everything was the same, but time passed more quickly. During the day, I had less time free for thinking and feeling the suffering. Between six and ten in the evening, however, the same misery began again. The heavy hours. Mute ones. The walls fell into silence. We didn't dare brave the nocturnal quiet, the militiawomen's inactivity. In order not to fall asleep, they had but one occupation: stick their eyes to the judas and sharpen their ears.

Drifting along one evening, verging on the limit of my solitude and despair, I unthinkingly began reciting a prayer. "Hail Mary, full of grace . . ." Once. Once again. Over and over. Gradually, the rhythm of the charming words became a drug. A haven of calm. Lulled by the cadences, thought subsided in a sort of void. I got lost in nonbeing. I was nowhere. Neither here nor somewhere else. I kept up the habit of it.

I had a shock of horror, however, when S. offered to teach me the prayer for the dead. What did she know? Why did she want to teach me the prayer for the dead? For whom? For what dead person should I invoke God's mercy? For my father? For my mother? This supposition alone was already a sacrilege. I hadn't the right to think of it. I could stand my life only by thinking of their life. They didn't have the right to go away. To abandon me.

With some difficulty, S. managed to calm me down. No special reason. For her, we were the dead. "*De profundis clamavi . . .*" What words, what other words could better express our plight? Thus, I learned her prayer for the dead and, then, when the need to complain overwhelmed me, it seemed to soothe my pain to murmur tirelessly: "*De profundis clamavi a te, Domine . . . a te clamavi . . . clamavi . . .*"

The chanted prayers mechanically insinuated themselves into my heart. A kind of faith, or rather, an ardor for faith. The desire to reach a port that my reason knew was an illusion.

I began to think of God.

I had always had a belief in the spirit. In prison this belief sustained me from the beginning. I couldn't believe that man is merely measurable matter. No. I was a piece of the eternal and infinite spirit that floated everywhere from time immemorial and without end, and which men called God. Thus, a piece, as tiny as it was, was also necessarily infinite. No force could bury it in my grave with my decaying flesh. How could pure spirit decay? Who could bury the flame of a candle? The fragrance of a rose? Even a wilted rose?

As a child I had broken a thermometer. The little pearls of mercury had scattered on the ground. I had fun making them roll around, and when two silver pearls touched each other, they became one, a bit larger. They had swallowed each other up. I went on with the game, and in the end there was only a single large, shining pearl. For me, an image symbolizing my piece of spirit, the candle gone out, binding with the great mass of universal spirit.

I thus finally arrived at incarnation. Not in the total transition from the piece of spirit freed by a dead body into another barely nascent body. But as though from the height of a cloud, a condensation of steam rising from all over, falling on the arid earth, at random, drops of rain giving life to grass, flowers, and fruits. Thus I imagined that every human being is endowed with some of the innumerable fragments condensed in the great mass of universal spirit. Thus for me incarnation was the explanation for the multiple faces of the human character. For its unforeseeable reactions. For good and evil in turn possessing us. I managed to accept the cruelty of a guard and sometimes his inexplicable good will. An obtuse peasant woman's delicacy of heart. For hours, the twists and turns of these thoughts followed my slow walk, step-by-step, from the door to the window, from the light to the darkness.

For despite the pains in my legs, I went on moving them continually, out of a fear of ankylosis. The walk warmed up my blood. Soothed the pain. Every time, however, I had to find the will to get myself walking. To have this will each day. Several times a day. To overcome the inertia several times every day. What was the use? To forget several times a day that the struggle would last much longer. To win, several times a day, for five more years, my essential victory.

Reflecting on impersonal problems helped me to live. I had studied neither philosophy nor the exact sciences. But I believe that prolonged solitude begets key questions. What are we? Why are we alive? Does life have any purpose other than life itself? All this "infinite," incommensurable but more acceptable than the "finite," who then had given it order? To what purpose? Wasn't the need for a purpose merely a prosaic and vulgar human need? The need of our physical weight?

To believe in God. I admitted the possibility of faith. To believe in the existence of God. But how could one admit the existence of the Devil? God and Satan, good and evil? A contradictory attribute? No. I could conceive only of an omnipotent and unique God, or nothing. God alone, encompassing everything. Evil, the shadow of good, being part of God. Any light, projected on an opaque object, creates the shadow of this object. The more intense the light, the darker the shadow. Or an uncut diamond. The light barely penetrates it. Cut, the light goes through, makes it glitter. There is no more shadow. I relate, at random, snatches of memories. But I know full well that it is as a consequence of my relations with human beings, after the monsters, that these problems monopolized my attention. I sharply recall that day in spring.

Even my cell was then almost bright. Was it late morning or early afternoon? A golden light came through the shutters. I get up on the bar of the bed. I look down at the courtyard of the barracks nearby. How can I express the soft yet dazzling green of that carpet of grass spattered by a profusion of sun-shaped dandelions? Flooded with a nearly unbearable joy, I felt a presence close by, around me. With such an intensity that I turned back toward my cell. Who was there? Someone had to be there. But there was no one. My cell was empty. For a few more moments the indefinable presence continued to dissolve me in its glory. I wanted to believe, no, I really did believe that God had given me the grace of his manifest presence.

It was still that same spring that I saw a very beautiful young woman in my cell dressed in a long, glittering white dress. She was there before me, standing tall, against the dark background of the door, but alas, I blinked and she was lost. I didn't want to talk about her to my neighbor, who would have hailed it as a miracle.

In the same climate of fervor, there occurred the episode of the child's dress.

The drama began in the cell just beneath mine, occupied by the legionnaires. My former neighbors from the ground floor. Two young women, P. and O., and two older ones. A very young militiawoman, a gallant girl still flabbergasted at finding herself as a prison guard, had just had a baby. The two legionnaires had befriended her because of her polite, almost respectful way of addressing them. O., who had a small piece of beautiful fabric, had decided to embroider a little child's dress and to offer it to the militiawoman. P. offered to help her. They were forced to work in the greatest secrecy.

One morning around ten o'clock, my neighbor's cell was opened and closed several times, for no apparent reason. I was surprised to hear S. talking aloud. Usually, respectful of the regulations, she spoke to the militiawomen in a whisper. Why, this time, was she raising her voice? No doubt to get my attention. But I got to the door too late. Already her voice was fading down the corridor. Where were they taking her? A few minutes later, I once again heard the sound of footsteps, whispering. Her door was opened, then closed, and the key turned in the bolt. Just enough time to allow the guard to go off, and my signal *L* (in Morse) sounded impatiently on the wall. Quickly I repeated the signal, that is: "I'm listening, speak!" and tapping quickly, my neighbor, my new neighbor, let me know what had happened. They were both working on the little dress when they were caught by the nastiest and sneakiest of the militiawomen. An investigation, of course. Two important questions: for whom and why? Confessing the truth was unthinkable. Giving pleasure to someone at the risk of a punishment? No other reason? No investigator would ever accept such a simple, humane explanation. The only reason he could understand would be self-interest. The dress was surely payment for some service rendered. Which one? For him, unhesitatingly, the only credible one, a connection with the outside. The fact that they were legionnaires compounded the case. For the new mother, a serious condemnation.

At the start, it was the penitentiary's political officer who conducted the investigation, but he was merely carrying out an order from the center. Separate the two guilty parties until the arrival of a senior officer.

While P. was allowed to remain in her cell, O. had been moved into S.'s cell. O. asked me to communicate downstairs to P., as quickly as possible, the story that she had told the political officer and that she would not budge from, for anything in the world, despite all the risks, in order to spare the militiawoman. With only a few more months of prison to go, thinking of her impending release, she had had the idea of making a little dress to offer to one of her many nieces likely to be the mother of a little girl. Ask P. to say the same thing for she, O., would rather be chopped into little pieces than talk of the militiawoman.

So while O. was glued to the door to intercept any enemy intrusion, I crouched down beneath the window and quickly sent the message. Just in time, for ten minutes later, one of the older legionnaires transmitted to me with a great deal of fear and effort that P. had just been taken off to the interrogation. In fact, the investigator from the capital arrived only two days later, but P. had been isolated in one of the little cells on the ground floor. For two days on end, O. and P. were in turn interrogated, threatened with an extended sentence, cursed at, but nothing could get them to change their statement. During this time, O. and I spoke as little as possible. She called me only to describe the process of the investigation, and I transmitted downstairs only two or three words to ease their minds. In addition, we were not under much surveillance. The women were lucky enough to benefit from my very good reputation. I had never been accused of the least thing and still less of the wall. To be caught now would have had tragic consequences for us all.

In the afternoon of the third day, a new shake-up and S. reappears at the wall, having understood nothing about her temporary removal. A bit later, a signal from downstairs. I am summoned by O., who has regained her cell, as well as P. Everyone is safe and sound. The two of them will not even be punished for the two hidden needles, unfortunately now confiscated. They wish to give thanks to heaven and would like the whole penitentiary to join in the ceremony. By "closing time" all the cells on the ground floor will murmur a hundred short thanksgivings, whose words she will communicate to me. She would be happy if most of the women joined the two of them in a great outburst of love and charity.

I transmit the words to S. She transmits it to cell 9, the one whose occupants are sentenced to life imprisonment. Cell 9 transmits it to cell 8, that is, to G. and some fifteen other legionnaires. Through the outside wall of the militia's little office, the text goes to cell 6. Through the wall of the gutter of the toilets, room 6 transmits it to the other cells, 5, 4, 3, 2, and 1. Everyone is agreed.

Two sisters, who are Jewish, make it known that they will take part in the ceremony. We wait impatiently for "closing time." In the great expectant silence of the entire penitentiary, the doors of the ground-floor cells slam one after another. Boots hammer on the stone steps, they are coming up. The commandant at the head, then the officers on duty, finally the crew of guards. The inspection goes from cell 6, the first to the right of the stairs, to cells 8, 9, 10, 11 (mine), 12, and going back up the corridor, continues through cells 5, 4, 3, 2, and finally 1. We hear the footsteps come back, go down the stairs, and at last a great silence reigns over the prison. The time has come. The hour of our solidarity.

I murmured the words of the prayer. It filled me with deep emotion to know that all these miserable cells, hundreds of women, starving, destitute, separated from their families, from their children, are thanking God for having saved a prison guard, one of those women who sadistically applied sadistic regulations, because this one guard among them could smile from time to time. It seemed to me that through the walls infiltrated the fervor of the others' prayers, that it suffused me entirely, doing away with evil and proclaiming hope.

Finally, I was pleased that my long years of wisdom could now be of service. The militiawomen, seeing me endlessly pace up and down the cell all day long, walking and moving my fingers nonsensically, could not imagine that I was counting syllables and mumbling verses. They thought I was a bit deranged from so many years of solitary confinement and let me peacefully attend to my clandestine occupations. Thanks to S., I was never caught at the wall, but even so, they managed to slap me with the seven days. Reason? As absurd as it was unbelievable. I was punished because of the revolt of the Hungarians.

The story begins in the barracks' courtyard. The soldiers would set off from the barracks in small groups to go for their military exercises in the vicinity. At dusk, nearly all of them returned at the same time. To get them to march in time despite their fatigue, they were ordered to sing. Marches, patriotic songs, popular songs, anything, provided it was bellowed out loudly, as loudly as possible. The meeting-up at the barracks' door of hundreds of voices, each group singing its own song, produced a wild and irresistibly comical polyphony. One evening, however, a last group arrived a little bit late. Its song rang out loud and clear. A popular Hungarian tune, sung in Hungarian. Nothing surprising about that. We were smack in the middle of the "autonomous Hungarian region." Nonetheless that evening, we were the auditory witnesses of an unheard-of fact. In Romanian, a commanding and even angry voice ordered the group to shut up. Not to sing that song. The voices broke off. A door slammed. A moment of silence. Then a stamping of boots, and that was all. But S. and I had already hurried together, that is, to the wall, to discuss the event. It was a sign. A sign of something serious. But what could it mean?

Two days went by. A new sign. Next to me, in cell 12, a common-law prisoner was doing a "seven days" punishment. One of those who, invisible to us, executed their sentence in the service of the penitentiary. The legionnaires on the ground floor had managed to start up relations with them through their window, which looked out on the rear courtyard, despite the new shutters. These male inmates did some small favors for them. A bit of pencil, cigarettes, a little salt. For their pleasure, while sawing wood under their window—hence under mine—they whistled or sang ballads, inserting short fragments of long-prohibited legionary anthems. The soldiers on duty in the watchtower were too young to be familiar with these songs, but for the two of us the sounds were full of horror.

The man now being punished was named Szabo. He had been there for three days and in Hungarian he let fly what must have been protests of his innocence each time his door opened for meals or the "program." On the third evening the commandant took part in the "closing time." When they opened his door, I once again heard Szabo's agitated voice, speaking in his native language as usual. Then came a thunderbolt: irately, the commandant ordered him to speak the language of this country. Today it is hard to grasp the incredibility of such an order. After the war the Party had done its utmost to tone down the chauvinism . . . of Romania. In Transylvania, both languages were equally valid for all transactions. We thus discussed at length the astonishing change. Outside, something serious was afoot. Some latent territorial demands? A breakoff in relations? War? How could we have imagined the unimaginable? The Hungarians' revolt against the Soviet Union?

Stimulated by fear of a possible contagion, violently felt by the rulers, by the hope of the whole people, of a change of regime, the upheaval of this tempest surged through our country and ended up striking even the walls of our penitentiary.

A few days later, startling news raced from one cell to another. An inscription on one of the walls of the toilets had had time to be read by several cells before being discovered and erased. There, someone had scribbled four words. Just four words, but how explosive! The prison management was at an impasse. Which of these hundreds of women had had the nerve to write "Down with the communists!" on a toilet wall? For the management, the challenge of these words was unmistakably connected with the Hungarian revolt. How to discover and punish the guilty party without publicly divulging the words of the graffiti? A pointless qualm, for we all knew through the intramural telephone system both the words and who'd written them.

The administration had an obligation. To punish. But punish whom? After a lengthy evening meeting, the ideal solution was hit upon. Punish the largest possible number of the potentially guilty. Even if the actual culprit slipped through the net, the suffering of her companions would be a humiliating punishment for her.

For the next three days an uneventful calm. On the fourth day, at five in the morning, just after the wake-up gong, a massive assault. Several militiawomen armed with paper and pencil went rapidly from one judas to another. The regulations were precise. From the first sound of the gong, the inmates all had to get out of bed at once. In the large cells, however, since the beds were stacked up in twos and threes, the women on the third level had to wait their turn after the women on the second level crawled between the iron bars to get down. The names of thirty-five women were written on the blacklist. At 7 days per inmate, there were 245 days of isolation, 70 of which featured the standard diet and 175 of starvation. A real windfall for the penitentiary's treasury.

I was on the list. Nevertheless all the guards knew that each morning I had to massage my ailing legs to get the circulation going before I set my feet on the floor. They had never forbidden this. Still I was punished, as was my next-door neighbor. They emptied my cell. Bed, mattress, bench, coatrack, pail, everything was set out in the corridor. They left behind only the chamber pot. Each evening at ten they gave back the mattress for the night. In my turn I received the three mess tins of tepid salted water and the cube of polenta on the first, second, fourth, fifth, and seventh days and the normal diet on the third and sixth days. I was used to the hunger. But to remain standing for the seventeen hours of the day was exhausting. I could have sat on the floor with no risk. An occasional rap on the door to get me to stand up and nothing else. But I didn't want to sprawl on the floor before them. I felt thus that I was defending my dignity. I managed to get some rest on the cover of the chamber pot. But I could only sit on one buttock, because of the raised wooden crosspiece holding together the boards of the cover.

My neighbor was luckier. All punishments had to be initialed by the doctor. He canceled my neighbor's "seven days." She had an illness, "purpura reumatica," and moreover she was Catholic. Except for this one refusal, the doctor always signed all the decrees for punishment. Without comment.

After the punishment, it was even harder for me to take the chamber pot and the pail out for the "program." The chamber pot was heavy on the way out, the pail on the return trip. Several times I was forced to set them down on the floor during the outing. The stairwell in particular, with its slippery steps, seemed to me endless. The forever rushed militiawomen grumbled and stamped their feet, but nothing could be done about it. They had to resign themselves to assigning this chore to cell 8. In the cell, some fifteen legionnaires, most of them very young. I now merely took the pail and the chamber pot out in front of my door. They would take turns, two at a time, coming to fetch them. I heard them running toward me. Sometimes a furtive "good morning." When the militiawoman had her back turned, they even opened the judas to see me. Holding out an arm to keep the judas open, they drew back a step to let me have a look at them as well. Then, through the two cells separating us, they transmitted to me the name of the one whose hasty smile I had seen. One of these young women had been my neighbor in cell 12 for seven days. We had chatted a long time together. She now considered herself my friend.

"The girls of number 8 are crazy," S. told me one day. "They want you to lift up your pail tomorrow for they are putting something on the bottom of it."

Easy to say. But to have the strength to lift the pail up to eye level, I was forced to pour out three-fourths of the contents into the wooden tub. The outer surface of the pail was a dark brown enamel. They had coated the bottom of the pail with lime, let it dry, and with a stylus one of the legionnaires had written me a letter. Each word stood out clearly in brown against the white background. For my reply, she asked me to empty out the pail completely the next morning, moisten and level off the surface and answer them with a broom straw as a pencil. This tiring game lasted some time. It ended only at the express request of my neighbor, who couldn't stand any more trembling and sweating for me at the prospect of some accidental tipping over of the pail and bringing our correspondence to light.

Finally, December 31, 1956 arrived. The last conversation of the year. We wished each other a better year for ourselves and our families, for us all, for the whole world. At ten o'clock, the final gong. I had had a friend this year. Sincere and devoted. I was no longer alone. The walls of my cell no longer separated me from the world. On the contrary. I was now certain I could see it all through to the end. I could always find in myself not only the desire but also the will to survive. I felt calm and yet sleep evaded me. Sadness seeped in. Like every night when I heard the trains go by, one after another, somewhere, at the edge of town. The nostalgic sounds of the thundering wheels, the whistles piercing the dark. It had to be midnight when a storm, a hurricane of whistles flooded over the town. High-pitched, piercing, shattering the last dark night of the year, screaming hope, it was the railway workers' greeting to the prisoners. It rang out the same in all the towns of Transylvania that had the ignoble honor of hiding a prison.

Days 2725, 2726, 2727, 2728, 2729, 2730, 2731, 2732, 2733, 2734, 2735, 2736, 2737, 2738, 2739, 2740, 2741, 2742, 2743, 2744, 2745, 2746, 2747, 2748, 2749, 2750, 2751, 2752, 2753, 2754, 2755, 2756, 2757, 2758, 2759, 2760, 2761, 2762, 2763, 2764, 2765, 2766, 2767, 2768, 2769, 2770, 2771, 2772, 2773, 2774, 2775, 2776, 2777, 2778, 2779, 2780, 2781, 2782, 2783, 2784, 2785, 2786, 2787, 2788, 2789, 2790, 2791, 2792, 2793, 2794, 2795, 2796, 2797, 2798, 2799, 2800, 2801, 2802, 2803,

2804, 2805, 2806, 2807, 2808, 2809, 2810, 2811,
2812, 2813, 2814, 2815, 2816, 2817, 2818, 2819,
2820, 2821, 2822, 2823, 2824, 2825, 2826, 2827,
2828, 2829, 2830, 2831, 2832, 2833, 2834, 2835,
2836, 2837, 2838, 2839, 2840, 2841, 2842, 2843,
2844, 2845, 2846, 2847, 2848, 2849, 2850, 2851,
2852, 2853, 2854, 2855, 2856, 2857, 2858, 2859,
2860, 2861, 2862, 2863, 2864, 2865, 2866, 2867,
2868, 2869, 2870, 2871, 2872, 2873, 2874, 2875,
2876, 2877, 2878, 2879, 2880, 2881, 2882, 2883,
2884, 2885, 2886, 2887, 2888, 2889, 2890, 2891,
2892, 2893, 2894, 2895, 2896, 2897, 2898, 2899,
2900, 2901, 2902, 2903, 2904, 2905, 2906, 2907,
2908, 2909, 2910, 2911, 2912, 2913, 2914, 2915,
2916, 2917, 2918, 2919, 2920, 2921, 2922, 2923,
2924, 2925, 2926, 2927, 2928, 2929, 2930, 2931,
2932, 2933, 2934, 2935, 2936, 2937, 2938, 2939,
2940, 2941, 2942, 2943, 2944, 2945, 2946, 2947,
2948, 2949, 2950, 2951, 2952, 2953, 2954, 2955,
2956, 2957, 2958, 2959, 2960, 2961, 2962, 2963,
2964, 2965, 2966, 2967, 2968, 2969, 2970, 2971,
2972, 2973, 2974, 2975, 2976, 2977, 2978, 2979,
2980, 2981, 2982, 2983, 2984, 2985, 2986, 2987,
2988, 2989, 2990, 2991, 2992, 2993, 2994, 2995,
2996, 2997, 2998, 2999, 3000 of detention—
October 1, 1957

Numbers. Many numbers. Do they state the number of months, weeks, minutes experienced during those nine months?

What happened in the course of those nine lost months? In some fashion or other I must have lived the 9 months, 39 weeks, 275 days, 6,576 hours, those 394,560 minutes.

Wake up at five in the morning, as always. The routine of daily gestures. The same dull ache in my legs. The same insistent hunger. The same anxiety about my parents and sisters. The weather was cold, the weather was hot. Sometimes sunlight filtered through the shutters.

But I no longer lived withdrawn into myself. I participated with interest in the life of the penitentiary. Through the punishment-and-quarantine cell number 12, I entered into contact with many inmates. I transmitted their messages through the walls. I received their secrets. Requests for advice.

New prisoners often showed up in number 12. They brought us news of the country, which then made the rounds of the cells. A good deal of my time was taken up relaying the "mail." Written with a sliver of wood for a pen and methylene blue for ink, on small squares of cloth provided by our tattered linen, coated with wet soap, we had to stick them here or there, along the stairs, in the courtyard, or in the latrines when we went down in single file for the walk or the "program." Finally transmit through the walls the exact spot to the person to whom it was addressed. All this with extreme caution. Letting oneself get caught was to be subjected to the "seven days."

I transmitted the rare political news, the fear that prevailed over the country, the cost of meat, eggs, or butter. One fine day, some sensational news reached me! Women of every class no longer covered their heads with the *basma*, a square of fabric that only peasant women had worn before. Another startling piece of news: a textile factory had even arranged a fashion show. Impossible? No, since one of the two extremely elderly ladies newly arrived had been sentenced to five years for having written on a postcard—handed out at the entrance to the fashion show for noting down one's impressions of it—that evening gowns seemed to her premature as long as the lines at the state food stores—and there were no other kind—were still so long.

In 1957, we were given prisoners' uniforms. All our clothes had turned to rags. So they had no other choice but to go to this expense. Being the last served, I could not get a skirt in my size. They were thus obliged to give me two narrow skirts, scissors, needle, and thread. Making my skirt slightly wider, I became the most elegantly turned-out woman in the prison.

It was that same year that in the morning they began giving us, besides the three ounces of bread and cup of darkish liquid they called coffee, a little square of dense marmalade, sufficient to bring an end to the dreams of food.

I also recall the wretched story of the mattress. Undoing a few inches of the stitching of that rough canvas bag, I had hidden a piece of fabric I'd found in one of the trash cans in the toilets. I needed it one day, but couldn't find it. Futilely I stuck my arm as far as I could into the broken straw of the mattress. I was forced to empty it out completely and the whole cell was filled with an acrid cloud of dust. With my heart pounding, coughing as if about to die, I had to stuff large handfuls of straw and dust back into the mattress at top speed so as not to be surprised by the militiawoman on duty.

The searches continued. I could never understand what they were so determined to find. What could they be trying to find when a militiawoman with a rubber-gloved hand subjected us to a gynecological search? How can I describe the horror of my neighbor the virgin?

Somehow, the time went by.

At the beginning of fall, one morning I received slightly sweetened coffee, a large hunk of bread weighing over a pound, and a double portion of marmalade. At noon, in addition to the mess tin of soup, noodles with cheese. This went on for about two weeks. I also received some semolina, one day a little margarine, and from time to time some milk. Why were they once again giving me a TBC diet?

A short time earlier, I had told my neighbor that I would very much like to have two minor illnesses, tuberculosis and syphilis. "Minor" because even so I didn't want to be gravely ill. According to one legend from my youth, the great poets all suffered from syphilis. It was said that this was the cause of their genius. I was not claiming to be able to reach the level of genius, of course, but a small talent would have been a great help in the difficult working out of my verses.

"So," my neighbor tells me, "I understand this foolish wish, for since I have known you, I have noticed that wisdom often fails you, but tuberculosis?"

"That's much more understandable. With tuberculosis officially declared, I would receive a special diet and this diet would do something to calm the hunger pangs that prevent me from achieving the total escape created by the intensity of my work."

Now that this kind of diet was provided, however, I was not as pleased as I had thought I would be. It was the official recognition of my state of ill health. But at the end of two days, my hunger appeased, the delectable taste of the bits of cheese in the noodles, that of the milk, sugar, and coffee consoled me. I decided to take the best possible care of myself. The air in my cell was pure—I would keep the window open most of the time—and with the help of the food, I was certain to get well.

Only . . . two weeks later, the militiawoman on duty entered, all smiles, and announced that the commandant had decided to have me change cells. After eight years of solitary confinement, eight-and-a-half if my first arrest is included, the next morning I was to enter a cell inhabited by fourteen women.

I was floored.

I don't know how the rest of the day went by or whether I managed to sleep that night. I was frightened. Frightened of the new. Frightened of humans. Frightened of these unknown women, of these strangers who seemed like so many potential enemies.

What's more, my neighbor was also desperate. They had announced the same switch to her. She had already lived for some years with the lack of privacy of the large cells and had suffered from it.

Both of us were whimpering, and at the very time when my ardent desire for social life was finally going to be granted, I was once again mortally afraid!

I cannot end this story without paying homage today to all these unknown women who very soon became my friends. All of them knew that in one of the cells of their penitentiary lived, for years, a woman even more miserable than they. Moreover, I had spoken with some of them at the wall.

They took me in with great friendship and helped me, with all their might, to adjust to this new environment.

My three-and-a-half years of communal life are really a whole other story.

Despite outrageous privations of every kind, the lack of basic hygiene, the confinement, illness, the barbarous punishments, or perhaps because of all this, it is a fine story of human solidarity, of feminine solidarity in suffering.

Afterword

It was in Paris, in 1977, that I began writing this book, and the work lasted for some time.

I didn't have much spare time in Bucharest. Most of my time was taken up with my tapestries. If they had been paintings, I might have been able to do one a week. I didn't even manage to do one tapestry a month. Far from it. So I did my writing during my trips abroad. Each time, I took what I had managed to write and transcribed it in tiny letters in a notebook, with very thin pages. So I could more easily hide my manuscript. My memoirs are not a political text. Nevertheless, to provide a better understanding of the circumstances of our trial, I shall try to summarize the political situation in Romania in 1944.

August 23, 1944. After secret meetings between King Michael, the three heads of the historical parties—Brătianu of the Liberal party, Maniu of the Peasant party, Petrescu of the Socialist party—and Pătrăşcanu—representing the hitherto outlawed Communist party—Marshal Antonescu, the dictator who led the country during the war years, was arrested as an ally of Hitler.

The Soviet Red army had already crossed the Romanian border. In Moscow a coalition of the parties signed an armistice. The Romanian army went over to the side of the Allies, to fight against Germany on Romanian soil and to carry on the struggle on the

Hungarian and Czech fronts. To lose some four hundred thousand soldiers.

Though Romania thus avoided military occupation, the Soviet Union was to impose on this deeply nationalistic and anticommunist country a regime of harsh communist dictatorship.

Under the screen of a Romanian communist government, the USSR then imposed on Romania disproportionate war reparations, the arrest and conviction of the party heads who had nevertheless signed the armistice, the exile of King Michael after elections that were one hundred percent rigged, hundreds of thousands of arbitrary arrests, and finally Pătrășcanu's trial and death sentence. A trial similar to those imposed by the USSR in all the newly created socialist republics in the East.

The communist government was headed by the party secretary, Gheorghiu-Dej—who was freed from prison after August 23—and the communists Ana Pauker, Luca, and Kisinevsky—who had returned from the USSR where they had sought refuge during the war. They hastily improvised a party, soliciting members by force, fear, and opportunism. Many former members of the Iron Guard, the pro-Nazi party, found a haven in it.

A bourgeois by birth and education, Pătrășcanu was not one of them. But he was probably the most honest, idealistic, and also naive of the "pure" communists. He had imagined that the war that had opened the borders of the USSR would also open the eyes and minds of the Soviets and would establish in all of the East a new communism, based on social justice for all and not on a new dictatorship of hatred and murders.

At the trial, he was accused of having been an agent for the old State Securitate (the prewar police who had hunted down communists), a spy in the pay of the "imperialists," and a counterrevolutionary. The accusations were totally untrue. But, although he wasn't guilty in words or deeds, he was in fact guilty in thought. Before the war, he had spent I don't know exactly how much time in Moscow, but enough to return deeply anti-Soviet and anti-Stalinist.

He would have liked to keep the Communist party for a few more years in the opposition, leaving the historical parties with the heavy burden of getting the country back on its feet. He would also have liked an end to the revenge, an end to the trials presided over by the new people's courts. Arrested in 1948 and kept under house arrest for two years in the countryside near Bucharest, incarcerated in 1950, he was tried in 1954—after a long, hard investigation, and a change of minister of the interior.

Stalin's death and the subsequent de-Stalinization of the USSR had frightened Gheorghiu-Dej. Even in 1949, he had reinstated the death penalty, which had not existed under the old monarchist regime, with the obvious intention of eliminating Pătrășcanu. He now had to move up the trial date, driven by fear that Khrushchev, the new secretary of the CPSU, would replace him with a Pătrășcanu released from prison.

In April 1954, the trial was hurriedly dispatched. One hundred fifty perjuring witnesses, six days of trial, a spurious court, and Pătrășcanu was "legally" murdered.

By what unfortunate chance were my friend Harry Brauner and I involved in this trial? Because, after the war, Pătrășcanu's wife, a set designer by profession, had decided to set up a marionette theater in Bucharest. Because she had chosen me from among many other artists to collaborate in the creation of this theater. Because Harry had gone to Pătrășcanu to reconstruct the Romanian folklore archives—founded before the war by professor Constantin Brăiloiu (who crossed over into Switzerland toward the end of the war)—and received from him all the help needed to create a new institute, the one currently operating in Bucharest. We were only two pawns on the chessboard of this plot made up out of whole cloth.

Like me, Harry was sentenced to twelve years. Released at the end of those twelve years, I was returned to freedom but prohibited from living in Bucharest or any other large city. Utterly arbitrarily, he was sentenced to two more years of house arrest in a pitiful hamlet lost in the Baragan, the vast agricultural region in the southern part of the country. He lived there in a tiny adobe house, with an earthen floor and a thatched roof.

Stricken with tuberculosis while in prison, I was settled by my family in the small town of Breaza, nestled in the foothills of the Carpathian Mountains. The climate there was very mild, very beneficial for my ailing lungs. My parents were both still living in Bucharest. From time to time, I came to spend two or three days with them, trying not to be seen by the neighbor, who was "Moscow's eye" on their peaceful street.

To go spend a few days with Harry involved a long journey.

Not because of the actual distance, but because of the difficulties of transport. Leaving Breaza at nine in the evening, I went down a winding road as far as the station, followed in the darkness by a pack of dogs that I kept at a distance by shouting with all my strength. After an hour's train ride, I reached Ploieşti. There, I spent the night on a bench in the station's waiting room, and a second train took me in three to four hours to Slobozia. From there, a bus, and finally almost two miles on foot through a forest and rice fields. If I missed the bus, my trip was prolonged by several hours.

Finally, I would arrive, loaded with two heavy sacks of food. I did the housework and some cooking while listening to the marvelous lieder Harry had composed during his imprisonment, like mine, in solitary confinement.

After a few days, because of the hostile climate, my fever would rise and I would have to leave again, to our great chagrin.

It was there that we were married. It was an extraordinary, tragicomic ceremony performed by a half-illiterate town hall secretary. Arriving at the town hall at three in the afternoon, and following some hilarious scenes, we left, husband and wife, at eight in the evening. But back at the house, a wedding meal and two guests—two former convicts like ourselves—awaited us.

The sight of the white tablecloth, two plates of prettily decorated sandwiches, the bottle of champagne, the cake my mother had given me, and some flowers adorning the table so moved our guests that they were in tears as they congratulated and embraced us.

Despite my many approaches to the Central Committee, there was no way for me to earn a living. I was supported by my sister, who was married to professor Grigore Moisil, a member of the Romanian Academy. Two years later, I finally received permission to sell craft work at the official Artists' Union store in Bucharest. Paintings, no. They decreed that I was undeserving of it.

I began making folk dolls. To make them more artistic, I had the idea of dressing them with real peasant embroidery, the remains of worn-out blouses.

A childhood friend, the great actress Clodi Bertola, invited me to accompany her on a motor tour of the country. We thus arrived in Hunedoara, in Transylvania, on a market day. Coming from the villages in the hills nearby, the peasants wore gorgeous blouses embroidered with a thousand more or less stylized geometrical and floweret patterns, in every color against a background of black or red. I gave my address to a group of women from the village of Cerişor, asking them to send me some of their cast-off blouses instead of selling them by the pound to itinerant rag dealers, usually gypsies.

I had always been a painter, but on that day my future changed. In 1974, ten years later, thanks to Cosana—one of the peasants who had become my friend and collaborator in the village—my first exhibition of tapestries took place. They were all composed of embroideries from this tiny village, and they caused a scandal in Bucharest. Some of my fellow tapestry weavers accused me, backed up by the newly created "Preservation Commission," "of destroying precious evidence of the country's artistic patrimony."

This conspiracy lasted more than two years.

In 1964, after two years of house arrest, Harry returned to Bucharest. New legal proceedings, new futile waits. It took him more than a year before he was hired at an institute of art history, at a minimal salary and work that was not in his field.

Thanks to our marriage, I succeeded in effecting a return to Bucharest, and we moved into a little garret above my parents' apartment. After my arrest and the confiscation of my studio, my parents also had been punished. They were forced to share their four-room apartment with a family—a man, his wife, and child. Hence, no room for us.

In 1965, after the death of Gheorghiu-Dej, a feud among the Party bigwigs had "provisionally" elevated Nicolae Ceauşescu to the head of the Party. This "provisional" arrangement lasted exactly twenty-five years and ended only with the country's rebellion in December 1989.

The man they had thought was ready to allow himself to be led resorted to the cunning of a peasant, an acute sense of diplomacy, and a diabolical thirst for power.

To ruin the legacy of the former Party secretary, he had a brilliant idea. Retry the Pătrăşcanu case, prove the man's innocence, and accuse Gheorghiu-Dej of murder.

In 1968 we were thus retried by the Supreme Military Court, and all of us were exonerated. Pătrăşcanu was buried near the other dead communist "eminences" around a monument to the dead in which the murderer's coffin continues to lie enthroned.

This revised judgment was doubly advantageous for Ceauşescu. For, a short time later, the armies of the Warsaw Pact invaded Czechoslovakia and stifled the springtime of Prague. Romania remained neutral. Even more, Ceauşescu used blackmail to
force the members of the pro-Soviet Central Committee to support him. They had all signed an innocent man's death sentence.

After the second trial, the country's Constitution gave us the
right to ask for our former salaries corresponding to twelve years'
imprisonment. About a million *lei* in current value. It was quietly
made known to us that it would be better to refrain from doing so.
For all our goods that had been confiscated, Harry's manuscripts,
my canvases, our books, the furniture, his piano, which alone was
worth 30,000 *lei*, really for all our possessions, we received altogether only 27,000 *lei*!

Thus, upon leaving prison, and even for some years after
1968, we were extremely poor. In 1970, they finally housed us in a
neighborhood of low-income high rises rather far from the center
of town.

Harry got back his former job at the Conservatory and could
once again do research and make recordings of music and folk
songs in the villages, and he published numerous articles support-
ing the preservation of authentic folklore, which was threatened
with what he called "folklore pollution," the new Party directives.

However, from 1968 on, we more easily obtained permission
to travel. Harry's brother, the painter Victor Brauner, had died in
1966, but Harry could see his sister in Geneva and his remaining
brother Theodor, who lived with his wife and two daughters in the
Paris suburb of Fontenay-aux-Roses.

In 1982, I had a brief exhibition of tapestries in Paris, thanks
to the generosity of Claude Braband, owner of the L'Usine picture
gallery on the Boulevard de la Villette, and a second exhibition at
the Palace of Culture in Rennes.

On March 11, 1988, with keen regret at being able to make
known only very little of his musical work, Harry took his leave of
this world.

In 1985, after I had read some passages from my text to two
highly educated Romanians living in Paris, they offered me their
help in securing immediate publication.

How could I have accepted? Upon its publication we would
have had to put up with the gravest consequences in Bucharest.

Thus, choose freedom? But we wanted at all costs to remain in our own country. And then, what freedom? Since I had succeeded in feeling free, as it were, in prison, I would go on feeling free in Romania. For us, the country and the country's government were two distinct entities. It is the Romanian land that we didn't want to leave, its villages, its peasants, our language.

It is true that I have written this memoir in French with the intent, or rather the dream, of publishing it in Paris, but I could not decide to do this at the time. Could Harry have, in Paris, worked with all his might to defend Romanian folk music? Was it in Paris or elsewhere that I could have gone on making my tapestries? The tapestries that had become a passion for me?

So I ended up writing this book with no hope of ever seeing it published. The miracle of December 1989 was required to enable me to reconcile my attachment to the country with a desire to bear witness.

Perhaps this personal testimony will make clearer the difficult times we all lived through, our despair and our terror. The terror that penetrated deeply into each of us.

To someone who has not, day after day, for years, suffered humiliation, slavery, repressed resentments, the permanent, powerless desire for revenge, the cold, malnutrition, the total lack of horizon, it will be impossible to have a perfect understanding of us.

This book is not the story of an isolated case. We were not the only ones to suffer. The great mass of the Romanian people was crushed under the weight of an inhuman and aberrant regime, and hundreds of thousands of Romanians suffered oppressive years of prison. But I must recognize that I am the only woman in the country who endured eight-and-a-half years of total isolation. I hope that no reader will consider this to be a glorious distinction.

Paris, April 1990

SOCIETY AND CULTURE IN EAST-CENTRAL EUROPE
Irena Grudzinska Gross and Jan T. Gross, General Editors

Compositor:	Prestige Typography
Text:	10.5/13 Galliard
Display:	Galliard
Printer:	Haddon Craftsmen, Inc.
Binder:	Haddon Craftsmen, Inc.

4